Meals in a Social Context

Aarhus Studies in Mediterranean Antiquity (*ASMA*)

I

ASMA is a series which will be published approximately once a year by The Centre for the Study of Antiquity, University of Aarhus, Denmark.

The Centre is a network of cooperating departments: Greek and Latin, Classical Archaeology, History, and the Faculty of Theology. The objective of the series is to advance the interdisciplinary study of Antiquity by publishing articles, e.g., conference papers, or independant monographs, which among other things reflect the current activities of the Centre.

Meals in a Social Context

Aspects of the Communal Meal
in the Hellenistic and Roman World

*Edited by Inge Nielsen
and Hanne Sigismund Nielsen*

AARHUS UNIVERSITY PRESS

Copyright: Aarhus University Press, 1998
Printed in England by The Alden Press, Oxford
ISBN 87 7288 697 8

AARHUS UNIVERSITY PRESS
University of Aarhus
DK-8000 Aarhus C
Fax (+ 45) 8619 8433

73 Lime Walk
Headington, Oxford OX3 7AD
Fax (+ 44) 1865 750 079

Box 511
Oakville, CT 06779
Fax (+ 1) 860 945 9468

ANSI/NISO
Z39.48-1992

Contents

Abbreviations	7
Inge Nielsen & Hanne Sigismund Nielsen Introduction	9
Peter Ørsted Salt, Fish, and the Sea in the Roman Empire	13
Keith Bradley The Roman Family at Dinner	36
Hanne Sigismund Nielsen Roman Children at Mealtimes	56
Hugh Lindsay Eating with the Dead: the Roman Funerary Banquet	67
Katherine Dunbabin Ut Greaco More Biberetur: Greeks and Romans on the Dining Couch	81
Inge Nielsen Royal Banquets: the Development of Royal Banquets and Banqueting Halls from Alexander to the Tetrarchs	102
David Noy The Sixth Hour is the Mealtime for Scholars: Jewish Meals in the Roman world	134
Per Bilde The Common Meal in the Qumran-Essene Communities	145
Geert Hallbäck Sacred Meal and Social Meeting: Paul's Argument in 1 Cor. 11.17-34	167

Contents

L. Michael White
Regulating Fellowship in the Communal Meal:
Early Jewish and Christian Evidence   *177*

Bibliography   *206*

Contributors   *223*

Index of Names   *225*

Index Locorum   *234*

Abbreviations

AE	*L'Année épigraphique*
BAR	British Archaeological Reports
BdI	*Bollettino dell'Istituto*
CCSL	*Corpus Christianorum. Series Latina*
CEFR	*Collection de l'École française de Rome*
CGL	*Corpus glossariorum Latinorum*. Götz
CIL	*Corpus Insciptionum Latinarum*
CIJ	*The Classical Journal*
CPJ	*Corpus papyrorum judaicarum*
ESAR	T. Frank (ed.), *An Economic Survey of Ancient Rome 1-6*, 1933-40
IDR	*Inscriptiile Daciei Romane*
IG	*Inscriptiones Graecae*
ILS	H. Dessau (ed.), *Inscriptiones Latinae Selectae*
JAAR	*Journal of the American Academy of Religion*
JIWE	*Jewish Inscriptions of Western Europe*
LTUR	*Lexicon Topographicum Urbis Romae*
LCL	*Loeb Classical Library*
RE	Pauly, A. & Wissowa, G. *Real-Encyclopädie der classischen Altertumswissenschaft*
SEG	*Supplementum epigraphicum Graecum*
SHA	*Scriptores Historiae Augustae*
SHC	Studies in Hellenistic Civilization. Aarhus 1990-

Introduction

Inge Nielsen & Hanne Sigismund Nielsen

In August 1995 an international conference on "Meals in Social Context. The communal meal as a reflection of religion and society in the Hellenistic and Roman world" was held at Fuglsang Manor in Denmark. Scholars from various fields of research participated, and the aim was to illuminate the communal meals in the complex societies constituting the Mediterranean world in the Hellenistic and Roman period. As many aspects of eating together as possible have been analyzed, ranging from the possibility for the poor of getting anything to eat at all, through meals in the family or family-like groups, to banquets among the élites and the kings. Further, religious meals among Jews and Christians are included.

At the conference, each paper was followed by a very lively discussion that reflected the different methodological backgrounds and source materials of the participants. It was interesting to observe that interdisciplinarity implies the necessity of defining fundamental terms of relevance for our common starting point, the ancient Mediterranean world. This observation, of course, holds true not only for eating habits of the ancient world, but is a general problem. This is banal, but important to remember, when a subject is viewed on the background of different scholarly traditions. This will be clear to the reader of this book, whenever terms like Greek, Hellenistic Roman, family, Jewish, Christian, crop up, as well as in the use of the sources available.

The present book contains the revised versions of most of the papers given at this conference. The intention of publishing the papers has been to give the reader a possibility of participating in the current discussion among scholars working with social structures in general, in this context specifically the dining-habits, in antiquity. Rather than being a book of answers, it raises questions about the common interpretations of eating habits. You will find authors of the articles here reaching conflicting results, frequently on the basis of the same sources.

The book can be used both as a collection of articles each illuminating one specific topic, and as a general work of reference (with common bibliography, indices, etc.). It has, however, unfortunately not been possible to take all aspects of communal meals in Antiquity into consideration. Thus we have not been able to cover the following fields: esoteric meals in connection with Greek, Roman and Oriental cults, meals in the context of *koina* and *collegia*, commemorative meals among Jews and Christians, and finally installations for funerary banquets.

The first part of the book covers the communal meal in the pagan world. In the first article, however, Ørsted provides the reader with an insight into the economical and social aspects of providing food at all for those living at subsistence level. Ørsted poses the basic question: what happened to persons who for some reason were excluded from the social provisions made for the poor in the Roman empire. Especially the greyzone between private and public property i.e. the resources accessible to all (*res nullius*): salt and fish from the sea, has been treated here. It is crucial that this *res nullius* was physically situated within the Roman Empire and thus had to be defined legally. On the basis of the evidence of these legal sources it is discussed whether the existence of *res nullius* was a consequence of an active policy of the state towards the poor living in the country, as was the *annona* and *congiaria* for those living in the cities of the Empire.

The next two articles treat the dining habits of the Roman family. Primarily on the basis of the literary material concerning the eating practices of the Roman élite, Bradley analyzes the hierarchical structure of social relations in the upper classes of society. Bradley defines the *cena* and *convivium* as occasions for convivial, relaxed conversation between a host and his male friends. Thus the *cena* had nothing to do with dinner in our sense of the word, but was seen as a means of social display rather than as the educational institution for children as we know it in western civilization. Thus the children of the ancient élite family were not allowed to participate in dinner until they reached the age of 15-16 years. Further, Bradley argues that the important function of dinners among the Roman aristocracy was to enhance the individual male's reputation (*fama*) in society.

Sigismund Nielsen concentrates on the lower status groups of Roman society not normally represented in literature. On the basis of epigraphic material from Rome and Isola Sacra she argues for a general lack of interest in the close biological family in pagan Rome as one reason why family dinners, in our sense of the word, are only very infrequently found in the ancient sources. In early Christian literature and funerary inscriptions, however, there is an emphasis on the importance of the close biological family also where eating habits are concerned. It is suggested that the nuclear family did not become an ideal until early Christianity.

Lindsay studies the complex and biased sources on the Roman funeral habits and the offerings and meals related to it. He starts his investigation by treating the ancient Greek burial customs to decide whether there were common features between Greek and Roman norms. Also, he introduces the comparative anthropological method by including burial traditions in modern Taiwan. In his analysis Lindsay emphasizes the regenerative fertility aspect behind the various rituals. Finally he gives an example of the widespread use in Roman society of funeral *collegia* which were of great importance for the persons of small means to obtain a decent burial.

Dunbabin and Nielsen both places the focus on the preserved dining halls from Hellenistic and Roman times. Dunbabin concentrates on dining installations in private houses and uses these dining rooms as a means of comparing the dining habits of Greek and Roman society. While the dining rooms of the *andron* type, known from Greece, connotes social equality, the Pi-formed dining rooms occurring first on Hellenistic Delos, and soon also in Italy, do not. Thus the Roman *triclinium*, although relatively small, at least in the Republican period, still presupposed a strict hierarchy. Only very little is known of dining room architecture in the Greek areas in the first century BC and first century AD, but at least from the second century AD the Roman *triclinium* was in use here, too, which must mean that the Roman hierarchial type of dining was taken over, as well.

A similar picture appears when royal dining-hall architecture is concerned, as shown by Nielsen. Like Dunbabin, her aim is to trace a development from the Greek to the Roman period. It is proposed that the open dining-hall of the Pi-type existed already in the Hellenistic royal palaces, and that it was here that the Roman aristocracy found their models for the creation and development of the *triclinium* in the Republican and Imperial period respectively. Thus hierarchy was always important in palaces, including in their banqueting rooms. Contra Dunbabin it is suggested that the Roman dining halls of the east was inspired from those of the Hellenistic palaces directly, and not via Rome.

In the second part of the book the focus is on Jewish and Christian communal meals. Noy treats the sources on the Jewish meals, both in Palestine and the Diaspora, consisting primarily of Rabbinic writings, since pagan sources are hard to come by. Noy focuses in particular on the Rabbinic meal, and concludes that the way the rabbis dined together was related to the Greek and Roman social hierarchical meals in many ways, for example did they recline on couches; but the blessings said and the things eaten were different, and also, no women were present. The dining together of close family members was apparently not very important for the rabbis, since they very rarely mention it in their writings.

Bilde, who treats the communal meals of the Essenes, poses the questions whether this meal was considered sacred and even sacramental, and whether this meal did, in fact, replace, in a spiritual way, the sacrificial cult of the Temple in Jerusalem. He analyzes the pertinent sources and emphasizes the initiation of members as reflected in the communal meal of the Essenes, the importance of purity, as well as the priestly and hierarchical organization of the community, the latter in opposition to the Therapeutes, treated only by Philo. Bilde concludes that the Qumran Essene common meal was indeed sacramental and manifested the congregation as the only legitimate expression of Jewish faith, and as a replacement of the Temple cult after the usurpation of the highpriesthood by the Hasmoneans.

Hallbäck analyzes the very important pericope, 1 Cor. 11.17-34, in which Paul goes over a number of problems concerning the communal meal and the Eucharist in the Corinthian community. According to Hallbäck, Paul does not worry about the different kinds of food taken, reflecting the social status of the Christians in Corinth as such, but admonishes them that they, by exposing their eating practices publicly, reveal a contempt for the Church of God. Instead, they ought to appear as a unity in the eyes of outsiders. Examining whether this is a question of a regulation of the meal practice or rather a promotion of the significance of the Eucharist as a religious ritual, Hallbäck argues for the latter. He concludes that "the communal meal is the context of the Eucharist and should thus be taken seriously as the Eucharist itself", and that the focus of the text shifts from treating the meal as a communal occasion to an understanding of the Lord's Supper.

Finally, White discusses the development in time of communal dining practices among early Jews and Christians in the cities of the Diaspora. The article focuses on how the communal meal regulated fellowship among these groups and how that regulation evolved. In this context, the relationship between the communal meal and the Eucharist by the Christians is treated as well. Primarily on the basis of the epigraphical and archaeological material White shows that while among Jews the communal meal preserved its social and sacred character, the Christian communal meal developed into an exclusively social and private occasion taking place outside the church buildings. As White aptly concludes his article: "The adaptation of dining practice, symbolically, ritually, and architecturally, is an important indicator of the cultural roots as well as the historic development, of the Jewish and Christian traditions". One might add that this holds true also for the pagans!

The editors wish to thank the Danish Research Council for the Humanities and the Aarhus University Research Foundation for their economic support in connection with the publication of this volume.

Salt, Fish and the Sea in the Roman Empire

Peter Ørsted

The discussion

It is almost impossible to conceive of an agrarian society which has not developed a well-defined — albeit primitive — social structure: a hierarchy tightly connected to and supported by private ownership of land, safeguarded and secured by some sort of state. Seemingly naturally, a distinction arises between those who own land and those who do not, between rich and poor, between people who are able to support themselves, and those who are not. And if a certain number do not manage to survive, so what?

Many years ago, A.R. Hands wrote a book which he somewhat provocatively called *Charities and Social Aid*.[1] These days topics of this type would be discussed under quite different headings. Even if we allow for a shift from man-to-man relations to man-to-nature relations stressing the ecological aspects and soft-pedalling the political ones, the dichotomy in the title of Hands' book is still a fundamental, maybe even an eternal one. As the Lord said to Moses (Lev. 23.22):

... and when you reap the harvest in your land, you shall not reap right into the edges of your field, neither shall you glean the fallen ears. You shall leave them for the poor, and for the alien.

But as the poor and strangers were apparently not totally abandoned by the Lord, neither were they by the Romans. In his *De officiis* (2.73) Cicero wrote of Philippus, when he introduced his agrarian bill, that ...

In his public speeches on the measure he (Philippus) often played the demagogue, ... when he said "there were not in the state two thousand people who owned any property". That speech deserves unqualified condemnation, for it favoured an equal distribution of property; and what more ruinous policy than that could be conceived? For the chief purpose in the establishment of constitutional state and municipal government was that individual property rights might be secure (Translation by Miller, *LCL*).[2]

That this point of view must create problems for people without means, Cicero clearly saw. A little later he comes up with the following comment:

> ... and it will also be the duty of those who direct the affairs of the state to take measures that there shall be an abundance of the necessities of life (Translation by Miller, LCL).[3]

Two models or attitudes, then, both existing in ancient societies, but of course not of equal importance. The Roman "city-state" intervened and provided food under different headings such as the *cenae* in Roman municipal charters,[4] the *annona* of big cities, the *congiaria*[5] of emperors and more or less privately inspired *munera*. As a matter of fact it would be difficult to find societies which have not established some sort of organized system for supplying food,[6] although insufficient compared to modern, western standards. Pure charity did exist in Jewish and later on in Christian moral behaviour, but was somehow un-Roman. Roman attitudes in this field seemed — apart from the possible social implications of the concept of *clientela*[7] — to be framed and delimited by the concept of *familia*. But excluded for one reason or another from either the private (*agri privati*) or the public (*agri publici/bona civitatium*) space, poor people were actually lost, if they were not allowed to draw on a third area, a greyzone, in between. This third area will be my concern in the following.

Roman law, the *res nullius*

Our sources for questions like this are as usual in Roman social and economic history a highly problematic blend of legal texts, philosophy, inscriptions, archaeological evidence and often strange literary texts.[8] As suggested above, I will take my starting point in the first-mentioned group of sources. Next I will try to exemplify what might have gone on in such greyzones in the Roman economy through a brief examination of the relation between access to the sea, fishing and salt-extraction. The evidence indicates implicitly a chronological limitation to early imperial times.

In the *Digest* we find not only the key notions defined, but the *Digest* also allows for some glimpse of the more important social and economic consequences. The problem, however, seems to be that these same notions to some extent overlap, which sometimes forces the lawyers to make quite unambiguous statements to avoid misunderstanding. Gaius and Marcianus do this. But first we find the overall divisions:

Hae autem res, quae humani iuris sunt, aut publicae sunt, aut privatae; quae publicae sunt, nullius in bonis esse creduntur; ipsius enim universitatis esse creduntur (Dig. 1.8.1). Again, those things that are under Roman law are either public or private. Those which are public are held to be the property of no one, and are considered to belong to the entire community (Translation by Scott, 1973).

And Marcianus continues

... *Quaedam naturali iure communia sunt omnium, quaedam universitatis, quaedam nullius, pleraque singulorum, quae variis ex causis cuique acquiruntur.* Certain things are common to all by natural law, some belong to the entire community, some to no one, and the greater number to individuals, these are acquired in various ways respectively (Translation by Scott, 1973).

... and finally the "user's handbook"

... *Et quidem naturali iure omnium communia sunt illa: aër, aqua profluens et mare, et per hoc litora maris* (Marcianus, *Dig*. 1.8.2.1).[9] Again, all the following things are common by natural law, namely the air, running water, the sea, and hence the shores of the sea (Translation by Scott, 1973).

This last piece of evidence I consider crucial, and a closer examination will — I think — prevent often repeated misunderstandings as to Roman intervention in public space. Focusing on the *jus humanum*, the law of property, the *dominium* or *possessio* is of course essential. It is what it is all about here. As stated, the *res, quae humani iuris sunt* ... are divided into *res privatae* and *res publicae*.[10] Leaving the *res privatae* out here, we are left with the *res publicae*, which as the *Digest* goes on to say, are believed to belong to nobody: they are ... *nullius res*, because — or rather when — they belong to *universitas*. I think *universitas* is here used to denote a difference between what is *publicum* according to *jus civile* (for *cives Romani* only) and what is *publicum*, i.e. *commune omnium* according to *jus gentium* and *jus naturale*.[11] No doubt *universitas* is here used in an explanatory manner and is in practice synonymous with *res communes omnium*, i.e. *res nullius*.[12] To prevent misunderstanding Marcianus goes on *expressis verbis* in order to underline precisely what are *res nullius*, namely the air, running? water, the sea and the coastline. Decisive for these distinctions seems to be the dividing line Aristotle draws between what was made by nature (*physikon*), and what was created by man (*nomikon*).[13] The above quote from the *Digest* is concerned only with the *physikon*, reflected in the double stressing of the *jus naturale*. In this context it is almost impossible to translate the Latin *universitas*. Returning, however, to Aristotle, it seems close to the Latin translation of the Greek *koinon*,[14] i.e. to the modern notion of community. Thus it is distinct from the ancient one of *civitas*, the organized body of citizens. In the first place the problem is to discern *publica* in the broad sense of "belonging" to nobody from *publica* in the more restricted meaning of "belonging" to a (specific) Roman city state and thereby — in principle — to everyone in the body of citizens.

To clarify and to advance the argument, we may sum up as follows: seen from the viewpoint of the Romans there existed in practice three categories of property:

1. We have the *bona singulorum*. They are in private ownership (*dominium e jure quiritium*) secured by the *jus civile*, which in this case is *proprium civium romanorum* — valid only for Roman citizens.[15] In principle, however, it will be the same in any other city-state in the Roman empire, according to its specific system of law.
2. We have the *bona civitatis*. These things are owned by the city-state in common. They are defined as *publica* or *communia* according to *jus civile*, i.e. for the body of citizens. They are *in dominio populi Romani*, which means that everybody has an *usus publicus*. Due to her *dominium*, the city-state (e.g. Rome) derives her income from these *publica*[16] when used, primarily of course from the *agri publici*, from land use. Seen from Rome, private persons cannot personally have *dominium*, only *possessio*, so consequently — in the case of public land — a tax, *vectigal*, was payable for the right to till it.[17] That is, of course, crucial to my whole argument: collection of *vectigal* proves indirectly *publica* understood as *bona civitatis*.
3. Without using strict terminology one might call this third category *bona naturae*, the property of nature, common then by definition to all men. They are regarded as *nullius res*, albeit they somewhat confusingly are *publica*. But here it means that everyone has free access to these areas, to enjoy *ususfructus* justified by a basic *naturalis ratio*, codified and underlined in Roman law. This *naturalis ratio* has coloured Roman law in certain restricted areas. It comprises all human beings, whatever their personal status, i.e. not *cives romani* only, but *peregrini* as well.[18] Seen from this point of view, the *res nullius* comprises that part of nature, including the resources to be found there, i.e. fish, salt, birds, to which the Romans *a priori* did not extend the concept of *dominium*. You might call it a residual category of space. It was no doubt a problem that these *res nullius* were physically located inside the Roman Empire. Consequently they had to be separated clearly not only from the *bona civitatum*, but also from the *agri publici/provinciales* of Rome, from *agri exempti* (e.g. mining-areas) and from privately owned property.

The classification and registration of these different categories of land were a constant preoccupation of hundreds of *agrimensores* and have caused thousands of *cippi* and inscriptions to be found all over the empire. The reason for these huge efforts was of course that this cadastration was decisive for Roman financial administration. The exact location of the different types of land was closely connected with the collecting of *vectigalia*,[19] the income of the Roman people, the *nervi rei publicae*, as Cicero termed it.[20] All this is summed up in the famous statement of Ulpian:

> ... *Inter publica habemus non sacra, nec religiosa, nec quae publicis usibus destinata sunt, sed si qua sunt civitatium velut bona ... Publica vectigalia intellegere debemus, ex quibus vectigal fiscus capit; quale est vectigal portus, vel venalium rerum, item salinarum et metallorum et pi(s?)cariarum*[21] (*Dig.* 50.16.17). We include among public property not only such as is sacred and religious, and intended for the use of the people ... We must understand public taxes to mean those which the Treasury levies on certain articles, among which are the tax on merchandise in a harbor, or goods which are sold, as well as those on saltpits, mines, and (places where pitch is produced ?) (Translation by Scott, 1973).

This quote must be the next logical step, reflecting indirectly the problems discussed above. In the Roman Empire revenue was collected through a public leasing system, the *locatio publicorum*, as stated and discussed elsewhere.[22] But why does this listing seemingly comprise *vectigalia*, which according to the *jus naturale* ought to be *nullius res* and thereby free?[23]

I will end this part of my paper with a quote from Gaius, who indirectly reflects my point of view, stressing at the same time the core of the problem. Writing on how to acquire private ownership (*dominium*) of certain *res*, he makes the following statements:

> ... *Quarundam rerum dominium nanciscimur iure gentium, quod ratione naturali inter omnes homines peraeque servatur, quarundam iure civili, id est iure proprio civitatis nostrae. et quia antiquius ius gentium cum ipso genere humano proditum est, opus est, ut de hoc prius referendum sit. Omnia igitur animalia, quae terra mari caelo capiuntur, id est ferae bestiae et volucres [et] pisces, capientium fiunt* ... (We) obtain the ownership of certain property by the Law of Nations which is everywhere observed among men, according to the dictates of natural reason; and we obtain the ownership of other things by the Civil Law, that is to say, by the law of our own "country". And because the Law of the Nations is the more ancient, as it is promulgated at the time of the origin of the human race, it is proper that it should be examined first. Therefore, all animals which are captured on land, on sea, or in the air, that is to say, wild beasts and birds, as well as fish, become the property of those who take them (Translation by Scott, 1973).

and a little later the central quote:

> ... *Quod enim nullius est, id ratione naturali occupanti conceditur* ... (*Dig.* 41.1.1-3).[24] For what does not belong to anyone, by natural law becomes the property of the person who first acquires it (Translation by Scott, 1973).

Now, is the free access to this space to be understood as part of an ancient social aid-scheme? Can we imagine a deliberate substitute for public intervention and thereby perhaps even a means whereby poor people could survive? If really so, how did that work in practice?

The sea, fish and salt. The epigraphical evidence

The sea

The physical link between the sea, fish and salt is the *litus*, the beach. The *litus* is considered a part of the sea,[25] which not only means that you can have what you find there, for example pearls, but also that you can fish from the beach and use it for different purposes typically associated with fishing.[26] As far as the sea might extend — and this would probably have taken account of the tides — the *litus* is *publicum* in the sense of *nullius res*, which allows for building small houses, construction of *moles*, piers from the beach into the sea, small huts (*casae*) for shelter, and the drying of nets. It is worth noting here, however, that the jurists distinguish between the sea and rivers. The *flumina* and the ports are *publica* in the sense of *bona civitatum*. The same is the case with certain lakes, *lacus* and *stagna*.[27] Albeit access here is free and a *usus publicus* is possible, you have, according to this status to pay a *vectigal*. The difference can be explained through the different notions of *usus* and *ususfructus*. For fishing the rivers then, you might pay *piscaria(?)*, for using the harbours, a *portus/portorium* such as we were told by Ulpianus above.[28] Consequently we here find the public lease system at work and with it the *publicani*. The reason for that, I think, is that the rivers and lakes have their origin in the land, not in the sea. The harbours[29] are considered *loci publici*, public installations.[30]

Free access to the sea and its resources did not mean that it was uncontrolled or rather unsupervised. The coastline of the empire was of course sub *imperio populi romani*[31] and the Roman authorities had to keep order and see to that no one was bothered. Moreover, where the *litus* stopped, private land — either genuine *agri privati* or leased *ager provincialis* — began,[32] and the provincial governors or the different *praefecti/procuratores orae* or *ripae*[33] had to maintain law and order. Most parts of the quotations in the notes are about protecting landowners close to the sea or securing free fishing. There existed accordingly an *actio*, which quite logically was not about *res*, that is ownership of the different sorts of catch, but *de injuria*. You are able to sue persons who in one way or another have done something, which might disturb (*nocere*) you. This *actio* is to the Roman lawyers the same as that open to people who are bothered by noisy behaviour in the city area, in the public baths, theatres, etc.[34] So, to sum up, there existed a free "*jus piscandi*" in the sea including a free *ususfructus* as well as a free *usus*. On rivers and lakes, we find an *usus publicus*, but this *usus* is limited to transport and does not include a free *ususfructus*.[35]

Fishing

It is obvious to direct our attention towards three very common types of installations: the installations for salting and processing of fish and those for extraction of salt from the sea, the *salinae*. This scenario is often in its entirety labelled an "industry" and discussed under the heading of *garum* or fish sauce.[36]

I will start in the negative. As support for the *communis opinio*, that fishing was a monopoly of the state, it is worth noting that there exists one inscription on that subject — and one only — from the western part of the Empire. All the rest is from the eastern part of the Empire. This fact gives some methodological problems. Apparently, the general attitude to the sea was the same in Greece as in Rome. Plato closes his chapter on hunting, fowling and fishing with the following conclusion:

... The fowler no man shall hinder on fallow land or mountain; but he that finds him on tilled fields or on scared glebes shall drive him off. The fisherman shall be allowed to hunt in all waters except havens and sacred rivers and pools and lakes ... (Translation by Bury, LCL).

In the wording of the *Institutiones* the same distinction is expressed in this way:

flumina autem omnia et portus publica sunt. Ideoque ius piscandi omnibus commune est in portubus fluminibusque.[37] All rivers and ports are also public, and therefore the right of fishing in a harbor or in streams is common to all (Translation by Scott, 1973).

With considerable care, then, it is possible to deduce that neither in Greece nor in Rome did fishing in rivers and harbours (and public lakes) entail direct ownership of the catch. The same attitude is expressed in two different ways, but the result seems to be the same: the payment of a fee. We are informed about the collection of fees in that respect, for example in the grand inscription found in Histria[38] on the Black Sea. Without going into detail, it seems quite clear that fish(ing) is subject to a fee, but it is as clear in the context that it is to be related to the collection of *portorium*. It is worth stressing this point, because part of the remaining evidence from the east actually seems to relate either to rivers or lakes, which in this case are all the property of temples, cities or the Roman state. Consequently we find *publicani* or leaseholders involved.[39] Apparently they were constantly trying to usurp *vectigalia* from Asiatic land or lakes/rivers. As a consequence most of our information stems from complaints concerning these *publicani*, often — it is worth noting — *conductores publici portorii*.[40] In two cases, however, that of Kyzikos[41] and of Byzantium,[42] there seems to be a clear relation to fishing the sea *(mare)* and not a *portus, lacus* or *flumina*. Here we meet an *arkon*, in Latin a *manceps* or *publicanus*. This must refer to either Roman state property — or better here — city-state property, leasing and tax (a *synergasia* was formed for the collection), but a collection for/to whom? As these are the only examples, the explanation might lie in the fact that Kyzikos — here in the first century BC according to the dating of the inscription — was a *civitas foederata*, i.e. a free city governed by its own laws and with its own financial administration.[43] The other case, that of Byzantium, rests solely on the description of Strabo,[44] and it is not possible to deduce precisely what the situation was. The explanation, however, might be exactly the same as in the case of Kyzikos. On the other hand, it is clear from Strabo that Byzantium sells her fishing-rights i.e. that fishing the open sea as a matter of fact was a monopoly of this city state. In that case the explanation might be that the city owned the installation at the seashore (towers for watching the tunny) and the quite expensive fixed nets and piers installed on the bottom of the sea (close to the shore). According to the reconstruction in Dumont,[45] these installations for the *madrague* were substantial and no doubt expensive and might have involved some sort of ownership of the seabed.

Seen in this perspective, this evidence rather corroborates — than the opposite — that Roman law is respected. Fishing in lakes and rivers is regulated,[46] not fishing from the beach, i.e. in *mare* except where fishing rights might have been transferred to a given city-state according — presumably — to old traditional rights or special privileges as we often find in the eastern part of the empire.[47] It might be what is mirrored in the rather enigmatic quotation from the *Digest*, where we read that the sea *(mare)* in some cases might be *proprium*, that is regarded as private property.[48] The methodological problem, however, remains. Caused by lack of clearcut positive evidence, it is possible to argue for either 1) free status (and privilege) of the city-state in question, 2) *publica* in the sense of *bona civitatis*, or 3) the fee collected is not a *vectigal* proving *dominium* but a *portorium*, as seems to be the case, for example, with purple-snails landed in the harbours of Asia[49] and in the inscription from Histria.[50]

The highlight, however, in the argumentation for Roman intervention and taxation of fishing comes from the western part of the Empire. It is an inscription found in Beetgum, in the marshy area of northern Holland.[51] It runs:

Deae Hludanae/ conductores /piscatus mancipe/ Q(uinto) Valerio secu/ndo v(otum) s(olverunt) l(ibentes) m(erito), to be rendered: The sub-leaseholders of fishing with Quintus Valerius Secundus as their chief-leaseholder *(manceps)* happily redeemed their promise to Dea Hludana (Translation by Scott, 1973).

This inscription, which dates from the second century AD, was found just west of Leeuwarden in the Frisian area, that is in barbarian territory. By chance, we seem to know this same Valerius from an inscription found in Bonn,[52] and the only plausible explanation I am able to find is that Quintus Valerius Secundus has taken a lease from the Roman state, such as the notion of *manceps* indicates, in order to supply the Roman army and/or administration on the Lower Rhine with fish. So what Valerius leased was in this case an *ultro tributum* — a delivery — and not a *vectigal*. To organize that he has made, what is quite normal, a sub-lease according to private law with some Frisians(?) no doubt *peregrini*, fishermen. The correct terminology for that is a *locatio-conductio*, which makes the sub-leasers *conductores*, not *mancipes*. Probably we have to imagine that the fish was salted or might even have been further processed into some sort of local *garum*.

In this interpretation one avoids the *crux* of arguing for *vectigalia*-collection in barbarian territory and thereby indirectly at the same time for some sort of a *vectigal piscatus*, which — as I have tried to demonstrate above — should be contrary to Roman law — if fished in *mare* and not in *flumina publica*. I must conclude that the epigraphical evidence cannot positively support the prevailing opinion in this field.[53]

If we return to the *Digest* and the seemingly positive evidence there, we have two quotations only, both establishing a link between *publicani* and *salinae*. The problem then, seems to be the same as above, still assuming that salt is extracted from the (free) sea. But if so, what then, are the *publicani* doing here? Salt is undeniably a product of the sea, as is fish, and the *salinae* seem to be placed for natural reasons on *litus*, i.e. as far as the sea (tide) will come. Gaius, however, informs us quite clearly that

> ... *et hi, qui salinas et cretifodinas et metalla habent, publicanorum loco sunt*,[54] ... they are also included under the term farmers of the revenue who lease the income from salt pits, quarries, and mines belonging to the State (Translation by Scott, 1973),

and Ulpianus — as quoted above — has the same message, namely that *salinae* as well as *metalla* are *vectigalia publica*. So twice we find *salinae* listed as a *publicum* leased to *publicani*, who moreover in exactly this same field are allowed to form *societates* or *collegia* ... *vectigalium publicorum sociis permissum est corpus habere, vel aurifodinarum vel argentifodinarum et salinarum.*[55] *Metalla* are here more closely defined, but still we find *salinae* included.

To explain this contradiction, I think it is important from the very outset to distinguish between two different ways of obtaining salt: from the sea on the one hand and from the land, i.e. from mining, on the other. The

Romans themselves, I think, made this distinction,[56] but the confusion stems from using the same word for both sources, namely *salinae*.[57] I think it quite simply has been overlooked that all mention in the *Digest* of *salinae* comes up in connection with mining. Crystalline salt then, as we have it for example in the Hallstatt area,[58] is a *vectigal publicum* in the same sense as the production of iron, gold, silver and marble. The working of inland *salinae* is land use and not — so to speak — fishing.

In support of this view it is worth noting that we know of only three *conductores salinarum*, which are all listed as inland, in Roman Dacia.[59] No *conductor* from the hundreds of *salinae* on the coastline of the Roman Empire is attested — surprisingly, although an *argumentum e silentio*. What we do have, however, are different designations of persons, who in one way or another are associated with the extraction of salt. In the broad narrative of Livy[60] we learn that the *institutor* of a *vectigal* on salt received the *cognomen salinator*, and later on we meet those *salinatores* in a different context. But no doubt it is difficult — if not impossible — to draw secure conclusions from the technical terminology involved. Often it is heavily abbreviated, but as far as I can see we are not able to relate any of these persons who actually seem to be associated with salt in one way or another to the collection of a *vectigal* on the *salinae* themselves. Clearly, a *salinator* cannot be a *conductor* or *manceps salinarum*, and all other designations are almost exclusively associated with trade in salt or salted products.[61]

Garum

For several and obvious reasons fish, salt and *garum* production has to be understood as a whole, as a production where all the factors are closely interrelated. The locations of the so-called *garum* factories or salteries stress this point; for example the two most famous ones, the site at Troia[62] and that at Lixus.[63] It is quite clear that we do not have a single, large industrial complex before us. Each site is a composite of perhaps hundreds of small units. Travellers tell us that the *garum*-installations at the peninsula of Troia extended for at least some three kilometers along the coastline as late as a few hundred years ago.[64] We find the same pattern in the coast of North Africa,[65] southern Spain, Portugal,[66] along the coast of Brittany and Normandy in France[67] and even further to the north in present-day Belgium.[68] The vats so typical for the salting seem to be everywhere, exactly as is the case with the *salinae*, even though the extraction of salt north of Bordeaux had to rely on the use of fire as well,[69] which demands another technique and thereby gives other types of remains. When one takes the inland salt deposits into consideration it is apparent that salt was abundant throughout the Empire.[70]

There is one problem, however. The vats used for the manufacture of *garum* are never to be found on the *litus* itself. The reason for that is the obvious one that the *litus* — by definition — must be regularly inundated in stormy weather or by the tide. The legal status of the *garum*-installations must then be another. This fact may lead to another conclusion as well, namely that even though salt-extraction and fishing might be carried out by the same persons, the owners of the *garum*-installations were probably quite different people. The installations, and in some cases the houses, and even baths around them — often with mosaic floors — were certainly not *casae* analogous to those of the fishermen.[71] The *garum*-installations are placed as close as possible to the *litus*, but on privately owned land such as several times is to be deduced from the *Digest*.[72] Edmondson suggests that the *garum*-installations are to be seen in relation to the *praedia* and *villae* further inland.[73] It is interesting in this connection to note that in medieval times the monasteries close to the coast in Southern France owned the *salinae*, and as Benoît has showed, there actually seems to be a connection between the grand *villae* of late Antiquity and the monasteries of early medieval times.[74] If so, the owners or the bailiffs of these small units are not to be included directly in that group of persons which is my concern here. They are either landowners or to be attached to the households of such landowners. These problems, however, raise the question of the interrelation in the production itself between fishermen, salt-extractors, the salteries, trade and consumption.

The organization of production

The production of *garum* has its own inner and almost natural logic. At least 4 stages are to be defined separately:

1st stage:
As reflected in the almost poetic descriptions by both Oppianos[75] and Manilius,[76] we find common fishermen all over the Empire living in some sort of a subsistence economy. The term seems to be *piscatores*.[77] They might extract some salt in a rather primitive way, just to cover their own needs. The fish does not leave the coastal area and the production consequently brings no money into circulation through sales. As a matter of fact, we are dealing with an *oikos*-economy in the sense of Bücher/Weber.

2nd stage:
The catch produces a surplus, which demands a more organized salting. Some sort of collaboration is needed both among the fishermen, especially

if the catch is tunny, where fixed nets etc., are used, the madrague (F), tonnara (I), almadraba (Sp), armacao (Por).[78] Now both *salinae* and *cetariae* are involved,[79] but the terminology here is unfortunately vague. They formed *collegia*, about which we know quite a lot for the eastern part of the Empire[80] and some for the Western parts.[81]

Two much discussed inscriptions are relevant for a possible procedure on this level. They are both found in Rimini. Here we meet some *salinatores* from the *civitates* of the Menapii and the Morini, who honour a certain Lucius Lepidius Proculus, a native of Rimini. He has served as a *centurio* in the legions on the Rhine in the second half of the first century AD.[82] I think we in principle find the same relationship here as in the inscription from Beetgum. The difference lies in the organization only. As a *centurio*, Lepidius was in charge of supplying the Roman army and had contracted for salt/salted fish (or meat) with the Gallic *salinatores*. They were, then independent, free men, who must have occupied the land close to the *litus* of the Atlantic.[83] As an army officer, Proculus cannot have been a *manceps*, but an *emptor*.[84] Consequently the *salinatores* are not *conductores* but *venditores*. We then face an *emptio-venditio* and not a *locatio-conductio*. The use of *salinatores* cannot, then, be a direct terminological parallel to the Republican *salinatores aerarii*, who in my opinion — as suggested above — purchased the salt on behalf of the state and organized its sale plus the collection of a *vectigal* on that same sale.

On the other hand the similarity seems obvious. The Gallic *salinatores* must have been independent, free persons with *dominium* to their salt/salted fish. So again we have an *ultro tributum* (seen from the viewpoint of Proculus/the Roman state) and not a *vectigal*. The *salinatores* acquired (purchased) their fish from the local fishermen or did the fishing themselves. Anyhow, they had to organize their installations for salting (the vats) where the sea could not reach them, so they must have been able to occupy the land lying between the *litus* and the centuriated (and taxed) hinterland, the *subseciva*.[85] Without having almost any positive evidence,[86] the *salinatores* we know from imperial times seem only to have covered the last one of the two first stages, that is the processing of the fish and — probably out of season — meat (the famous Gallic ham)[87] as well. In that case they had to buy the fish one way or another. The *Digest*[88] offers an interesting clue here: You could lease a *jactum retis*, a throw with the net from a *piscator*. This means that the *piscator* owned the nets.[89] As far as I can see the *conductores* from Beetgum explicitly defined as *piscatus* fit perfectly into this quotation. Valerius contracted for fresh fish, Proculus for salted fish. The structure of production, however is the same. We encounter two separate stages: fishing and salting, and neither of them seem to entail the collection of a *vectigal*.

3rd stage:
We have met two types of purchasers up till now, both linking a coastal economy to Roman Imperial administration and the army. But trade in a wider sense apparently took place on a large scale, as described and analysed by both Edmondson and Curtis. From the same area as discussed above, we find several *negotiatores salarii* attested to in the monuments recovered from the Schelde estuary at Colijnplaat in 1970.[90] They represent the third possibility, private trade with *salaria*, salted meat and fish and not, I am convinced, necessarily with salt only. Finds from the vats of the *garum-*installations show that it was not only fish that were salted.[91] Unfortunately, it is not possible to say where most of the *negotiatores* and shippers documented in the Schelde estuary came from, nor where they went. *Origo* in cities like Cologne and Trier does not explain trade routes satisfactorily, and especially discussing the trade in salt — or rather here — *salaria* — it is hard to imagine a genuine Britannic market, and the same process reversed is even harder to imagine. I still think that the key to the understanding of the trade and transportation pattern in and around Colijnsplaat and Domburg is to be found in the upper reaches of the rivers from the Garonne to the Rhine and along the Atlantic coastline. The often repeated formula ... *ob merces conservatas* ...[92] must mean that at least some of the items traded were landed there or transported there from the hinterland. The *nautae* from Fectio[93] (although the Rhine) and the many Celtic names in the inscriptions from the Schelde area suggest in my opinion a much more sophisticated pattern than usually described. Still, I think the Romans and the Roman legions on the Rhine were the prime movers.

I am convinced that the scale of production was decisive for the way in which the actual production took shape. To the north it is difficult to imagine how the producers of salted fish obtained enough salt to match the abundance of fish — and meet the demand. I have suggested that it might be this which can explain the *negotiatores salarii* in the Schelde estuary. That, of course, does not exclude low-scale local salt extraction, corresponding to my 1st stage. Production, however, which took place to the south, especially in present-day Spain and Portugal, appears to have been on a grand scale, an industry-like production, organized from the top of a hierarchy. We have no *negotiatores*, who are likely to have headed the production itself, but we do find the *socii*, who apparently organized the *garum-*production in Cartagena,[94] and we have already envisaged other *socii*, albeit only a few.[95] If I dare use the label "industry", the *socii* from Cartagena may be taken as an example of building up a structure from which the participant at least in my first and second stage must have profited. But a *societas* like that cannot possibly have been a *societas vectigalium*. *Garum sociorum* must mean that the *garum* belonged to the *societas* and was sold by them either to consumers or to *mercatores* or *negotiatores*. No such thing as *gari vectigal* ever existed. So where we actually meet *socii*, they might somewhat confusingly point to 1) public ownership in a city-state, especially in the east 2) to Roman state ownership such as for example the inland *salinae* (mining) in Dacia, or 3) purely private enterprises. To choose between these three possibilities is often very difficult and is in fact a question of how far you dare push your argument. What the Cartagena *socii* had in common was the production of *garum*, that is some sort of collaboration between several minor salteries. Without any evidence, it is difficult to say whether they had occupied the *salinae* and through ownership of the costly nets and installations for the madrague controlled the fishing as well. By analogy, however, to more recent times, they probably did.[96] A private enterprise, then, which brings them closer to the *salinatores* in Gaul than to the *salinatores* of Minturnae.

Conclusion

If I am right in interpreting the sources in this way, two key areas were laid open to total private enterprise: fish and salt from the sea, in addition to fowling and some hunting, not discussed here. If you lived by the sea then, you could draw on these resources freely for yourself and for your family. You were offered a free — so to speak — social dinner by the state, but you had either to cook it yourself or sell it. These rather poor people did not leave many traces, but at least at the level just above subsistence economy, the system must have brought some money into circulation in the marginal areas between the cities, along the sea and the cultivated hinterland of the coastline. As discussed, this might have happened in several ways in proportion to the potential of the coastline and the market. According to level, the production became more and more sophisticated and specialized, including *piscatores, salinatores, negotiatores* and even *socii*. No doubt there existed a huge market, and it is not to be forgotten that the, as I would imagine, relatively poor *salinatores* from Gaul became rich enough to celebrate their benefactor in two costly inscriptions in far away Rimini. But certainly most fish was caught and processed close to urban centres and was sold on the nearby market. We know that fresh fish does not remain fresh long, which was certainly reflected in the prices.[97] The same procedure was possible, where you were able to go upstream by boat to urban centres. The inscriptions concerning that sort of trade stem solely, however, from the rivers of Baetis and the Tiber.[98]

Compared to the situation of poor people living inland, the sea and beach seem after all to offer considerably better prospects. Inland you were left with wild animals and birds. You might even be forced to go to Rome or other cities and to rely on the emperor and the *annona*. Seen in this perspective the *annona* and *congiaria* of the cities had the same function for the poor city-dwellers as had the sea, coast and sky for the poor living in the countryside.

To sum up, I have tried in this paper to discuss two different, but interconnected items, both to show the concern for the livelihood of poor people in the Roman Empire. Certain resources were left free and excluded from Roman taxation and management. Whether this was rooted in some *naturalis ratio*, which the Romans did not consider very much, or whether it was a deliberate policy intended to keep poor people alive, is not to be decided here. Taking the sources into consideration it might not be possible to decide at all. Personally, I think this concern was within the frame of antique thinking and culture, but even so, it did not originate in some sort of social consciousness, but was rather a reminiscence of a society and a way of life which preceded the agrarian one.

Notes

1. Hands 1967.
2. Cic. *Off.* 2.73 ... *sed cum in agendo multa populariter, tum illud male, "non esse in civitate duo milia hominum, qui rem haberent". Capitalis oratio est, ad aequationum bonorum pertinens; qua peste quae potest esse maior? Hanc enim ob causam maxime, ut sua tenerentur, res publicae civitatesque constitutae sunt.*
3. Cic. *Off.* 2.74 ... *Atque etiam omnes, qui rem publicam gubernabunt, consulere debebunt, ut earum rerum copia sit, quae sunt necessariae.*
4. E.g. *Lex Irnitana*, LXXVII.
5. Quite substantial amounts, see Duncan-Jones 1994, 248ff. with references.
6. E.g. Rickman 1980.
7. E.g. dinners in the houses of rich *patroni* or the like, see e.g. Juv. 5 passim.
8. Discussed in general by Curtis 1991, passim, but especially 6ff, 191ff; Edmondson 1987, 270-73 has collected the most important evidence. Ponsich and Tarradell 1965 primarily stress the archaeological evidence (i.e. the *garum* factories); Bohlen 1937, 55f. See also Martin-Kilcher 1990.
9. Neither *aqua profluens* nor *aër* will be discussed here. I consider *aqua profluens* distinct from *flumen*, i.e. as rainwater, which you can catch in cisterns for different purposes (for drinking/irrigation, etc.)
10. See Kaser 1972, esp. vol. 1, 376ff, 425ff.
11. Jolowitz & Nicholas 1972 do not allow for any significant difference between *jus gentium* and *jus naturale* in this respect, 35 and 102-77. "Res communium omnium ist nichts als eine confuse Bezeichnung derjenigen *res publicae*, deren Occupation von rechts wegen jedem frei steht", is the opinion of Mommsen published by Zangemeister 1889, 223, no. 127. Kaser 1972, 381, no. 59 ... *Res universitatis* ist untechnisch Gebrauch ... (= *ad Dig.* 1.8.2, *praef.*)
12. See Kaser 1972, 380 "... Das Meer und seine Ufer sind *publica*. Die noch flüssige Terminilogie der Klassiker versteht darunter hier nicht die Staatseigentum,

13. sondern einen vom *Jus gentium* anerkannten Gemeingebrauch an Sachen die selbst herrenlos sind ..." See also Bohlen 1937, 44-51, Curtis 1991, 149ff, Edmondson 1987, 117. The best discussion is as a matter of fact that in Zangemeister 1889, n. 11.
13. Arist. *Eth. Nic.* 5.7.1. See in general Jolowitz & Nicholas 1972, 102-7. See also the interesting quotation: Plato, *Leg.* 823 and Stöckle 1924.
14. Arist. *Rh.* 1.13.2
15. The implication is probably that no one but Roman citizens can enter a public (state) lease, see Ørsted 1985, 157ff.
16. It seems that *communia* are foremost used in relation to *municipia*, and *publica* directly to Roman state-property (or *coloniae civium Romanorum*) *Dig.* 18.1.6, *praef.*, and 41.1.14, *praef.*, 50.16.15. For a discussion and references, see Ørsted 1985, 73, n. 41 and 98, Kaser 1972, 304.
17. See Ørsted 1994, 115-27.
18. For that same reason we find these conceptions and the problems related to them reflected in the *jus gentium*, which has the same relation to the *jus civile* as has the *jus naturale*. Therefore the Roman jurists are forced to be quite explicit in defining precisely what is public for all people and what is public for citizens only, because the terminology will here often be identical. Cic. *Off.* 3.69. Jolowitz & Nicholas 1972, 103f.
19. The general opinion is that the Romans obtained huge income from, for example, fishing. See e.g. Kaser 1972, 381, Curtis 1991, 150. Basic for Bohlen 1937, but in quite another sense. He stresses the indirect revenues stemming from *portorium*, etc., 62f.
20. Cic. *De imp. Cn. Pomp.* 8.17 ... *vectigalia nervos esse rei publicae semper duximus.*
21. The reading *piscariarum* must — if upheld — be interpreted as income from fishing, i.e. some sort of a *vectigal piscatus* (otherwise not attested), if seen from the viewpoint of the Roman state (I exclude here the evidence from fully independent city-states). If so, it must stem from the leasing of fishing rights in *flumina* or *lacus/stagna* (see later), which all are *publica* in the sense *bona civitatium*. The most likely reading, however, is *picariarum*, which gets support from Cic. *Brut.* 22.85-86: *liberi societatis eius, quae picarias de p. Cornelio L. Mummio censoribus redemisset ...*, and *AE* 1934.254: ... *pic(ariorum) soc(iorum) s(ervus)* ... See Johnson 1935, 126. See furthermore Cimma 1981, 22.
22. For a discussion and the relevant evidence, see Ørsted 1985, esp. 61-171.
23. So both fishing and salt extraction are considered monopolies of the state, a point of view which as a matter of fact underlies all analysis, see for example Hirschfeld 1905, 150, Benoît 1959, 95, Will 1962, 1651, Jones & Mattingly 1990, 224f.
24. This is repeated several times: *Dominiumque rerum ex naturali possessione coepisse Nerva filius ait, eiusque rei vestigium remanere in his quae terra, mari caeloque capiuntur; nam haec protinus eorum fiunt, qui primi possessionem eorum adprehenderint. Item bello capta, et insula in mari enata, et gemmae, lapilli, margaritae in litoribus inventae eius fiunt, qui primus eorum possessionem nanctus est* (*Dig.* 41.2.1, *praef.*). And: ... *Et quidem mare commune omnium est, et litora, sicuti aër, et est saepissime rescriptum, non posse quem piscari prohiberi; sed nec aucupari* (*Dig.* 47.10.13.7). *CIL* 14.4328 from Ostia has a ... *conductor aucupiorum* ... Compared with *Dig.* 7.1.9.5 and

47.10.13.7. I believe that this *sacerdos Liberi*, P. Luscius Bergilianus has leased fowling on private, i.e. temple land. It is not, then, a *vectigal publicum*.

25. *Litus publicum est eatenus, qua maxime fluctus exaestuat; idemque iuris est in lacu, nisi is totus privatus est* (*Dig.* 50.16.112). And: *Litus est, quousque maximus fluctus a mari pervenit; idque Marcum Tullium aiunt, quum arbiter esset, primum constituisse* (*Dig.* 50.16.96); Just. *Inst.* 2.1.1-7.

26. *Praetor ait: quo minus illi in flumine publico navem, ratem agere, quove minus per ripam onerare, exonerare liceat, vim fieri veto. Item ut per lacum, fossam, stagnum publicum navigare liceat, interdicam.* §.1. *Hoc interdicto prospicitur, ne quis flumine publico navigare prohibeatur; sicuti enim ei, qui via publica uti prohibeatur, interdictum supra propositum est, ita hoc quoque proponendum Praetor putavit* ... 7. *Publicano plane, qui lacum vel stagnum conduxit, si piscari prohibeatur, utile interdictum competere, Sabinus consentit; et ita Labeo. Ergo et si a municipibus conductum habeat, aequissimum erit, ob vectigalis favorem interdicto eum tueri* (*Dig.* 43.14.1-7). And: *Item lapilli, gemmae, ceteraque, quae in litore invenimus, iure naturali nostra statim fiunt ... Nemo igitur ad litus maris accedere prohibetur piscandi causa, dum tamen villis, et aedificiis, et monumentis abstineatur, quia non sunt iuris gentium, sicut et mare; idque et Divus Pius piscatoribus Formianis et Capenatis rescripsit.* §.1. *Sed flumina paene omnia et portus publica sunt* (*Dig.* 1.8.3-4).

27. See note 26 and Servius (Verg. *G.* 2.161): *Lacus ... Lucrinus et Avernus, qui olim propter copiam piscium vectigalia magna praestabant*, Festus, 121: *Lacus Lucrinus in vectigalibus publicis primus locatur*, *CIL* 6.9854, Strabo 4.188, Cic. *Leg. Agr.* 2.40, *Dig.* 43.14.1, praef, *Dig.* 43.14.1.7: *Publicano plane, qui lacum vel stagnum conduxit ...* but some lakes might be private, *Dig.* 50.15.4.6. See Bohlen 1937, 44-46. ... *flumina autem omnia et portus publica sunt: ideoque ius piscandi omnibus commune est in portubus fluminibusque* (*Inst.Iust.* 2.1.2).

28. *Publica vectigalia ... quale est vectigal portus, vel venalium rerum, item salinarum et metallorum et pi(s)cariarum* (*Dig.* 50.16.16-17).

29. One can imagine a fee for using the harbour (*scapharii* etc., see below) one for *portorium* (import/export) and one for fishing. Juvenal mentions a *conductor portus* and a *conductor fluminis* (Juv. 3.30ff). The famous mosaic from Toledo (see *Hispania Antiqua. Denkmäler der Römerzeit*, Trillmich 1993, 242, with illustrations) shows fishing (of tunny?) in a habour, a procedure which some years ago could still be seen. The tunny is chased into the bassin. This way of using the habour might have been easy to control and it might have been the job of a *conductor portus* (or *portuum*) to control that, among other things, and to collect a fee. See again *Inst.Iust.* 2.1.2. That was perhaps the task of the *promagister portuum* in Sicily (*CIL* 3.6065) perhaps assisted by a *vilicus portus* (*AE* 1989, 341), even though it is difficult (and open to dispute) whether *portus* and *portorium* are used synonymously or not. See Carlsen 1995, 48. That might be the case for Pompeius Potens, the ... *conductor portus Lirensis* ... although a problematic interpretation. See Nesselhauf 1937, 161 and Johnson 1935, 127. This will have been contrary, then, to a rather unorganized fishing from the *ripae* of hundreds of rivers, where collection of a *vectigal* might be justified and legitimate, but was seemingly never carried out.

30. See n. 27 and *Dig.* 1.8.4-6: ... *Riparum usus publicus est iure gentium, sicut ipsius fluminis. Itaque navem ad eas appellere, funes ex arboribus ibi natis religare, retia sic-*

care et ex mari reducere, onus aliquid in his reponere cuilibet liberum est, sicuti per ipsum flumen navigare. Sed proprietas illorum est, quorum praediis haerent; qua de causa arbores quoque in his natae eorumdem sunt. §.1. In mari piscantibus liberum est casam in litore ponere, in qua se recipiant ... Flumina paene omnia et portus publica sunt.

31. Dig. 43.8.3, praef. *Litora in quae populus Romanus imperium habet esse arbitror. 1. Maris communem usum omnibus hominibus, ut aeris ...* etc.
32. The dividing line will often coincide with the limit of the grid of centuriation. I imagine — if centuriated at all — that these areas had a status akin to that of the *subseciva* or the *agri occupatorii*, i.e. a regulated *jus occupandi* was allowed. See Ørsted 1985, n. 17. To be parallelled — although in another context — with CIL 2.2242 (from la Sierra de Cordoba) where ... *L Valerius Kapito alvari locum occupavit*.
33. For a listing of these *praefecti*, see Saddington 1988, 299-313. For *procuratores* who might have had a task like that, see for example AE 1988.664. Also n. 96.
34. *Quamvis quod in litore publico vel in mari exstruxerimus nostrum fiat, tamen decretum Praetoris adhibendum est ut id facere liceat; immo etiam manu prohibendus est, ut id facere liceat; imo etiam manu prohibendus est, si cum incommodo ceterorum id faciat; nam civilem eum actionem de faciendo nullam habere non dubito* (Dig. 41.1.50, praef.) This is repeated more explicitly: *Adversus eum, qui molem in mare proiecit, interdictum utile competit ei, cui forte haec res nocitura sit; si autem nemo damnum sentit, tuendus est is, qui in litore aedificat, vel molem in mare iacit. §.9. Si quis in mari piscari, aut navigare prohibeatur, non habebit interdictum, quemadmodum nec is, qui in campo publico ludere, vel in publico balneo lavare, aut in theatro spectare arceatur; sed in omnibus his casibus iniuriarum actione utendum est* (Dig. 43.8.8-9).
35. Dig. 7.1.9.5: *Aucupiorum quoque et venationum reditum Cassius ait libro octavo Iuris civilis ad fructuarium pertinere; ergo et piscationum*, Dig. 43.7, Dig. 43.8, Dig. 43.14.1.7. For *usus* and *usufructus*, see Kaser 1972, esp. 447-55.
36. See in general Curtis 1991, especially 38-148, Edmondson 1987, 100-52, Ponsich & Tarradell 1965, especially 93ff, Traina 1992, 363-79, Alarcao 1988, 87ff.
37. See Dumont 1977, 53-7, and Dumont 1976-77, 96-120. For a listing of the evidence, see Höppener 1931, 150ff. See also Stöckle 1924, col. 458, Plato, *Leg.* 7.824C, *Inst.Iust.* 2.1.2.
38. AE 1919.10, Strabo 7.6.2, Curtis 1991, 150f, 127f, Ørsted 1985, 270 with references, Étienne 1970, 305, n. 3, Laet 1949, 355, n. 1 (and for Istria, 206-9), ILS 8858.
39. See in general Nicolet 1976, and 351f.
40. The *Monumentum Ephesenum* (see n. 43 below) reflects obvious problems in distinguishing *vectigalia publica* from *portorium*.
41. See Bohlen 1937, 47 and 59, Rostovtzeff 1902, 509. Furthermore the explanation might be that Kyzikos (as well as Byzantium) following Strabo 12.576, had the fishing rights to Manyas Gölü (lake), Stöckle 1924, col. 459.
42. For the right of the state, see Arist. *Oec.* 2.2.3, Strabo 7.320, Bohlen 1937, 47. Byzantium was a *civitas libera et foederata* until Vespasian. The evidence might refer to this period. See Dumont 1976-77, passim.
43. The *Lex Antonia de Termessibus* might offer a parallel here. It is clearly indicated that this city-state in its own right could collect *portorium* of its own, CIL

1(2).589. See Ørsted 1985, 87f. Exactly the same was the case for Alexandria Troas (as *colonia* Augusta Troas was endowed with *jus Italicum*) following lines 103-5 in *Monumentum Ephesenum*. For the text, see Engelmann & Knibbe 1989.
44. 7.320. See Dumont 1976-77, passim.
45. Dumont 1976-77, 107f, 109f.
46. See *Dig.* 43.14.1.7, *Dig.* 43.14.2.
47. See Dumont 1976-77. For evidence concerning fishing and collection of fees for fishing in individual and independent city-states, see Rostovzeff 1902, 509, Bohlen 1937, 48, 56, Höppener 1931, 150ff, Edmondson 1987, 116ff.
48. *Dig.* 47.10.13. *Sane si maris proprium ius ad aliquem pertineat, uti possidetis interdictum ei competit, si prohibeatur ius suum exercere, quoniam ad privatam iam causam pertinet, non ad publicam haec res, utpote cum de iure fruendo agatur, quod ex privata causa contingat, non ex publica; ad privatas enim causas accommodata interdicta sunt, non ad publicas.* As I see it, this clause is necessitated by traditional rights in the East. Analogous are those *salinae* and *lacus piscatorii* which happen to be situated on private land and in consequence are *in dominio* of a private person (*bona singulorum*) or a free city-state. See *Dig.* 43.14.1.7, *Dig.* 50.15.4.7-8.
49. See *Monumentum Ephesenum* lines 20 and 122-23 (commentary pp. 53 and 122).
50. See further n. 29 on *portorium*.
51. *CIL* 13.8830 (*ILS* 1461). See Zangemeister 1889, (with photo) the reading of whom I follow, Curtis 1991, 150, Bohlen 1937, 46, Rostovtzeff 1902, 375, 414, Cimma 1981, 207, Ørsted 1985, 108. According to the discussion of Zangemeister (and Mommsen) (both *Westd. korr. Blatt* 1889 (p. 4 and p. 223 respectively) nothing seems to indicate that the stone has been removed from somewhere else. *Dea Hludana* is attested at Xanten (*CIL* 13.8611) and at Holtedoorn (*CIL* 13.8723), but apparently nowhere else. See *Beihefte der Bonner Jahrbücher*, 44, 1987 (Matronen und verwandte Gottheiten) 60. If the fishing had taken place in a *flumen publicum* (Flevo?) or a *lacus*, the *conductores* might have been *conductores vectigalium*. The findspot and the suggested physical conditions in that area in antiquity (see Zangemeister 1889, with references) do not exclude this possibility. But after AD 47 the Romans could not possibly claim any *dominium* north of the Rhine. One might dispute the dating of the inscription (Zangemeister allows without any enthusiasm for a doubtful dating to the period Vespasian-Trajan and certainly not before AD 47). A fair suggestion is mid/late second century AD. See Beek 1983, 6.
52. See Lehner 1930, 14, no. 27: *Matronis/Aufaniabus/Q Valerius/Secundus /pro se et suis/ ex imp(erio) ipsarum/ s l m*. This inscription is dated to the second half of the second century AD by Nesselhauf (and Lehner) and regarded as contemporaneous with the Beetgum-inscription. See also Ørsted 1985, 108, n. 125.
53. Leaving aside here inscriptions mentioning *salinatores, salsarii* etc. (see below n. 61) there is to my knowledge only one more inscription taken as evidence of Roman control. It was found on the beach at Ris close to Douarnenez in Amorica. See Sanquer & Galliou 1972. The reading (as restored by Sanquer 1973, 215-36) runs: *n(umini)Aug(usti)/ Neptuno Hippio/ C(aius) Varenius Voltin(ia tribu)/ Varus c(urator) c(ivium) R(omanorum)IIII/posuit*. See *AE* 1952.22 for the former reading. If any connection to fishing and salting at all (what I deem likely), it

must be trade. See e.g. *CIL* 2.1944 (*ILS* 6914), *AE* 1969-70.270, Haley 1990. See in general Jacobsen 1995, Curtis 1991, 150.
54. *Dig.* 39.4.13., *praef.*
55. *Dig.* 50.16.16.17 and *Dig.* 3.4.1., *praef.*
56. Vitr. *De Arch.* 7.3.7: *Salifodinae.* Solinus 5.19: *salinarum metalla.* And of course we find the distinction in the more technical descriptions: *Sal fossicius* (Varro *Rust.* 1.7.8, 2.11.6, Pliny *HN* 31.73, 77 and 81) and *sal maritimus* (Varro *Rust.* 1.7.8, 2.11.6). See Blümmer 1920, col. 2076f.
57. Traina 1992, passim. The early history of Roman salt-extraction is obscure, which seems to have complicated the discussion: Pliny *HN* 31.89 ... *salinas primus instituit* (Ancus Marcius). Aur. Victor, *De Vir.* 5 ... *salinarum vectigal instituit* disputed by Blümmer 1920, col. 2096f. Livy, 1.33 ... *In ore Tiberis ostia urbs condita salinae circa factae.* This does not mean, however, that the *salinae* were necessarily the property of the king and certainly not that they after 509 BC were the property of the state. See Kniep 1896, 74 for a discussion.
58. Ørsted 1985, 289 with references. See also Scherrer 1985, 255-58.
59. *CIL* 3.1209, 3.1363 (= *IDR.* 3.3, no. 119) *Publius Aelius Marus ... conductor pascui et salinar(um), AE* 1937.141 ... *Gajus Julius Valentinus ... c(onductor salinar(um).* Vitr. *De Arch.* 8.3.7, Ørsted 1985, 346f, Traina 1992, passim.
60. Livy (29.37.3) tells us that in 204 BC ... *vectigal etiam novum ... ex salaria annona statuerunt.* I think it is clear that it is not the *salinae* at Ostia, as normally suggested, which are leased from now, but a new tax, a *vectigal*, on trade with salt — an antique forerunner for the famous *Gabelle.* This *vectigal* — for how long we do not know — was considered an indirect tax such as the *portorium,* the *venalium rerum,* etc., and the collection was leased to publicans. It was the buyer then, and not the producer, who had to pay. See Hirschfeld 1905, 150, and Cimma 1981, 31f for a different view. To collect this *vectigal* we find — in my view — the *salinatores aerarii* (maybe a parallel to the *redemptores ab aerario,* see Ørsted 1985, 118ff). Now in Republican times at least a *salinator* seems to denote someone who is engaged in *vectigal* on trade and not in the actual running of the salt pans. This *vectigal*, then, cannot prove state ownership more than any other indirect taxes can (e.g. *portorium* or *centesima venalium rerum*). Kniep 1896, 75, Mommsen, *StR.* II 370, Blümmer 1920, col. 2097, Johnson 1935, 125-28, Benoît 1959, 95.
61. Responsible for a possible misinterpretation of the evidence on this crucial point, seems to be Marquardt 1876, vol. 2, 154ff. He is, however, right, I think, in his definition of the *salinatores*: "Denn in den ersten Jahren der Republik erreichte der Salzpreis durch die Spekulation der Händler eine so unverhältmässige Höhe, dass der Staat beschloss den Verkauf des Salzes zum Monopol zu Machen (=Livy 2.9.6, in 246 BC.) Die Beamten ... scheinen den Titel *salinatores aerarii* geführt zu haben ... während die Pächter *salarii* heissen" (Marquardt 1876, vol. 2, 155). But Marquardt did not — of course — know the inscriptions from Colijnsplaat, from which it is clear that the epithet *salarius* denotes a trader in salt or in salted products (see below n. 90). Benoît 1959, 95 has *salinatores* = *conductores.* Already by Blümmer 1920, however, col. 2095 "der Salzhändler heisst salarius". Will 1962, 1651 has *salinator ... qui salem facit.* Cf. Kniep 1896, 69, 72, 74, 77, and especially 85, Hirschfeld 1905, 150, Rostovtzeff 1902, 413,

Blümmer 1920, col. 2096f, Beek 1983, 9, Étienne 1994, 306. The very scanty evidence is as follows: *CIL* 12.5360 ... *Hilaro salinatori* (Peyriac-de-Mer), *CIL* 5.6670 *D M Batoni ... salario* (Vercellae), *CIL* 6.1152 ... *corpus salariorum* ... (Rome, to Constantine), *AE* 1888.65 ... *Genio saccariorum salariorum totius urbis*. And ("Glaspaste" im Berliner Museum, Kniep 1896, 69, Hirschfeld 1905, 150) ... *soc sal e scr* ... meaning, I guess ... *soc(ii) sal(inarum) e(t) scr(ipturae)* from the Dacian evidence, see n. 56 above. A parallel is here offered by the ... *sal soc s ... salinat soc s ... sal soc s ... salin soc s* ... from Minturnae, *AE* 1934.254. A total of four inscriptions from the first half of the first century BC, see Johnson 1935, nos. 13.3, 15.7, 20.12, 25.11. (Degrassi 732, 733, 738, 743). It is tempting (with Johnson 1972, 125-28) to suggest *salinatorum sociorum servi*, i.e. that these slaves are not necessarily *salarii*, but rather people collecting the *vectigal* on salt. They are then *servi* of the *redemptores* (= *salinatores*), and they are not, then, to be compared to the situation reflected in the evidence for the famous *garum sociorum* from Cartagena (see below) nor for the *[garum or liquamen] penuar(ium) iuniorum III s(ociorum)* = *AE* 1988.862. *CIL* 10.7856 ... *Cleon Salari(us) soc(iorum) s(ervus)* ... (Sardinia). See Sotgiu 1961, 93 = *AE* 1924.122 ... *im(munes?) salinarum pertinent[es]*. See also Mart. 1.41.8, 4.86.9. Cato (Serv. *Aen.* 4.244, Cic. *De Imp. Cn. Pomp.* 16 and for the late *mancipes salinarum, Cod. Just.* 4.61.11. The ... *salar(i)a(rius)* ... of *IDR*, 3.2.285 is difficult and might (see *ad loc.*) be compared to the *medicus salariarius* of *CIL* 11.3007. This listing does not give any clear picture, probably due to a change in the use of the original technical terminology. From denoting a purchaser of salt and collector of a *vectigal* on salt which apparently was abolished (albeit *e silentio*) in late republican or early imperial times, the designation *salinator* seems mainly to have been used for purchasers and traders in salt, i.e. some sort of middlemen between the people working the *salinae* and the *negotiatores* or Roman authorities directly. *Salarii* then is no technical terminus, but rather used very broadly to denote any relation to something concerning salt.
62. Étienne 1994.
63. See Ponsich & Tarradell 1965, 10-37 (with plans).
64. Étienne 1994, 11f (and map).
65. Lassère 1977, 366-70, Leveau 1984, 49f, 248ff, 396.
66. Ponsich & Tarradell 1965, 81-93, Edmondson 1987, 255-70.
67. Sanquer 1973, passim.
68. Thoen 1978, Thoen 1981, 245-57, Will 1962 and Beek 1983, passim. For Britain, see Jones & Mattingly 1990, 224-29 (with map).
69. For a description of the technology involved, see Ponsich & Tarradell 1965, 93ff. For procedures further north, see Will 1962, 1653. Beek 1983, 6ff, and especially Sanquer 1972, 220ff.
70. See for example the description by Pliny, *HN* 31.39-45, 73-105, Tac. *Ann.* 13.57, *ESAR*, vol. 3, 105.
71. A representative scenario — albeit clearly a Nilotic scene — might be reflected in the famous mosaic from El Alia in the Bardo museum, where fishermen draw in their nets from the beach with both cottages and *villae* nearby. See also, for example Sanquer 1972, 213 and Haley, 1990, 75, n. 22.
72. Indirectly *Dig.* 41.1.50, *praef.*, *Dig.* 43.8.8-9, *Dig.* 1.8.4-6 (although *ripa*).

73. Edmondson 1987, 116-17 and 128-134. Curtis 1991 supports this view, see 148, 151, and 146 and the general discussion, 38-148. Alarcao 1988, 62-73, Sanquer 1972, 219f. Rut. Namat. has ... *subjectas villae vacat aspectare salinas* (1.475).
74. Benoît 1959, 87-110, especially 106f.
75. Op. *Hal.* 3.620
76. Manil. *Astronomica* 5.656-81.
77. E.g. *AE* 1920.99, *CIL* 2.5929, *CIL* 4.826 (*piscicapi*), *CIL* 6.1872, Stöckle 1924, col. 460.
78. Ponsich & Tarradell 1965, 93.
79. The term *cetariae* is not much used, but seems to denote the fisherman as well as the salt extractor/salter. Varro (*Non.* p. 49.15), Columella *Rust.* 8.17.12. Sanquer 1972, 219 and especially Curtis 1991, 150 with n. 6.
80. Étienne 1994, 305. For a specific discussion concerning Corinth, see Robert 1960, 42-52.
81. *CIL* 14.409 (Ostia). *CIL* 2.5929 (Cartagena) with/or as *propolae* (fishmongers) at the same time. I suggest they sold fresh fish. Morover we find *corpora ... piscatorum et urinatorum ...* (for dyeing, I suggest (*murex*)) in *CIL* 6.29700, 29701 and 29702. See also *CIL* 6.1080 and the somewhat enigmatic *CIL* 5.8750 from Pedum.
82. *CIL* 11.390 and 11.391. *L Lepidio L f An Proculo* (his military carrier) *salinatores civitatis Menapiorum ob mer(ita) eius Septimina f(ilia) reponend(um) curavit.* And 391 with exactly the same wording except *... civitatis Morinorum ...* See Will 1962, 1649-57, Sanquer 1973, 235, Thoen 1978, 85, Thoen 1981, 250, Beek 1983, 7, Bohlen 1937, 33, 59, Blümmer 1920, col. 2098. See also *AE* 1994, 1279 ... *sal(inator?) Men(apiorum?)* ... from Tongres.
83. That land was *agri provinciales* and — untilled — everyone had the right to occupy it thereby acquiring a *jus colendi*. For Gaul, see Ferdiére 1988, 115-57, especially 147 (map). *AE* 1991.1024 (Baetica) brings *litus, portorium* and *vectigal* in a very interesting context, but is heavily fragmented and therefore difficult to use. See Fernandez Gómez 1991.
84. To my knowledge we find only one *conductor*, who might be attached to the army, see *CIL* 3.14356: 3a, Ørsted 1985, 342ff.
85. See Ørsted 1994, passim. Cf. again *CIL* 2.2242.
86. I am convinced that the salteries themselves were divided up into relatively small units: *officinae* (see the plans in, for example, Ponsich & Tarradell 1965, passim and especially 97 n. 7) *CIL* 2.537, 681, *AE* 1913.91. If so, mining (in for example Vipasca) offers a parallel. So I agree with Curtis 1991, 151 "... most salteries were *small* (my italics) privately owned industries ..." The evidence (especially *tituli picti* as well as the archaeological evidence) seems to underline this. See also Curtis 1991, 148f.
87. Strabo 4.4.2, Beek 1983, 7, Cabal 1973, 17-28.
88. *Si iactum retis emero, et iactare retem piscator noluit, incertum eius rei aestimandum est; si quod extraxit piscium, reddere mihi noluit, id aestimari debet, quod extraxit.* (*Dig.* 19.1.12)
89. Discussed by Ponsich & Tarradell 1965, 93ff, Edmondson 1987, 116ff, Étienne 1994, 305.
90. For the inscriptions, see Stuart & Bogears 1971 (with photos). No. 1 (p. 61) = *AE*

1973.362: *Negotiator salarius* from Trier. No. 4 (p. 62) = *AE* 1973.363: *Negotiator salarius* from Köln. No. 5 (p. 63) = *AE* 1973.365: *negotiatores allecari*. No. 22 (p. 70) = *AE* 1973.375: *Negotiator allecarius* from Trier. No. 25 (p. 71) = *AE* 1973.378: *Negotiator salarius*. Edmondson 1987, 152-99, Curtis 1991, 151ff, 157, Ètienne 1970, 297-313, Beek 1983, 7, Haley 1990, 76 with notes. In general on trade, see Jacobsen 1995, passim and more specifically 36ff, 127, 157ff.

91. See my note 87 above.
92. E.g. *AE* 1973.370, 1976.646 and *CIL* 13.8793.
93. *CIL* 13.8815.
94. Étienne 1970, 297-313, Pliny, *HN* 31.94 and *CIL* 4.5659 (*Garum sociorum* from Pompeii).
95. *AE* 1988.862, *AE* 1934.254 (Minturnae) and *CIL* 10.7856 (Sardinia).
96. "... en tout cas elle a pris en main à la fois la pêche du scombre et le marché du garum ...", Étienne 1970, 302. See also Strabo 3.11 and 3.4ff.
97. For prices, see Blümmer 1920, col. 2095, Bohlen 1937, 62, Curtis 1991, 170-75, Étienne 1970, 309f.
98. The *schaparii* are of interest here. See *Dig.* 9.2.29.2-7, 21.2.44, *CIL* 6.1872, *CIL* 14.409. From Spain we have *CIL* 2.1168, 1169, 1180, 1183 and 5929 (with *propolae*).

The Roman Family at Dinner

Keith Bradley

Early in the second century AD Plutarch asked of the Romans, "Why, in the old days, did they never dine abroad but they took with them their sons, when they were mere children?" He answered his question in Greek rather than in Roman terms, suggesting that the convention had begun with Lycurgus at Sparta. Its purpose was to inculcate good behaviour in boys under careful supervision of their fathers, and there was also the reciprocal benefit that the fathers themselves would be better behaved in the restraining company of their children. No less an authority than Plato could be invoked in support.[1]

Whether this explanation was true for Rome Plutarch evidently did not know. His enquiry is of interest, however, because it raises questions first of how regularly contemporary Roman fathers dined in the company of their sons, and secondly, given that Plutarch has nothing to say of them, of whether Roman fathers regularly dined with their wifes and daughters. The essential purpose of the modern daily dinner is to bring together around a common table all the family's members, with the emphasis falling on the all-embracing rather than the opposite. Dinner functions particularly as a means of training the young in the ways and values of their elders, and so it socialises children inclusively from the moment when they are first able to sit at table. Plutarch recognised the shaping potential of good company, but he was writing for an audience whose expectations of how children should be prepared for adulthood — and thus whose attitudes towards children at large — differed significantly from those of the modern western world.[2]

The consumption of food is essential to human survival. But the *manner* in which food is consumed and shared is a matter of cultural construction, and often the result of what a particular society judges most important in its general understanding and patterning of human and social relationships. So cultural anthropologists maintain, taking it as axiomatic, for example, that food incontrovertibly functions as a "medium through which a system of relationships *within the family* is expressed". In this paper I consider what Roman dining practices — all of which will be very familiar in and of themselves — suggest about the character of family life and family relations within the Roman *domus*. I shall be working in the context of recent studies of the Roman family, in which a privileged place is assigned to the core element of father, mother and children, "the sort of structure with which we are familiar today", on one (demographically derived) formulation. For the most part I shall discuss practices among the prosperous members of society. My interest lies in capturing the cultural bias in Roman family history, especially with regard to the history of children, and my principal focus will be the minimal involvement of groups of fathers, mothers and children in standard Roman dining procedures. The enquiry begins from the question, raised for a broader investigation of communal food rituals in the ancient world, of determining the conditions under which Roman family members dined together.[3]

Dinner

Dinner, the *cena*, eaten in the evening, was the main Roman meal of the day and as such was heavily charged with symbolic meaning. It could take various forms, ranging from the relatively simple situation of a head of household eating alone, as L. Licinius Lucullus is famously reported to have done on more than one occasion, to the more formal and lavish celebrations, of which Plutarch's grandfather disapproved, given in sumptuous dining rooms that could accommodate thirty or more dining couches. A mean is perhaps represented by the dinner Pliny (*Ep.* 2.6) describes when protesting a host's practice of serving graded food and drink to match the differing statuses of those present: the top people, the host, Pliny and some others, fared much better than the "lesser friends" and freedmen present at the table, the group as a whole probably totalling nine people. Nine at least was the number, ideal in Varro's view, provided for by the traditional appointment of the Roman *triclinium*, in which three couches forming three sides of a square allowed space for three diners each.[4]

At the formal *cena*, or the more elaborate *convivium* which it might become, various types of entertainment accompanied the food. Pliny the Elder usually had a book read aloud to him while he was dining from which he made notes, while the aged Vestricius Spurinna was diverted by performances of comedy. Other amusements could be provided by mimes, clowns or exotic dancers. But the *cena* was also, and particularly, an occasion for convivial, relaxed conversation. According to Varro, worrisome and complex subjects were to be avoided in favour of the pleasant, the diverting, the useful and the improving. The topics of Plutarch's *Table-Talk*, a work dedicated to a Roman friend (Sosius Senecio), illustrate the type: "Whether wrestling is the oldest of the sports", "Whether the sea is richer in delicacies than the land", "Why the Pythagoreans used to abstain from fish more strictly than from any other living creature".[5]

To mention the variable numbers of diners and the entertainments they enjoyed is at once to begin to see that the *cena* was not an affair that had anything of the familial about it in any modern sense. Rather, it was in essence an occasion for a man and his friends, his male friends above all, to pursue ease, well-being and conversational refinement while consuming food and drink. "But the most truly godlike seasoning at the dining-table", Plutarch remarked (*Mor.* 697D), "is the presence of a friend or companion or intimate acquaintance — not because of his eating and drinking with us, but because he participates in the give-and-take of conversation, at least if there is something profitable and probable and relevant in what is said".[6]

Women were not of course completely excluded. Drawing a comparison with Greek practices, Cornelius Nepos (*Praef.* 6) indicates that in his day it was perfectly acceptable for a wife to accompany her husband "*in convivium*", and Pliny (*Ep.* 9.36.4) makes clear that he sometimes dined just with Calpurnia at Tifernum Tiberinum. The response of Poppaea Sabina's husband to Claudius when asked why his wife had not accompanied him to dinner — because she was dead — is an indication of custom within the Julio-Claudian court. Nor were children altogether barred. Cicero (*QFr.* 21.19) mentions in a letter to his brother, absent on campaign with Caesar in Britain, that the young Quintus had dined with him one evening when Pomponia had dined out, and Plutarch (*Mor.* 725F-726A) refers to an occasion when his own sons were late for a dinner attended also by the sons of a guest. A passage in the Augustan life of Septimius Severus (S.H.A. *Sev.* 4.6) shows Severus eating a "*parca cena*" out of doors in a garden with his young sons and other children (but no wife). Passing literary indications of this sort are matched by iconographic evidence, especially the evidence of funerary art, where representations of men, women and children sharing in a funeral meal, perhaps modelled on ordinary social practice, are common. None of the sources suggests, however, that the presence of wives and children at the *cena* was a fixed convention so much as an *option* sometimes followed, and most Roman families in any case would not have had nine members to occupy the couches of the standard *triclinium*. At the banquet described at enormous length by Athenaeus there were twenty-three guests, all adult men, while Juvenal's Trebius, in search of a host to feed him dinner, was more than content to leave his wife at home. (I recognise of course that the sources themselves derive predominantly from men and that there is no way of reconstituting a female or a child's perspective.)[7]

Behaviour at Dinner

No matter who was in attendance, there were certain proprieties that the *cena* demanded of its participants, protocols that offer considerable help in understanding the culturally unique character of Roman dining behaviour.

Diners arriving at a host's house changed clothes, substituting for their outdoor dress a looser fitting, more comfortable, set of garments, the *synthesis* or *vestis cenatoria*. Shoes were taken off — an expression of leaving dirt outside — and rings were removed from fingers. For eating, spoons and knives might be used, but the fork was unknown and the prevalent mode was to eat with the fingers. Not surprisingly, hands had to be washed between courses, in clear or sometimes perfumed water. It was acceptable to toss unwanted or inedible bits of food on the floor, and it was essential to have a napkin and to know how to use it (but not for stealing food to take home and eat, or, worse, to sell later). In sum, there was an etiquette that governed the Roman *cena* — or, to use Ovid's words (*Ars Am.* 3.755-56) as he pointed out to a female audience that you did not make a good impression by smearing your face with a food-stained hand, a "*quiddam gestus edendi*".[8]

One element of the protocol package of course was that diners reclined to eat, resting on the left elbow and taking food from a serving table with the right hand. The custom was a mark of high status, inappropriate for lesser men. Thus Columella (*Rust.* 11.1.19), recommending that the farm bailiff should eat in the presence of the farm hands, said that the bailiff should recline only on days of religious observance, meaning that normally a man of servile stock should sit to eat. Similarly the story was told of Terence, a man of servile background, that when he went to read the *Andria* to the great Caecilius, he found the poet at dinner and so read the first few lines sitting on a bench next to Caecilius' couch; Caecilius then invited him to recline and to eat with him, a sign of favour and approval, after which the reading of the play was completed. The positions of the diners, moreover, were determined by the understanding that one reclined "above" or "below" one's companions, and that the guest of honour sat in a special place, the "consul's spot". The *cena* thus naturally implicated diners in a hierarchical and competitive environment, to the coded nuances of which all had to be alert. The obnoxious senator M. Favonius was remembered, after a dinner given in 42 BC by Cassius for his fellow conspirator Brutus and friends, first for arriving without an invitation and then for unceremoniously trampling over the servants who had been instructed to escort him to the uppermost couch and rudely making his way to a place on the more favoured central couch.[9]

The seriousness with which these rules and the behaviour dependent on them was taken is very well illustrated by Lucian's essay, *On Salaried Posts in Great Houses* (*De Mercede conductis potentium familiaribus*), in which advice is given to a young Greek contemplating a position as a tutor in the household of a Roman grandee. The depths of indignity to which the young man will have to sink if he does so is the main theme. Lucian evokes a scene in which the young man is invited to dinner in the great man's house for the first time, itemising the problems, and the deep anxieties they will produce, with which the candidate will have to contend. First, the time of arrival (14): it is gauche to arrive before anyone else and unmannerly to arrive last, so you will have to hang around outside at first, biding your time for the right time to enter. Once inside (15; cf. 29), it is a great mistake to stare across the room at the grandee's wife or sons because you might be suspected of ogling; so you must be very careful not to incur the host's wrath by an untoward glance. Next (15), enormous trepidation can result from not knowing in what order to eat the dishes served, when to reach out your hand for which food and so on; so you will have to keep a surreptitious eye on your neighbour and follow his lead. Further (16-17), if you are to avoid a reputation for boorishness, you will have to know how to respond to a toast in your honour, and if you are well treated and given a favoured place at table you will have to be ready to deal with the veteran household retainers who resent your intrusive presence. Finally (17), if you eat or drink too freely, you will be criticised for having no manners at all.

"Polite behaviour", it has been said, "is ritual performed for the sake of other people, and for the sake of our relationship with other people. Its purpose is to please and soothe them, especially where a rough passage is to be feared; to recognize and supply their need for esteem and comfort, to get one's way with them without arousing resentment". In modern society, learning how to be polite is an experience of childhood, and training children in the rules of behaviour appropriate to a "structured social event" such as dinner is largely a parental responsibility. As fully incorporated members of the modern family dinner, children are expected to learn the rules in a setting that is often prepared with their socialisation uppermost in mind. Consider for instance this view of the importance of teaching children the art of good conversation:

Parents who are so busy that they are coming to wonder whether they should go on "staging" family meals at all often continue the tradition almost entirely because they feel that children need these meals: they must learn how to converse. Our cultural tradition expects us to bring up children to ask why; and where people's lives are lived so separately, dinner-table conversation becomes a unique opportunity for the family to find out what all its members are thinking and doing.[10]

Romans were also expected to learn how to behave at table as children. Having oddly worn a dark coloured toga at a funerary banquet, which apparently was a breach of religious etiquette, P. Vatinius, the tribune of 59 BC, was confronted with the withering sarcasm of Cicero (*Vatin.* 32): "Did you not know the custom? Had you never seen a feast? *As a boy or young man* had you never been one of the cooks?" (In other words, did you never learn the rules of social comportment as a child?). Similarly, Apuleius in the *Apologia* (41.2) can assume that his stepson Sicinius Pudens is learning how to separate the inedible from the edible parts of a cooked fish as a boy. There was in fact a real sensitivity to the need to habituate children to good behaviour: so Plutarch (*Mor.* 99D) spoke of instructing children to "take their meat with the right hand and hold their bread in the left", and (*Mor.* 5A) of correcting them should they happen to reach out with the left hand instead of the right. But if Romans learned the rules of polite behaviour in childhood, the circumstances under which they did so were rather different from the modern situation.[11]

As I have noted, Roman boys sometimes attended *cenae*. Perhaps therefore some learned the rules of acceptable adult deportment from simple observation or from instruction from their fathers. Given the keen interest in children his writings evince, Plutarch for example could well have been a father who took a strong personal interest in the social formation of his own offspring. Yet it was more customary in the central era for such teaching to be given by the slave attendants who filled the lives of élite children from infancy on, their nurses and, especially in this case, their pedagogues. The correct number of fingers to use for different sorts of dishes, how to respond to dishes offered by lifting the head to signify no and lowering the head to indicate yes, the all-important technique of how to recline ("*mensam accumbere suffixo cubito*") — these were the kinds of graces that slave childminders instilled in their charges so that children would be properly equipped to take their places in the *triclinium* as adults. The training was part of a long process of child care which incorporated not just practical tasks but, particularly through the activities of play and storytelling, interaction of a very important socialising kind as well. It took place within the household, through the agency of women and men who comprised part of the *paterfamilias' familia*, but it was not given by parents. Even in very late Antiquity Augustine could tell in the *Confessions* (9.8) how his mother and her sisters had as children been handed over by their parents to the care of a "*famula decrepita*" who had combined moral instruction with the ordinary tasks of child care. One of the lessons she taught was the need for moderation in drinking, anticipating the time when as adults the girls would be able to drink wine; now they drank simply water, but not on demand, only when the old woman said so. The amount of time, quite simply, that children spent in the company of childminders was enormous, and perhaps often far greater than the time spent with parents. The indications in the late schoolbooks known as *colloquia* of how nurses or pedagogues, having spent the night with their charges escorted them at the beginning of the day to greet their parents, comprise just one sign of how relatively uninvolved in children's daily lives parents might be

— of how unoriented towards children Roman family structures were: it was not the parents who came to see their children at the beginning of the day.¹²

A sense of how complex the external training of children in the "*gestus edendi*" may have been is conveyed by a Christian tract from the late second century, Clement of Alexandria's *Paedagogus*. It was Clement's mission to instruct converts and the young in Christian morality and decorum, his ultimate goal being to lead his audience to a life of serene and perfect virtue marked by simplicity, moderation and prudence. With a figure recalling Paul's statement in *Philippians* (2.7) that Jesus had taken "the form of a slave", he presents Christ to his readers as their divine pedagogue, their teacher and moral instructor, from whose instruction perfection will result. The teachings include directives on how Christians (both men and women incidentally) should physically comport themselves in their daily lives as well as instructions on matters of the spirit, and in the second book especially Clement devotes his attention to Christian behaviour at dinner, giving counsel on the importance of exhibiting temperance and politeness at all times. Primarily this was to be part of the Christian's cultivation of the self for the sake of attaining virtue, but Clement links his teachings to the *raison d'être* of all rules of polite table behaviour (as just defined), the need to avoid giving offence to one's dining companions: "We must consider the feelings of our companions at table, and avoid disgusting or nauseating them by our crude conduct, testifying to our own lack of self-control" (*Paedagogus* 2.60.1). From his quite extensive remarks on eating and drinking a selective list of injunctions can be drawn up which constitute a guide to correct behaviour at dinner in the élite, highly sophisticated circle in Alexandria to which Clement belonged. But given the conceit of the pedagogue on which Clement's tract is based, the list may also, I think, be taken as illustrating the sort of detailed instructions the pedagogue in Greco-Roman society at large normally conveyed to those in his care. Many of his rules have a familiar ring:

— keep your hands, chin and couch clean while eating (2.13.1)
— take only small amounts of food and drink (2.55.1)
— eat slowly (2.55.1)
— be first to finish, though be indifferent about it (2.55.1)
— do not contort your face while swallowing your food (2.13.1)
— reach for the food when it's your turn and then only occasionally (2.13.1)
— do not lean forward to take the first serving (2.55.3)

- do not talk while you are eating (2.13.1)
- do not eat and drink at the same time (2.13.2)
- when drinking, do not swallow the largest amount possible (2.31.1)
- do not turn your head while drinking (2.31.1)
- do not roll your eyes around while drinking (2.31.1)
- do not drain your cup in one gulp (2.31.1)
- drink slowly, by sipping only small amounts (2.31.3)
- summon servants with words, not by whistling, hissing or snapping fingers (2.60.1)
- do not spit (2.60.1)
- do not cough (2.60.1)
- do not blow your nose while drinking (2.60.1)
- if you must belch, do so silently with your mouth closed (2.60.2-3)
- if you must sneeze, do so quietly, holding your breath and suppressing it (2.60.2-3)
- do not induce a sneeze (2.60.4)
- do not scratch your ears (2.60.4).[13]

This is a list of general directives; but to specific constituencies Clement addresses further injunctions. A married woman, if she must be present at all, should wear a cloak, in contrast Clement means to the more revealing *synthesis* of non-Christians, so that she will not appear seductive (2.54.2; cf. 2.33.4; 3.79.4). (There is great anxiety over what might follow from sharing a couch with another man's wife (2.54.1)). The young man — the sort of young man Lucian had in mind — is to keep his eyes modestly fixed on his own couch, to recline on his elbow without unnecessary fidgeting, and to eat in silence, listening only to his elders (2.54.3). Perhaps in all of this, in what seems almost a fixation with matters of bodily control, Clement shows an extreme fastidiousness, inspired by his Christian zeal, that others did not share. The manner at least in which he gives advice suggests that his rules were often broken: he inveighs for example against sloppy drinking which results in a wet chin or wet clothes (2.31.1), against noisily guzzling drinks from taking in too much air and hard swallowing (2.31.2), against excessive scraping of the teeth which produces bloody gums (2.60.4), items of behaviour, or misbehaviour, he must have observed in real life around him. He was especially sensitive — the *frisson* of excitement is palpable — to the lack of propriety in women, whose every gesture he saw as a temptation to illicit sex (2.33.1):

As for women ... if only they would not keep their lips wide open as they drink from big cups, with their mouths distorted out of shape! And if only they would not lean their heads back when they drain vessels narrow of neck, thereby exposing their throats with — or so it seems to me — such immodesty! They hold their chins high as they pour the drink down, as if they were trying to reveal as much of themselves as they can to their companions at table; then they belch like men, or rather, like slaves, and at their carousals begin to play the coquet.[14]

Clement's rules, however, were not invented out of whole cloth. One of the reasons a diner might snap his fingers at a slave, as evidence from Martial (3.82.15-17; 6.89.1-2) shows, was to call for a chamber-pot, and perhaps the semi-public emptying of the bladder that followed was not a tradition that Clement wanted to endorse. (He has something to say (2.39.2), incidentally, about the extravagant use of chamber-pots and similar receptacles made from gold, silver and other costly materials). It might be recalled, too, that Pliny (*Pan.* 49.6) thought it worthy of public praise and advertisement that Trajan did not belch during dinners he gave in the palace (contrary to the habit of Domitian, Pliny implies); rather (*Pan.* 49.7), Trajan could be commended for his elegant table behaviour, his *suavitas* and, indeed, his *iucunditas*. The dangers of sexual impropriety, moreover, were not matters of Christian concern alone: an inscription (*CIL* 4.7698b) from a Pompeian dining-room gave the following instructions to its occupants: "*lascivos voltus et blandos aufer ocellos coniuge ab alterius, sit tibi in ore pudor*". Quintilian (*Inst.* 1.2.8), also, declaimed against the corruptiveness of the *convivium* (if not the *cena*), making clear by referring to the obscene songs and the guests' lovers to be found there, both female and male, that in his view children were not at all to be exposed to such an event. Clement would have agreed; in fact (2.53.5) he did so. The rules were part of a process by which the child was civilised and acquired culture, and while here they form part of a much wider moral concern they can clearly be recognised as forerunners of the collections of rules known from the "manners books" of the mediaeval era and beyond. Reflecting a longstanding belief that table manners gave indications of individual character, the second book of the *Paedagogus* is in itelf such a book in many respects.[15]

The *Paedagogus* is steeped in a profound knowledge of classical Greek literature and philosophy, and Clement has thus been described as "un représentant qualifié de la *hellenistische-römische Kultur*". One of the more recent influences on his moral thought was the Roman Stoic Musonius Rufus, who in the first century had shown a similar concern for temperance in eating and drinking, which is evidence enough that Clement's concern for propriety was not a matter of local relevance alone; "exercizing moderation and decorum", Musonius had said, and "demonstrating one's self-control" was "not an easy thing to do", but something "that requires much attention and practice". Nonetheless, "at table one should have regard for a fitting decorum and moderation, and most of all should be superior to the common vices of filth and greedy haste". Earlier still Cicero (*Off.* 1.106) had urged the importance of moderating the appetite for food, as for all sensual pleasures, in his disquision on the decorous. But if Clement's evidence further demonstrates how a code of refined adult behaviour at table was widely recognisable — there were fixed rules of table behaviour, and they had to be learned if social unease were to be avoided — it is more important still in my view for confirming the role played by slaves and freedmen in teaching the rules to children. For Clement's divine pedagogue was to perfect his Christian disciples as, for all their faults, a Phoenix to Achilles, an Adrastus to the children of Croesus, a Leonidas to Alexander, a Nausithoon to Philip, a Zopyrus to Alcibiades (1.55.1). Here of course a Christian moralist addresses an audience of adults, but in the metaphor that underlies the treatise those adults were equally the "children of God" (e.g. 2.2.1), akin to the young Achilles, Alexander and all the rest. So from the certain knowledge, enhanced in my view by Clement's directives, that the real-life pedagogue was required to teach etiquette, it follows that the "uncomfortable" notion with which I began finds itself amply confirmed, and a significant difference in cultural orientation between Roman past and modern present can therefore be expressed: the *cena* was indeed an event for which the child at Rome had to be externally prepared before full participation was possible, not an event, as in the modern idiom, by which the child was inclusively and constantly socialised from a very early age.[16]

Why was this so?

There is abundant evidence that élite Romans highly valued their children. But that they had a special regard for older children is equally clear. Two items make the point. First, adoption, where the norm was to choose not infants but much older, even adult, children. A classic example is provided by the two older sons of L. Aemilius Paullus, the conqueror of Perseus, who were given away in adoption after the birth of Aemilius' two younger sons. Secondly, and quite differently, a literary illustration, namely, Ovid's tendency in the *Metamorphoses* to ignore the lives of the mythical children whose births he records until they reach the stage of early adulthood. Thus (*Met.* 3.341-55) Narcissus, a darling child born of the nymph Liriope after her rape by the river Cephisus is suddenly and typically in his sixteenth year, at once *"puer iuvenisque"* (352), and the delight of all around him. This tendency to favour the older child was in my view a function of the harsh demographic regime that prevailed in antiquity, in which, as recent important studies have revealed, infant mortality was excessive and the likelihood of any infant surviving to adulthood very precarious. Probably more than 25% of all children born in Roman antiquity died within their first year of life and approximately 50% before the age of 10, a regime that is to say in which children died not so much prematurely as predictably, as a natural matter of course. The degree of parental "investment" in their children, consequently, tended to increase in proportion to the degree of viability, quite literally understood, their children demonstrated over time, which explains the statement of Plutarch (*Mor.* 113D; cf. 102E) that the deaths of infant children were much more easily borne than the deaths of older offspring whose lives had carried the promise of adult durability. A *paterfamilias* seeking to adopt quite obviously preferred the older child whose future seemed guaranteed to the infant who might not last the year. Until that crucial stage of adulthood had been reached, the child was in many ways kept at a social distance, a liminal being rather than a fully incorporated member of a core triad.[17]

To the extent that a turning-point might be guaranteed, the disappearance of the Roman boy's vulnerability to death coincided, around the age of fifteen or sixteen, with his assumption of the *toga virilis*, a rite of passage which thus marked the crossing of a boundary in more ways than one. This was also the time when the *bulla*, the amulet that since infancy had protected the child against the Evil Eye, could safely be set aside. At dinner, the boy, now a man, was permitted to recline, whereas previously, if present at all, he had sat. Suetonius (*Aug.* 64.3) reports that Augustus had his grandsons Gaius and Lucius sit at or on the bottom of the emperor's couch when they dined together, and (*Claud.* 32) that Claudius, habitually including the sons and daughters of the Roman upper class at his dinner-parties, followed an ancient custom in having them sit on the arms ("*fulcra*") of the couches adults used. According to Tacitus (*Ann.* 13.16), in Nero's palace the children of the imperial family and of other prominent families sat together at a separate table of their own within view of the adults. The practices of the palace were not necessarily representative of those in prosperous society at large, though Clement (2.54.3) knew of special rules that were to apply to sitting boys: they were not to put their feet on top of each other, to cross their legs, or to hold their chins in their hands. Some confirmation, however, of the inferior positioning of children at *cenae* is evident in iconographic material, as for instance the tombstone of Aelia Aeliana from York in Britain, where in a funerary banqueting scene the daughter of the deceased woman is shown standing at the foot of the couch on which her mother and father both recline. Far more than in any modern setting, therefore, the effect of these arrangements was to mark off children, both physically and symbolically, as inferior beings, individuals incomplete as yet in their physical and social formation who could not be fully integrated into the dining company. They might even have to eat, as Tacitus (*Ann.* 13.16) indicates for the Neronian court, a suitably inferior, "more frugal" type of food. It follows that no matter how frequently they attended *cenae*, children were never admitted as full and equal members of a family group, and never as the focal element of the proceedings.[18]

The distance between children and adult males that the physical positioning at dinner symbolised was matched by a similar symbolic marking off of wives from husbands. Traditionally wives did not recline at table at all, but like children sat, often, to judge from the evidence of art, in high-backed and sometimes very ornate chairs (the so-called "throne" type). On a relief from Byzantium commemorating a couple named Meniskos and Hymnis, a simple block is enough for the woman to sit on. In literature, when Lucius arrives at the house of the miserly money-lender Milo in Apuleius' *Metamorphoses* (1.22-23) he finds dinner is just beginning, with Milo reclining on an appropriately small couch and his wife Pamphile sitting on a chair at her husband's feet; to make way for the guest Pamphile is more or less ejected from the chair at once by Milo, though Lucius is not given any food. Even in the peasant household of Dio Chrysostom's *Euboean Discourse* (7.65-67), men recline and women sit to eat their dinner. In both literature and art women are of course sometimes found reclining. Suetonius (*Calig.* 24.1) refers to Caligula's wife and sisters reclining with him at dinner, but that is a detail to be construed in the light of Cicero's experience in November, 46 BC, when at a dinner given by a friend he found to his not altogether unpleasant surprise that one of his reclining companions was the notorious Cytheris. She was an actress, and for a woman of her profession, or that of a *meretrix*, the conventions of respectable society did not apply. Again, at her final dinner with Nero, truly a family affair, the younger Agrippina reclined above her son, at his invitation; and in Petronius' *Satyricon* (67.5), Scintilla, the wife of Habinnas, is also seen reclining when joined by Fortunata. Conventions may have changed from generation to generation, from class to class, from region to region, and, controlled by the amount of formality involved, from occasion to occasion. The Aelia Aeliana just mentioned, and other reclining women depicted in funerary monuments, cannot all have been comparable to Cytheris. The point remains, however, that in strict protocol the reclining position of ease, in which you might quite literally rub shoulders, if not other parts, with your neighbour, was the prerogative of the superior husband, and the more modest sitting position was the place of the dutiful, and subordinate, wife. It kept her confined, isolated and observable.[19]

The arrangement and positioning of the diners' bodies at dinner gave physical expression to the asymmetrical institutional relationships between father and children and husband and wife that typified Roman society. When women and children participated in the *cena*, they did so in a manner which made all the participants conscious of their relative standing in the familial hierarchy (as also conscious that they were but one element in a network of relationships constituting their husbands' or fathers' social world). An obvious analogy can be found in the way Roman theatre audiences reflected the social hierarchy at large, with the best seats being reserved for those of highest status and slaves, if they were present at all, being confined to the topmost limits of the building. The occasion of eating together, therefore, was not so much, as it tends to be in modern western societies, an occasion for family sharing — by which I mean sharing, around a common table, of both a supply of food and social intercourse — as for accentuating and confirming the conventional social order, rigidly patriarchal, and the disparities of status on which that order was built. The fact is that for the Roman family at dinner, there was no common table.[20]

The Table

"The idea, which we take for granted, that everyone usually sits round a table to eat is in fact very specific to our own culture." So again a modern commentator, in a clear demonstration of how the traditional dining-table acts in modern society as a device to bring the various members of a family together at meal times, at dinner especially, or else to remind parents once their children have grown up and left the family home of earlier dramas in which parents and children had once been closely engaged. Even in an age when on an ordinary daily basis eating in the kitchen has become customary for many families, the dining-table still retains its value as a symbol of familial unity and cohesion: "it is still the same table that gave us the word 'commensality', meaning 'togetherness arising out of the fact that we eat at one table'".[21]

According to Varro (*Ling.* 5.118), Romans had once used square dining-tables of a kind that could still be seen in military usage, but generally preferred round tables. In art, in fact, both types are well-represented and a more significant distinction therefore is that between moveable and immoveable tables. The former might be made of wood, marble or bronze, whereas the latter were masonry structures, permanently built into place with surrounding couches. In view of the fixed conventions of men reclining, which took up more space than sitting at table in the modern fashion, and women and children sitting apart, neither type, it seems to me, can have fulfilled the same social function as the modern dining-table.[22]

Whether round or rectangular, the moveable table was not an item of furniture that was replenished with food as diners proceeded from one course to another; instead the Roman practice was to remove the table altogether when one course was finished and to bring in another for the next. Hence the use of the phrase *"secundae mensae"* to signify dessert. As that phrase also indicates, because they were relatively small it was often the case that there were several tables in the *triclinium*, not one, with diners having their own tables from which to eat their food individually, as North Americans today sometimes eat from so-called TV tables. Children, as already seen, might have a completely separate table. There was nothing comparable therefore to the modern table with its series of place-settings to draw diners together and unite them. So, with diners constantly moving their recumbent bodies towards and then away from private tables, it might be questioned whether Roman habits could encourage anything quite comparable to the commensality of the modern situation, despite the intimacies that might follow from proximity on the couches. This is not to say that the Roman table was devoid of all symbolic significance. Some thought that the very word "*mensa*" conveyed an idea of centrality, though how widely this antiquarian speculation circulated is unknown. Others regarded the loaded table as a symbol of nature's beneficence, with the table itself — round, stable and nurturing — representing the earth. To others it was simply a token of civilised living. In none of this, however, is there anything remotely close to the idea of "commensality" as defined above, a word, incidentally, for which there is no analogue in classical Latin.[23]

Matters were no different with immoveable tables. I quote an archaeologist's description of a *triclinium* in the House of the Cryptoporticus at Pompeii, typical of many others:

Three sloping couches of masonry covered with red plaster run in a horse-shoe around the walls, with higher *fulcra* at the two ends; the central couch is 4.41 m long, the other two 4.68 m. Along the front runs a ledge where cups could be put down, leaving only a small space free for access at the end of the *imus lectus*. Low benches run along the ends of the couches and the walls in front, where children or other inferior persons could sit. There is a single small round table between the couches, and a stand against the wall to the right, where the service for the wine could be set.

Here the table is again very small in relation to the couches, and cannot possibly have drawn the reclining diners inwards and towards one other. It could hold neither a full course of food nor all the diners' tableware. The running ledge perhaps compensated in part, but temporary tables must also have been needed to accommodate a full group of diners. The "inferior persons" on the low benches could not even reach the main table, so that their marginality was again quite literally, and even structurally, built into the dining-room. The room was not perhaps overly spacious, but the *mensa* did not function as a focal point for the diners spread out around it.[24]

If the evidence of Roman art is any guide, the dining practices described in the literary sources may well have been emulated far and wide in those sectors of Italian and provincial society prosperous enough to afford funerary monuments of the sort to which I have referred, or to inhabit houses as large as the House of the Cryptoporticus at Pompeii. That in turn implies that the symbolic ordering and social distancing that I have commented on in élite dining behaviour was also normative and widespread among the prosperous classes of Roman imperial society. How deeply in society those habits penetrated it is difficult to say, and not my concern here. But to account for those practices, I want in conclusion to introduce the well-known anecdote that Plutarch (*Mor.* 800) recounts about the radical tribune Livius Drusus: "He had a house", Plutarch says, "many parts of which were overlooked by his neighbours". An architect undertook to remove this disadvantage at a cost of only five talents. "'Make it ten,' said Drusus, 'and make my whole house open, so that my fellow citizens can see how I live'." The story illustrates how for élite men devoted to the pursuit of honours and rank, no aspect of their lives was irrelevant to the goal, how the strict dichotomy between the public world and the private sphere that is so central to modern mentality was far less strict at Rome, and how the domestic was deeply implicated in the public profile of the individual aspirant to power.[25]

Above all, it seems to me, the *cena* has to be understood as an aspect of the competition for public recognition and increase in *fama* that obsessed the Roman ruling classes throughout the central era. Like the military triumph, the provision of benefits to the civic community, or the demonstration of rhetorical prowess, the *cena* allowed the opportunity, if on a smaller scale, for a spectacular display of authority and power, which could be carefully orchestrated before a select audience of people envisaged as not just the beneficiaries of personal generosity but also the interpreters of the host's reputation to a wider social group. The number and character of the guests, the quality of the food and wines, the value of the plate and drinking vessels, the style of the tables, couches and furnishings, the presentation of the slaves, the setting of the *triclinium*, the subjects of conversation, the nature of the entertainments — these were the constituents of the spectacle on which the reputation of the host would depend when reports of the *cena* were disseminated, the themes in which the sources show the greatest concentration of interest. If the spectacle were successful, the potential for enhancement of reputation was very high, as Horace's Nasidienus Rufus poem (*Sat.* 2.8) famously reveals; but as Pliny's letter on the parsimonious host makes equally clear, there was no shortage of criticism if the spectacle were thought deficient in any way. The host had to steer a difficult course between the Scylla of tasteless extravagance and the Charybdis of cheap restraint. If the *cena* for a while gave the host a certain hold over his guests, it was an event nonetheless at which there was much at stake, and it should not be surprising therefore that a preoccupation with self-presentation, as evidenced by the fastidious concern for correct table behaviour seen earlier, would manifest itself in such a tension-laden environment.[26]

Conclusion

"The evidence is conclusive that patterns in the consumption of food are almost always governed by cultural symbols and that the ways in which food is distributed and consumed reflect a society's dominant modes of social relationships and groupings, especially those pertaining to kinship ties." So a standard sociological reference work. In other words, the way food is selected, consumed and shared can be regarded as a mirror of its primary values. At Rome, the bonds between husbands and wives and between parents and children were crucially important, as a host of testimony, especially the testimony of commemoration at death, indicates; for it is now axiomatic that patterns of commemorating the dead, as revealed by a great body of epigraphical evidence, prove the primacy of the core family in Roman social organisation at large. But *in life* those bonds were not important enough to demand a primary place, either real or symbolic, in the main food ritual of the day. I know no way of judging how on a daily basis a given individual, say Cicero or Seneca or Pliny in their respective eras, chose between a relatively simple or a more formal dinner. The scale of the *cena* must have varied from day to day, depending on where the individual found himself — in the city, on his rural estates, on military or administrative service in the provinces — and on the availability of resources, both material and human. Then as now, any number of personal contingencies (holidays, sickness) must also have played a part.

The overriding impression, however, which the sources leave — the prevailing ideology one might say — is that no matter whether modest or elaborate, dinner was a meal about which the individual male made an individual decision — to entertain, to eat alone, to respond to an invitation — in a world in which ties of *amicitia* and *hospitium* were paramount. Other household members, wives for example, responded to such decisions as appropriate. Dinner was not a meal at which the company of family members was automatically and invariably assumed essential or even desirable. Within innumerable élite households, therefore, many wives and children must have eaten completely apart, in time and place, from their husbands and fathers, and from one other — I think of Pliny (*Ep.* 6.20.2) eating separately from his mother while Vesuvius was erupting — and when husbands, wives and children did dine together, they did so in ways that continually reinscribed the subordination of the two latter to the former. Dinner was eaten in a dining-room, in Vitruvius' (6.5.1) schema one of the private rather than public rooms in the *domus*, but even so a room that cannot accurately be called a family room, for like other private rooms the *triclinium* was in the first instance a room associated with the *paterfamilias* alone. In Roman culture the centrality of the family core unit was never great enough to produce a tradition like that in European art where the family dinner was represented as one of the quintessential images of family life.[27]

One way to explain this is to recognise that the family relationships concerned were part of a much wider framework of reference, the kin network, by which Roman society arranged and conducted its familial life, which meant for instance that at any moment men like Cicero and Atticus could take an active, interventionist interest in the lives of kin members such as Quintus and Pomponia who happened to find themselves married to each other. Under these circumstances, a man might well prefer to dine with a brother or some other male relative from his extensive circle of kin members than with his wife or children. The affective bonds at Rome between a man and his wife and with his children were not bonds that had to be reinforced day after day through the sharing together of food. If a man did eat dinner with his wife or children, they were either alternatives to or the complements of friends; and they may even have been part of the spectacle for friends and visitors to behold. Because, in fact, the Roman dinner was constructed principally as a vehicle of display for the enhancement of an individual's reputation, it was the men comprising a host's circle of friends, real or potential, who were the primary focus of interest in the consumption and sharing of food, and relatives who participated were consequently assimilated to this category. To the extent, therefore, that the principal mode of food-sharing at Rome encoded society's most valued relations, the subordination of immediate kin ties to those of friendship, in a mental landscape far removed from that which privileges the modern family dinner and its seclusive environment, is, it seems to me, undeniably clear. The high valuation of nuclear kinship ties visible in certain aspects of Roman life (or death) was offset by a low valuation of those ties in the regular round of dining practices within the Roman *domus*.[28]

Notes

1. Plut. *Mor.* 272C (Trans. H.J. Rose).
2. Modern western perspective: on family dining and the training of the young, see Visser 1991, 40-56, 80-83, 264-67. I begin with a contemporary point of departure on the assumption that all historical investigation must inevitably derive from the prejudices and preoccupations of the present, cf. Bradley 1992.
3. Axiomatic: Cohen 1968, Douglas 1975, Douglas 1982, Douglas 1984, Goody 1982, 10-39. Quotation: Douglas 1982, 86 (my emphasis), in a study of British working-class diet in the 1970s. Formulation: Parkin 1994, 178. Cultural bias: cf. Benedict 1934, 235.
4. Lucullus: Plut. *Luc.* 41.2. Lavish celebrations: Plut. *Mor.* 679B. Varro's view: Gell. 13.11.2-3. For a concise description of the disposition of diners in the Roman *triclinium*, see Bek 1983, 83-84. Basic literary sources on the *cena* are compiled in Marquardt 1886, 297-331.

5. *Convivium*: on the communal nature of the *convivium*, observe Gowers 1993, 25-26. My interest here, however, to the extent that it can be recovered, lies not with the elaborate dinner party so much as the more prosaic, day to day dining behaviour of the Roman élite. Pliny the Elder: Pliny *Ep.* 3.5.11-12. Vestricius Spurinna: Pliny *Ep.* 3.1.9. Other amusements: see for example, Mart. 5.78, Pliny *Ep.* 1.15.2-3, 9.17.3, 9.36.4, Lucian *Merc. Cond.* 18. Cf. Jones 1991. Varro: Gell. 13.11.4-5. Topics: Plut. *Mor.* 638B-F, 667C-669E, 728C-730F. On Plutarch's *Table-Talk*, see Jones 1971, 54. I take Plutarch's evidence, as also that of Lucian, to reflect the social behaviour of the Graeco-Roman élite at large under the High Empire and not to be exclusively Greek in any narrow sense, cf. Purcell 1995, 165, observing how "closely intertwined were the cultural and ideological characteristics of the elites of the ancient Mediterranean by the Augustan period". It is true, however, that in some respects Roman dining practices retained their own individuality, no matter what the influence upon them of Greek practices; see Dunbabin 1993.
6. Note also Plut. *Cat. Mai.* 25.3.
7. Pliny: note also Tac. *Ann.* 15.60, Seneca dining with his wife and two friends, Plut. *Mor.* 140A, 461C, 528A-B. Perhaps modelled: the correspondence is clearly expressed by Toynbee 1964, 184. Trebius: Juv. 5.76-77. Option: for the presupposition that parents and children might sometimes dine together, see Cic. *QFr.* 21.19 (Shackleton Bailey), Suet. *Claud.* 24.2, August. *Conf.* 9.8, cf. Cic. *Att.* 94.3-4 (Shackleton Bailey), lunch not dinner.
8. Changed clothes: Mart. 5.79, 10.87.12. On the *synthesis*, see Brewster 1918, McDaniel 1925, cf. Goldman 1994, 235. Shoes: Petron. *Sat.* 65.4, 72.4, Mart. 2.50.3, cf. 8.59.13-14. Rings: Pliny *HN* 28.24. Spoons and knives: Petron. *Sat.* 33.6, Mart. 8.33.23-24, 8.71.9-10, 14.120, 14.121, Juv. 11.133. Fingers: Ath. 4.161d-e. Floor: Vitr. 7.4.5, Hor. *Sat.* 2.8, cf. *Epist.* 1.5.22-24, Sen. *Con.* 9.2.4, Pliny *HN* 28.26, 36.184, Quint. *Inst.* 8.3.66, cf. Mart. 7.20.17. Napkin: Varro *Ling.* 9.47, Catul. 90, Hor. *Sat.* 2.8, Mart. 2.37, 7.20, 8.59, Lucian *Merc. Cond.* 15. See in general, Deonna & Renard 1961, showing that the lines between etiquette and superstition could be very blurred.
9. Reclined: Plut. *Mor.* 679F. Terence: Suet. *Ter.* 2. Positions: Sen. *QNat.* 5.16.6. Coded nuances: see especially Douglas 1975. M. Favonius: Plut. *Brut.* 34.4. Observe Plut. *Cat. Min.* 56.4: Cato's habit of sitting to dine while the tyranny of Caesar endured.
10. "Polite behaviour": Visser 1991, 39. "Structured social event": Douglas 1975, 260. This view: Visser 1991, 49.
11. Cicero: cf. Haskell 1994, 141. Note that Plut. *Mor.* 5A is from a spurious work, the *De Liberis Educandis*, but for present purposes this is immaterial.
12. Plutarch: see for instance *Mor.* 38C, 447A, 458D, 554A, etc. For recollections of traditional parental supervision of children, see Plut. *Mor.* 272C, Ath. 6.275a (from Posidonius). Graces: Sen. *Ep.* 94.8, Plut. *Mor.* 439F, Apul. *Met.* 10.17 (quoted). Child care: Bradley 1986b, 1991a, 13-102, 1994. Schoolbooks: *CGL* III 646, 647, 652-54, cf. Dionisotti 1982, 87-98, 108. Unoriented: cf. Stone 1981, 326. Note Plut. *Mor.* 672F-673A on the eating regime of nurses.
13. Clement's mission: on Clement in general, see Chadwick 1966, 31-65, Brown 1988, 122-39; on the *Paed.* in particular, see de Faye 1906, 72-86, Marrou 1957,

Marrou & Hart 1960, 7-97. Christ: de Faye 1906, 75, 79: "Le Pédagogue, c'est le Logos ou la Raison de Dieu détachée de lui-même et devenue une personnalité indépendante." "Ce Pédagogue divin, c'est Jésus." For a good discussion of Clement on etiquette that stresses the relationship between etiquette and morality and the manner in which etiquette functions as a marker of both self-definition and group identity, see Leyerle 1995.

14. Translation from Wood 1954.
15. Chamber-pot: cf. Sen. *Ben.* 3.26. 2. "Manners books": see Elias 1978, 84-89, cf. Leyerle 1995, 137. For the likelihood that Roman manuals existed before Clement's day, see D'Arms 1990, 317, and observe also Pliny *HN* 28.26 (Servius Sulpicius' book on not leaving the table). Personality: Leyerle 1995, 140, who notes that "Theophrastus illustrated 20 out of his 30 character sketches by some description of food handling habits or table manners". For other evidence presupposing widespread rules of etiquette, see Plut. *Mor.* 14F (the need for decorum among the young), *Mor.* 42F (a guest at dinner is to eat what he is served without complaint), Ath. 4.161d-e (a proper way to eat with the fingers), cf. Plut. *Mor.* 45E, 50D.
16. Described: Marrou 1957, 184. Musonius Rufus: Marrou 1957, 194, 198-199. Quotations: Lutz 1947, 116-21, see also 113-15. The decorous: see D'Arms 1995, 307-08.
17. Adoption: cf. Dixon 1992, 112. L. Aemilius Paullus: Plut. *Aem.* 5.3 (cf. Livy 45.41.12) with Astin 1967, 13. For other cases of adoption, see Prévost 1949. Ovid's tendency: see also *Met.* 4.288-95 (Hermaphroditus, aged 15), 5.47-52 (Athis, aged 16), 8.241-3 (Daedalus' nephew, aged 12), 9.702-17 (Iphis, aged 13), 11.301-2 (Chione, aged 14), 13.753-4 (Acis, aged 16). Important studies: Parkin 1992, especially 92-98, Bagnall & Frier 1995, especially 332-6, Saller 1994, especially 21-25. Probably: cf. Bradley 1994, 143-44, with other references. Liminal: cf. Bradley 1991b, 262.
18. *Toga virilis*: see Wiedemann 1989, 86, 90. *Bulla*: see Gabelmann 1985; Goette 1986. The *bulla* was also used to mark children's free birth. Permitted to recline: Booth 1991, 107-10. Nero's palace: cf. Suet. *Tit.* 2. Aelia Aeliana: Tufi 1983, 24-25 (no. 40 & plate 13); see also from York the tombstones of Julia Velva and Mantinia Maerica: Tufi 1983, 27-29 (nos. 42, 43 & plates 13, 14), showing girls respectively sitting in a wicker chair and standing; cf. Toynbee 1964, 208-9. Note also Toynbee 1964, 201: the child Serapion, who died at the age of three, and the adult relative Flavius Callimorphus, who died aged forty-two, on a stele from Chester; the child "is perched full-face upon the man's left thigh".
19. Traditionally: Val. Max. 2.1.2: "*feminae cum viris cubantibus sedentes cenitabant. quae consuetudo ex hominum convictu ad divina penetrauit. nam Iovis epulo ipse in lectulum, Iuno et Minerua in sellas ad cenam invitabantur. quod genus severitatis aetas nostra diligentius in Capitolio quam in suis domibus conservat, videlicet quia magis ad rem pertinet dearum quam mulierum disciplinam contineri*", Isid. *Orig.* 20.11.9: "*apud veteres Romanos non erat usus accubandi, unde et considere dicebantur. postea, ut Varro ait de vita populi Romani, viri discumbere coeperunt, mulieres sedere, quia turpis visus est in muliere accubitus.*" Chairs: see Richter 1966, 98-102. Relief from Byzantium: Koch 1988, 95-96 (no. 34). Lucius: cf. Apul. *Met.* 2.11: Pamphile is present with Milo on another occasion when Lucius has been invited to dinner,

he now reclines. Peasant household: cf. Ov. *Met.* 8.655a-61: Jupiter and Mercury recline on the couch in the cottage of Baucis and Philemon. Cytheris: Cic. *Fam.* 197.2 (Shackleton Bailey), cf. Mart. 3.82.11. Agrippina: Tac. *Ann.* 14.4 Conventions: Val. Max. 2.1.2 (above) is crucial, cf. also Livy 39.43.3, Sen. *Con.* 9.2.2.

20. Analogy: see Rawson 1987.
21. "The idea": Visser 1991, 149, cf. 130. "Commensality": Visser 1991, 82-83.
22. Art: see Richter 1966, 98-102. Moveable and immoveable: see Dunbabin 1991, 123-24.
23. *"Secundae mensae"*: Gell. 13.11.6. Several tables: Pliny *HN* 28.26-27, Pliny *Ep.* 9.17.1. Proximity: cf. Plut. *Mor.* 679B. Centrality: Varro *Ling.* 5.118. Others: Plut. *Mor.* 158C, 704B, 727A. On the extravagant qualities of dining tables, see Pliny *HN* 13.91-99, with Meiggs 1982, 287-96, and Juv. 11.117-27, with Courtney 1980, 506.
24. Archaeologist's description: Dunbabin 1991, 123. The subject of "the common table" seems to me to need more detailed investigation. I know of no comprehensive study of dining scenes in art historical sources, but this is clearly needed as a starting point. Note the contrast in two *stibadium* scenes discussed in Dunbabin 1993, 120 (figure 6) and 139 (figure 28).
25. On the competitiveness of the Roman élite, see Hopkins 1983, 107-16, 150, 154, 170-71.
26. Constituents: on the *triclinium*, see Bek 1983; on dining-room decorations, see Ling 1995; on slaves, see D'Arms 1991. Note that children perform the role of slaves in the household of Dio Chrys. 7.65-67. A certain hold: Hudson 1989, 83. Tension-laden: observe Plut. *Mor.* 511D-E on the orator Pupius Piso (cos. 61 BC) anxiously awaiting the arrival of his guest of honour, P. Clodius Pulcher. Presumably, also, the impressions to be made on "shadows" (Hor. *Sat.* 2.8, Plut. *Mor.* 706F-710A) might cause concern. On the role of the *domus* as a vehicle for élite display in general, see Wiseman 1987.
27. Reference work: Cohen 1968, 513. Commemoration at death: Saller & Shaw 1984. Ties of *amicitia*: D'Arms 1984. Family room: Elsner 1995, 60-61. European art: see for instance the images in Schama 1987, 47, 157, 159.
28. Kin network: Bradley 1991a.

Roman Children at Mealtimes

Hanne Sigismund Nielsen

"Meals can be seen as symbolising the important social relations of power and subordination that exist within the family. They function as a means of maintaining and reproducing a specific aspect of the social order, the family and the age and gender divisions which characterise it."[1]

Like all generations before us, classicists in modern Western society try to reflect the ideals and norms of life in antiquity in their own ideals. It is not many years ago — on the background of the studies of epitaphs — when it was advocated that the Roman family was nuclear rather than extended as had previously been claimed.[2] But only recently a new movement has begun to modify this (to my mind) biased picture of the Roman "nuclear" family.[3] This paper will further contribute to modifying the former viewpoint.

One of the fundamental ideals (perhaps the most fundamental) for the modern western nuclear family is that its members eat at least one meal together per day, usually the evening meal.[4] The quotation above speaks its own clear language. Thus it would not be strange to expect this basic tradition to also be found in ancient sources describing early Roman families. For example, if we had a better knowledge about how Roman children participated in the daily meals of a family, our knowledge of the Roman family structure would be greater, insofar as we would be enlightened as to the educational and emotional sides of relations whether inside or outside the biological family. The actual descriptions of meals in both the pagan and early Christian literature of the Romans, combined with other types of evidence, renders it possible to make some interesting conjectures about the ideal and real structures of family life both among the privileged and the poor.

The material

In an effort to look beyond the economically privileged levels of society, and being well aware of the difficulties involved, I have tried to acquire information not provided by Roman literature. Of course, in the following I will not avoid using the literary sources that primarily describe the conduct of the Roman upper-class males; but I have also included epitaphs from tombs still *in situ*, in order to gain information about the levels of society infrequently referred to in literature. Finally, I have included some examples from early Christian literature to show the possible development of the ideals and reality of the dining practices of Roman families from paganism to Christianity.

In order to find as many examples from literature as possible, I have examined all references to pagan Latin literature available on PHI CD-ROM #5.3 — i.e., the major part of literature available to us on the words *cena, mensa, convivium, epula, triclinium, jentaculum, prandium, taberna* and *popina* — words covering the most simple meals to grand and expensive banquets. I have likewise used the Christian equivalent to the pagan CD-ROM, namely the CETEDOC,[5] but restricted myself to the authors Tertullian, Ambrose, Augustine, and the letters of Jerome.

In Roman literature the word *prandium* usually indicates a meal around midday, while *cena* is the word most frequently used for dinner or supper in the evening, whether informal and private or sumptuous and formal.[6]

The habits of the élite

Roman literature abounds with references to meals both private and public. Cicero frequently refers to dinners especially in his letters to his friends and to Atticus. A well-known example is a family dinner at his brother Quintus' house that turned out to be unpleasant due to the miserable relationship between Quintus and his wife Pomponia, the sister of Atticus (*Att.* 14.10). Most of the meals Cicero refers to eaten together with friends and business relations were very pleasant and useful, he does mention, however, one meal which resulted in his being incapacitated for 2 weeks. He had attended a banquet at Lentulus' house and eaten mushrooms and other vegetables that were so heavily seasoned that they were "irresistibly delicious": *ut nihil possit esse suavius* (*Fam.* 7.26). The result was that Cicero was "seized with an attack of diarrhoea so persistent that not until this day (it) has shown any signs of stopping" (Translation by Williams, LCL). Perhaps Cicero like Horace should have stayed home — Horace describes (*Sat.* 1.6): "When I get home I have a meal of leeks, peas and a dish of pancakes (*lagani catinum*). My supper is served by three slaves, and a white stone slab supports two cups with a ladle. Further, there is a cheap salt-cellar, a jug and a dish (*gutus cum patera*)."[7] Pliny, who liked to describe his life and habits in his letters, writes a letter to Fuscus Salinator about how he usually spends summer in his Tuscan villa (9.36): "After a short sleep and another walk I read a Greek or Latin speech aloud and with emphasis, not so much for the sake of my voice as my digestion, though of course both are strengthened by this. Then I take another walk, am oiled, take exercise, and have a bath. If I am dining alone with my wife or with a few friends, a book is read aloud during the meal and afterwards we listen to a comedy or some music; then I walk again with the members of my household (*cum meis*) some of whom are well educated."[8]

Horace had no family in our sense of the word, Cicero had one; so did Pliny, although he did not have any children. The examples chosen here are typical of Roman literature, and it seems evident that meals were occasions of great importance both in the private and the public sphere, if this distinction is at all possible for the upper class males who have written the examples mentioned. Interestingly enough it is likewise evident from the literature that meals with spouses and children were of no importance or at least of minor importance. As a matter of fact handbooks indicate that children of the élite attended meals seated on chairs behind their father's couch. Suetonius and Tacitus are the sources of this piece of information. Suetonius writes in his biography of Augustus (64) that the Emperor did not have his meals alone but together with his children and grandchildren: *neque cenavit una, nisi ut in imo lecto assiderent* ...[9] Augustus wanted his family to live according to what was believed to be the *mores* of the early Republic, and his dinner habits are mentioned in the paragraph of his biography where Suetonius enumerates these *mores*. It is mentioned directly about Claudius (32) that this habit was considered to be an ancient one, the expression is *more veteri*.[10] In his account of the death of Brittannicus Tacitus[11] informs us that the habit was peculiar to the imperial family. Therefore I find it difficult to believe that the children of the élite in imperial times normally participated in the *cena* seated behind their father or at special tables (See, however, Bradley in this volume on other possible evidence).

There can be no doubt, however, that Roman children of the élite sometimes did attend or participate in the *cenae* of their parents. There are a few casual remarks referring to this in the material I have used. Pliny the Elder quotes Varro in his chapter on wine (14.96) saying that when L. Lucullus was a boy he never saw a formal banquet in his father's house at which Greek wine was served more than once. Pliny uses the term *puer* which must refer to the childhood of Lucullus. We are not informed whether this implied that the child Lucullus had actually attended his fathers banquets or just been around. But in any case the fact that Lucullus had any remembrance of the quality of the wine served in his father's home does not say anything about whether his father had felt that his presence was of importance. A more interesting example is found in Suetonius' biography of Caligula (24): After having lost his sister Drusilla Caligula decreed a period of public mourning; there was capital punishment for laughing, going to the baths, or for having dinner with parents, wife, and children.[12] Neither laughing nor going to the baths were unusual habits for the Romans, so we must conclude that dining with one's family cannot have been an extraordinary activity either. The interesting thing about Caligula's strange ban is that it is evidently directed against everybody without distinction. This — at least — gives an indication of how widespread common meals in the family were. It is interesting to note, and perhaps not easy to understand, why in Roman literature more emphasis was not put on these common meals. The Romans who wrote this literature obviously did not consider the common family meal to be a special characteristic of the family unit. This situation, with the exception of the information from Suetonius, just quoted, applies only to the élite. We still have not approached the major part of the population outside this group.

Status groups not belonging to the élite

It is extremely difficult to learn anything about the layers of society below the one which produced the literature. The literary references that can be found are indirect and seem unrealistic. Take for example Juvenal who in his fourteenth Satire, imagines what family life must have been like in the countryside in the old days far away from the vices of imperial Rome: "A little plot ... would feed the father himself and the crowd at the cottage where lay the wife in childbed, with four little ones playing around — one slaveborn (*vernula*) three the master's own; for their big brothers, on their return from ditch or furrow, a second and ampler supper of porridge would be smoking ..."[13] Note that Juvenal both comments on the frugal life of this ideal country family and on the size and structure of the family. The wife is very fertile. She is in childbed after having given birth to several children. This ideal was in all probability — both according to Juvenal[14] and modern demographic stipulations[15] — far from the realities of imperial Rome. Moreover a slavechild — a *verna*, that is a slave born in his master's house — is playing with the master's children. This theme is found in other idyllic descriptions of life in the country (for example Tibullus 1.5 and Martial 3.58) and emphasizes that the picture is quite unrealistic.

Usually the levels of society below the élite can be approached through the epigraphic material and to a certain extent through lawtexts. Where meals are concerned, however, this material gives no insight.

The conclusion at this point is that there is no evidence that the common meal of parents and their children played any role at all in constituting them as a family group, a nuclear family in our sense of the word. One reason may be that the nuclear family simply did not exist. There are several indications of this. One of the clearest indications is to be found on tombstones, both the ones marking single burials and the ones originally placed over the entrance to a so-called family tomb.

The evidence of the tombstones

On the Isola Sacra — the necropolis of Portus outside Rome — some inscriptions on family tombs are to be found still *in situ*.[16] Only on very few of them are there any traces of close kin relationships like the ones we would expect to find in a nuclear family. Tomb 87 is a typical example: It is dedicated by Publius Varius Ampelus and Varia Ennuchis to themselves, and to Varia Servanda their *patrona*, and to their freedmen of both sexes and their descendants; the formula *libertis libertabusque posterisque eorum* is used here as in most cases. Further, it is mentioned that no one outside the family could be buried in the tomb and that no heir outside the family could inherit it.[17] This is quite interesting since the most family-like relationship mentioned in the inscription is probably the marital one between Ampelus and Ennuchis. No children are mentioned, neither of the dedicators nor of the commemorated *patrona*. It is likewise unknown whether the *patrona* Varia Servanda had been married. The tomb contains several burials — about 46 — all of them, except Varia Servanda's, anonymous. Children might have been buried here anonymously to be sure, but then it is strange that they are not mentioned in a formulaic way in the inscription — for example with a *liberisque* — but this formula is only very infrequently found while the formula for freedmen is very usual.

The absence of family in our sense of the word is striking in these inscriptions — not only the ones from Isola Sacra, but also in inscriptions with a provenance from Rome. The impression that many of the dedicators of these inscriptions simply had no children is not easily dismissed.[18] Tomb 15 on Isola Sacra is another typical example (See Fig. 1). It is dedicated by Veria Zosime to herself and to her well-deserving husband, Lucius Verrius Eucharistus, and to their freedmen of both sexes, and it is added that no heir outside the family could inherit the tomb.[19] Tomb 64 is perfectly equivalent to tomb 15: It is dedicated by Betiliena Antiochis to her spouse, Publius Betilienus Synegdemus, and to their freedmen of both sexes and their descendants. But in this case we have very strong evidence that the couple actually had no children.[20] A funerary urn has been found that originally must have been put up inside the tomb. It commemorates both Publius Betilienus Synegdemus and Betiliena Antiochis and is dedicated by a certain Marcus Cosconius Hyginus.[21] Obviously Betilienus Synegdemus predeceased his wife Betiliena Antiochis and no close relatives were left to see to her funeral. Whatever the relationship had been between Betilienus Synegdemus, Betiliena Antiochis, and Cosconius Hyginus they cannot possibly have been parents and son or patron(s) and freedman/men. This is clearly indicated by their names.

In 1956 a necropolis under a parking ground in the Vatican was excavated by a Finnish team.[22] Also here, close family is hard to find. But like

Fig. 1. Tomb no. 15 on Isola Sacra between Ostia and Portus (Author's photo).

Isola Sacra, it is possible to discern if tombs are put up close to each other and thus if close kin or other close relations put up epitaphs beside each other. The best example I have found is the small plot belonging to Gaius Licinius Syneros. On one stele he has commemorated his freedman Gaius Licinius Felix who died at the age of 31 years.[23] On another stele his *patrona* Licinia Helena is commemorated[24] and on a third, his well-deserving slave Euphemus, who died at the age of 25 years is mentioned.[25] To my mind this looks like a well established quasi familial unit. There is a fourth stele on the plot of Licinius Syneros. It is dedicated by Marcus Masurius Pothinus to his wife Oculatia Daphne.[26] Fortunately an inscription in *CIL* 6 explains the relationship between Licinius Syneros and Masurius Pothinus. They must have been friends. They appear together with many others (from the *tribus Sucusana Iuniorum*) as dedicators of an honorary inscription to Vespasian and his family.[27]

Above I mentioned tomb 15 on Isola Sacra as a typical specimen of a so-called Roman family tomb without many traces of family — in our sense of the word — in the inscription. It was emphasized by the dedicator of tomb 15 that the tomb should not be alienated but remain in the hands of the family. The construction of the tomb proper explains why. There are *klinai* on each side of the entrance door designed for the very important meals shared by the living and the dead on the special festival days appointed to the cult of the dead.[28] If the inscription over tomb 15 on Isola Sacra is taken into consideration, it is unavoidable not to conclude that the *liberti* of Veria

Zosime and Verrius Eucharistus and their descendants must have been expected to take care of the cult of the dead. It did not matter whether the participants were related to each other by blood. The name would do. This concept of relationships within the *familia* has nothing to do with nuclear family, nothing to do with children and their parents.

It is striking how far the Roman ideas of family life are from our concepts. Our concepts of the family, on the other hand, is much more in accordance with the ideal presented by the early Christian writers.

The Christian evidence

As mentioned above I have looked up the same words relating to meals both in the PHI CD-ROM #5.3 where pagan literature is presented, and in the CETEDOC, where early Christian literature is presented. None of the three Christian authors that I have analyzed are particularly interested in families, children, or meals, but in the writings of Augustine there are some references to the nuclear family — parents and children — around the table. In his commentaries on the Psalms af David, Augustine makes mention of the family dinner table even though this is not referred to in the text on which he is commenting.[29] Further he mentions the fact that mothers nursed their children themselves. This virtue was particularly emphasized by the early Christians, and obviously some Christian mothers had changed the otherwise very prevalent habit of using wet-nurses and had nursed their children themselves.[30] There is epigraphic evidence of this fact: In *CIL* 6.32049 a Christian woman, Turtura, is commemorated by her husband. He describes her as *deo serviens, unice fidei, amica pacis, castis moribus ornata, communis fidelibus amicis, familiae grata, nutrix natorum et numquam amara marito* ("serving God, being of unique faith, a friend of peace, embellished with chastity, unpretentious towards all the faithful, agreeable to her household. She nursed her own children and was never unpleasant to her husband"). This inscription comes from Rome. A more precise provenance can unfortunately not be provided. In the comment to Psalm 130, Augustine describes that a mother feeds her infant child with her own milk which is nothing but meat and bread from the dinner table changed in the mother's body to a substance more suitable for an infant than meat and bread. The clearest indication of the Christian family around the table seems, to me, to be Augustine's sermon 117 where he uses the same picture of the mother transforming the food from the dinner table to milk for her infant: he writes: *nonne esca erat in mensa? sed invalidus est infans ad comedendam escam, quae in mensa est: quid facit mater?* ("Was there no food on the table? Yes, but the infant was not able to share it with the others: So, what does the mother do?") The keyword here is *comedendam*. It does not in Christian literature have the negative connotations found in pagan Latin literature (consume, devour), but means simply eat together. Thus, as far as I can see Augustine is showing us a table with a meal, a child who is too small to share this meal with the others around the table, and the child's mother who will take care of it. Examples like these from Augustine are never found in pagan Roman literature. It might be argued that the description of Christian family life in the commentaries and sermons of Augustine should be considered as ideal and idyllic like the picture found in the works of pagan Roman poets.[31] But the description in the *Confessiones* of his mother Monnica's childhood in a half Christian half pagan family, carries no idyllic connotations insofar as the family dinner is concerned.

Augustine was probably representative of a new Christian concept of what family life implied. The early Christian epigraphic material shows an interesting and conspicuous absence of relationships outside the close family,[32] while Christian literature emphasizes the importance of the marital and parental ties. As I pointed out above when I mentioned the inscriptional evidence from Isola Sacra, close relationships among the pagan Romans were not necessarily blood kin relationships, while these relations seem to have been the ones most important to the Christians.

In the Digest several passages deal with the problems of inheritance and legacies of masters of households because they had concubines by whom they had biological children who became slaves in the household. Ambrose in his discourse on Abraham (1.4) warns that this state of affairs would ruin marital love (*solvit caritatem coniugii*), make the slavewomen arrogant (*superbas ancillas facit*), wives angry (*matronas iracundas*), the spouses quarelling (*discordes coniuges*), the concubines impudent (*concubinas procaces*), and the husbands untrustworthy (*inverecundos maritos*). Therefore, it is perhaps not so strange that in pagan Latin literature it is difficult to find any mention of children at mealtimes. Children begin to be mentioned in early Christian literature, and it was not before that time that the ideal of the parents and children unit became established and cherished.

Notes

1. Charles & Kerr 1988, 17. Two feminist sociologists on the importance of the family's daily common meal in contemporary Western Society — and thus of the women who traditionally prepare these meals: "The most important meal she cooks in the day is the main meal which ideally should be eaten by the family *as a family*; i.e. they should eat it together sitting round a table, talking to each other and enjoying each other's company. This is seen as an important part of family life and something for which women are responsible." (p. 18).
2. See Saller & Shaw 1984
3. Cf. Dixon 1992, 4ff.
4. See DeVault 1991, 37-39 regarding the diminishing possibilities for members of the same nuclear family to share a meal together on a regular basis. I am grate-

ful to Lotte Holm, the Royal Veterinary and Agricultural High School of Denmark for references to modern sociological analyses of family and food in contemporary Western Society.

5. Based on the Christian authors published in the series *Corpus Scriptorum Ecclesiasticorum Latinorum*.

6. Suetonius gives in his life of *Vitellius* 13.1 a useful list of the meals of the day and their respective names: *Sed vel praecipue luxuriae saevitiaeque deditus epulas trifariam semper, interdum quadrifariam dispertiebat, in iantacula et prandia et cenas comisationesque, facile omnibus sufficiens vomitandi consuetudine*: "But his besetting sins were luxury and cruelty. He divided his feasts into three, sometimes into four a day, breakfast, luncheon, dinner, and a drinking bout; and he was readily able to do justice to all of them through his habit of taking emetics." (Translation by Rolfe, *LCL*).

7. *... inde domum me / ad porri et ciceris refero laganique catinum; / cena ministratur pueris tribus et lapis albus / pocula cum cyatho duo sustinet, adstat echinus / vilis, cum patera gutus, Campana supellex.*

8. *Cenanti mihi, si cum uxore vel paucis, liber legitur; post cenam comoedia aut lyristes; mox cum meis ambulo, quorum in numero sunt eruditi.* (Translation by Radice, *LCL*).

9. "... and he never dined in their company unless they sat beside him on the lowest couch ..." (Translation by Rolfe, *LCL*).

10. *Adhibebat omni cenae et liberos suos cum pueris puellisque nobilibus, qui more veteri ad fulcra lectorum sedentes vescerentur*: "He always invited his own children to dinner along with the sons and daughters of distinguished men, having them sit at the arms of the couches as they ate, after the old time custom." (Translation by Rolfe, *LCL*).

11. *Ann.* 13.16: *Mos habebatur principum cum ceteris idem aetatis nobilibus sedentes vesci in aspectu propinquorum, propria et parciore mensa*: "It was a custom that the emperor's children and others of the same age had their dinner seated at separate and more frugal tables supervised by their relatives."

12. *Eadem defuncta iustitium indixit, in quo rississe lavisse cenasse cum parentibus aut coniuge liberisve capital fuit*: "When she died, he appointed a season of public mourning, during which it was a capital offence to laugh, bathe, or dine in company with one's parents, wife, or children." (Translation by Rolfe, *LCL*)

13. *... saturabat glaebula talis / patrem ipsum turbamque casae, qua feta iacebat / uxor et infantes ludebant quattor, unus / vernula, tres domini; sed magnis fratribus horum / a scrobe vel sulco redeuntibus altera cena / amplior et grandes fumabant pultibus ollae ...* (Translation by Ramsay, *LCL*)

14. See Juv. 6.594-601: *sed iacet aurato vix ulla puerpera lecto. / tantum artes huius, tantum medicamena possunt, / quae steriles facit atque homines in ventre necandos / conducit. gaude, infelix, atque ipse bibendum / porrige quidque erit; nam si distendere vellet / et vexare uterum pueris salientibus, esses / Aethiopis fortasse pater, mox decolor heres / impleret tabulas numquam tibi mane videndus*"... but how often does a gilded bed contain a woman that is lying in? So great is the skill, so powerful the drugs, of the abortionist, paid to murder mankind within the womb. Rejoice, poor wretch; give her the stuff to drink whatever it be, with your own hand: for were she willing to get big and trouble her womb with bouncing babes, you might perhaps find yourself the father of an Ethiopian; and some day a coloured

heir, whom you would rather not meet by daylight, would fill all the places in your will." (Translation by Ramsay, *LCL*)
15. See Parkin 1992, 133.
16. Thylander 1952.
17. *P Varius Ampelus et Varia Ennuchis fecerunt sibi et Variae P(ublii) f(ilia) Servandae patronae et libert(is) libertabus posterisq(e) eorum ita ne in hoc monimento sarchophagum in feratur h(oc) m(onumentum) h(eredem) f(amiliae) ex(terae) non s(equetur) in fronte p(edes) decem s(emis) quadrans in agro p(edes) treginta tres*: "P. Varius Ampelus and Varia Ennuchis put up (this epitaph) to themselves and to Varia Servanda daughter of Publius, their *patrona* and to their freedmen of both sexes and to their descendants so that no sarcophagus may be placed in the monument. This monument will not follow an heir outside the family. The width of the monument is 10 and three quarters feet and the depth 33 feet."
18. See Sigismund Nielsen 1996, 47.
19. *D(is) M(anibus) Veria Zosime fecit sibi et L Verrio Eucharisto marito suo benemerenti libertis libertabusque suis posterisque eorum h(oc) m(onumentum) h(eredem) exterum n(on) s(equetur) in fronte p(edes) x in agro p(edes) x*: "Veria Zosime put up this memory to her well deserving husband L Verrius Eucharistus and to their freedmen of both sexes and their descendants. This monument will not follow an heir outside the family. It is 10 feet broad and 10 feet in depth."
20. *Dis Manibus P Betilieno Synegdemo Betiliena Antiochis coniugi bene merenti libertis libertabus posteris que eorum fecit*: "Betiliena Antiochis put up this epitaph to her well-deserving husband Betilienus Synegdemus and to their freedmen of both sexes and their descendants."
21. *D(is) M(anibus) P Betilieni Synegdemi et Betilienae Antiochidi cura M Cosconi Hygini*: "To the memory of P Betilienus Synegdemus and to Betilienae Antiochis. M Cosconius Hyginus put up this memory."
22. Väänänen 1973.
23. No 40: *C Licinio Felici C Licinius Syneros lib(erto) suo v(ixit) a(nnis) xxxi*: "C Licinius Syneros put up this memory to his freedman C Licinius Felix, who lived 31 years."
24. No 41: *Liciniae Helenae posuit C Licinius Syneros patronae in fro(nte) p(edes) x in agr(o) p(edes) vs*: "C Licinius Syneros put up (this memory) to his patrona Licinia Helena. The monument is 10 feet across and five and a half feet in depth."
25. No 43: *C Licinius Syneros Euphemo servo suo bene merent(i) v(ixit) a(nnis) xxv*: "C Licinius put up (this memory) to his well-deserving slave Euphemus, who lived 25 years."
26. *Oculatiae Dapinni posuit M Masurius Pothinus*: "M Masurius Pothinus put up this memory to Oculatiae Daphne (?)."
27. *CIL* 6.200 iv, 61 and 66. See Steinby 1987, 93-94.
28. See Bragantini 1990, 62 ff: Riti per il morto. She emphasizes that the habit of constructing graves with outdoor *klinai* probably was most popular in the Hadrianic and Antonine era (p. 67).
29. In his commentary to Psalm 127, Augustine quotes verse 3 of Psalm 128: *filii tui sicut novellatio olivarum, in circuitu mensae tuae*: "Like newly planted olives your sons sit around the table." The commentary is a sermon preached on the occasion of saint Felix' day on asceticism: *Ergo, fratres, Felix martyr et vere felix et*

nomine et corona, cuius hodie dies est, contemsit mundum (127.6): "In truth, brothers, Felix the martyr — and he was indeed lucky (*felix*) both in regard to his name and his martyrcrown — whose day we celebrate today, contempted this world." It might therefore be argued that the dinner table described must be far away from reality. On the other hand, Augustine mentions in the *Confessiones* his mother Monnica's childhood experiences with the family dinner: ... *Nam eas (filias) praeter illas horas, quibus ad mensam parentum moderatissime alebantur, etiamsi exardescerent siti, nec aquam bibere sinebat* ...: "For instance, except during those hours when they were receiving their frugal meals at their parents' table, she (the childminder) would not allow them to drink water, however parched with thirst they might be." (Translation by Warner, Penguin 1963). There can be no doubt that Augustine here refers to the habits of family life in Northern Africa in his own time. Unfortunately the material is too scarce to provide us with any information from other parts of the empire. Thus it cannot be taken for granted that the experiences of Augustine and his mother were shared by well-off members of the middle class in other parts of the empire.

30. The persons mainly responsible for infants and minor children in Imperial Rome were their wet-nurses. There is reason to believe that most children of almost all status groups spent more than the two first years of their life with their nurse. There is evidence of that both in the epigraphic material, in the lawtexts, and in literature, see Sigismund Nielsen 1987. Some children spent all their time with their nurse away from their biological family; in other cases we must assume that the nurse stayed in the household of the parents of the infant. But information on children's meals with the exception of the medical advice of Soranos of Ephesos is scarce, see *The Gynecology of Soranos* 2.21 (trans. O. Temkin 1956).
31. See above p. 59.
32. See Sigismund Nielsen (forthcoming).

Eating with the Dead:
The Roman Funerary Banquet

Hugh Lindsay

Roman funerary customs are in a sense relatively well known, but nevertheless details about the role of food at Roman funerals are not that easy to uncover. It may be helpful to start by looking at the other major Mediterranean civilisation to identify common ground as well as identifiable areas of difference. Where there are gaps in our knowledge, it may be possible to make a plausible reconstruction through the use of comparative materials. I have given a brief summary of Classical Greek practice for this purpose. Other comparative materials will also be canvassed, but necessarily treated with caution.

Food and the Greek funeral[1]

In Greek ritual before the *prothesis* wild marjoram, celery and other herbs were scattered on the funerary bier to ward off evil spirits. The corpse itself was laid on vine, myrtle or laurel leaves, and the head of the corpse was decorated with garlands of laurel and celery.[2] The aim may have been to dispel the unpleasant trappings of death, as well as to bestow honour and comfort on the deceased. This soft, aromatic and verdant bed on which the corpse was laid was appropriate for one who was about to be returned to nature.

There was an emphasis on the potential pollution of those who came into contact with the corpse, and a bowl of water was provided at the door to enable those who came into contact to engage in a physical purification. Ointment vessels would be placed beneath the bier.[3]

At the tomb the mourner would traditionally dedicate a lock of hair together with *choai*, libations of wine, oils and perfumes, accompanied by a prayer. This stage in the ritual was followed by offerings (*enagismata*) which included milk, honey, water, wine, celery, *pelanon* (meal, honey and oil) and *kollyba* (first fruits of the crops dried and fresh fruits). It seems unlikely that the mourners actually participated in the eating at these banquets, for fear of passing under the influence of the spirit world.[4]

Greek tombs never mimicked the magnificent materialism of Egypt, and other aspects of expenditure on the funerary rites were also kept in check.

Nevertheless an emphasis on catering for the needs of the deceased in the tomb remained quite prominent in the Myceneaean and Homeric worlds, and continued to have an impact on subsequent customs. In the Homeric world the most cruel form of vengeance on a foe was refusal of burial; the souls of those who were not buried were unable to cross to Hades and could turn malevolent. Those who refused in their duties to the deceased would raise the anger of the gods.[5] In the Classical period there is something of an imperfect reconciliation between material and spiritual values in Greek burial customs. Concern often centres on the spiritual welfare of the deceased at least as much as on their material comfort.

The sumptuary laws of Solon had forbidden a bull sacrifice at the graveside, but animals of other sorts remained a commonplace feature – sheep, lambs, kids, birds and fowl.[6] Bulls were still allowed in exceptional circumstances; the dead from Marathon are an example. An animal on this occasion would be killed over a trench (*eschara*) to allow blood to run into the earth and appease the souls of the dead. These offerings formed part of the feast for the dead, and the meal was burnt as a holocaust. Offerings to the dead could include other lifetime trappings such as lyres, ribbons, garlands and robes. The whole process was conducted amidst grieving. There was an important notion of renewal associated with the offerings. By burying the dead in the earth and making offerings of fruit, grain and flowers, it was believed that the earth could be repaid for the gift of life, since earth was the nurse and mother of all things and thus fertility could be promoted.

Purificatory rituals would ensue — the household and objects within it would be purified with sea-water and with hyssop. Then the ritual meal known as the *perideipnon* was shared by all the dead man's relatives around the hearth of his house.[7] This would be held normally immediately after burial on the third day after death. The bereaved would wear garlands and deliver eulogies. According to Artemidorus the dead man himself was believed to be present.[8] Even if this was what the Greeks thought, it is likely that the aim was for the survivors to form a united group in the aftermath of their loss.[9] This was an occasion to demonstrate that the living and the dead no longer share the same family circle.

The *perideipnon* probably occurred immediately after the return of the relatives from the *ekphora*. According to Lucian (admittedly a late authority), it brought an end to the fasting which lasted for three days from the time of decease.[10]

Offerings at the tomb were made on the 3rd, 9th and 30th days — also after one year, and on certain festivals when the emphasis was on propitiating the spirits of the dead.[11] There is some dispute as to whether the dates for these tomb offerings are calculated from death or burial.

At Athens the 30th day rites seem to have brought an end to the obsequies.[12] In late writers a meal known as the *kathedra* again shared by all the dead man's relatives is mentioned as marking the end of mourning and the resumption of normality.

Introduction to the Roman material

When we turn to the role of food in Roman death rites we find that here too there was a complicated ritual sequence. Within a traditional Roman funeral, there appear to have been specific requirements over the type of food to be consumed as well as the stage at which it should be prepared.[13]

Some caution is necessary over the universality of Roman customs. Status clearly had an important impact on every stage of commemoration of the dead, and it can also be expected that the diversity of belief about the fate of the soul would result in different practices.

In relation to high status funerals, I have therefore concentrated on the imperfectly preserved archaic material, most of which emerges from Cicero's *De Legibus* and especially from Festus, the antiquarian late 2nd century epitomizer of Verrius Flaccus' *De significatu verborum*, a work in turn epitomized in the 8th century by Paul the Deacon.[14] Thus we have through a dual filter remnants of an antiquarian work of the age of Augustus. In several instances it seems as though even Verrius Flaccus included items which no longer reflected contemporary practice. As a freedman in the imperial house entrusted with the teaching of the grandsons of the emperor he was perhaps encouraged to dig up materials with a strong link to *mos maiorum*.[15] He was interested in the calendar, and associated with the partially surviving Augustan calendar at Praeneste.[16] There are serious problems in using a source with a bias of this type, but it is to be hoped that it may provide some reflection of the earliest Roman procedures; it is only to be expected that with the passing of time funerary customs should be repeated without much appreciation of their original purpose.

Lower class funerals may in many instances have been seriously truncated on grounds of cost, and economic factors can also be expected to have had an impact on subsequent commemoration. In trying to gain some picture of more lowly practice, I will briefly discuss the feasting which occurred in conjunction with Roman funerary clubs. Here again I believe that the evidence shows quite a move away from this supposed superstitious world of the early city.

Ancient Rome and modern China

In other cultures the ritual use of food is closely linked to the process of transformation which is occurring between the time of death, and in extreme cases, the creation of an ancestor. I have argued elsewhere in favour of the notion that ancestor worship had been important at an earlier stage in Roman development (probably very much earlier), although it had already undergone serious decay by the time of the late Republic.[17] Nevertheless we might expect the antiquarian material to show signs of this earlier phase in Roman society.

If this hypothesis is correct (and not vitiated by its reliance on an evolutionary argument), valuable insights and supplements may be provided by considering the ritual sequence followed in another society where ancestor worship is still practised, one in which the purpose of each stage of the ritual may be easier to ascertain. Such a society is to be found in modern Taiwan; I am not suggesting that Taiwanese society is in any substantial sense similar to Roman society, merely that the process of settling the ghost of a dead person in a society which believes in the continuing power of the corpse over the lives of the living will have some similarities regardless of the more general cultural setting. I have been dependent on an article by Stuart Thompson entitled "Death, Food and Fertility" for the following observations on Chinese practice.[18]

The starting point is that in both cultures there appears to be a belief that beings in the netherworld require nourishment from the survivors in this world for their well-being. This topic has been thoroughly investigated by Emily Ahern who in discussing the purpose of funerary offerings by the living (again in a Chinese context) explains that "the living hope to inspire a reciprocal response from the ancestors, to obtain through them the good life as they perceive it: wealth, rice harvests, and offspring".[19] This can be summarised as a hope for fertility from the dead.[20] There are two underlying expectations involved in the process of feeding the dead. Firstly, that they will be transformed into beneficial ancestors and secondly, that a process of exchange is underway. Corpse and survivor are mutually dependent, and each expects a service from the other.

One interesting component of the Chinese picture which cannot be found in the Roman context is the notion that mourners should abstain from certain prestige foods as a mark of respect to the deceased. When a Chinese emperor died the whole court would abstain from eating flesh or strong smelling vegetables as well as from drinking wine. As Thompson points out this has a certain logic to it, since it is considered that the more the mourners abstain the more the deceased can feast.[21] What was done during a Roman *iustitium*? We might expect some signs of like conduct, but only know about the cessation of business.[22] A *iustitium* may in fact only have come to cover a *funus publicum* under the empire.[23] Nevertheless some impact on dietary behaviour is surely a likely inference: This seems to be one of the areas monitored by Caligula during the *iustitium* for Drusilla.[24]

In the Chinese context food appears at the following stages of the ritual:

1. Food is presented immediately upon death and at the moment of encoffining. These foods which are particular to the Chinese context, are thought to protect the deceased on his "journey".
2. After encoffining, food offerings are presented twice a day (corresponding to each normal mealtime) until the day of burial. In China these offerings are made by the daughter-in-law of the deceased.
3. A major farewell feast immediately precedes the burial. Now the food is chosen in preparation for transformation into an ancestor. This time offerings are made by a wide range of agnatic relatives, and meat dishes, especially pigs' heads are often regarded as the primary offerings. This is of special interest in view of the use of pork in the Roman purificatory rituals. In China neighbours and friends also bring offerings to satiate hungry ghosts who would otherwise thieve the food offerings intended for the deceased. The final rite for the encoffined corpse before it is removed from the community is the threefold presentation of libations of wine for the deceased.
4. Further offerings are carried out as far as the grave and are presented after interment. On return from the funeral procession further offerings are made in conjunction with the installation of the temporary ancestral tablet in the household altar room or ancestral hall. This is an area where Rome yields very slim pickings, since nothing is known about the process by which ancestral masks came to be installed in the *atrium* of an aristocrat's home.
5. A funeral banquet for the guests is then held, and subsequent offerings to the deceased vary greatly depending on particular circumstances.

The foods themselves are significant, but it may be more convenient to try to discuss this as we look at Roman practice and notice the main differences of emphasis.[25] A final point worth noting from the Chinese funeral is that there is a clear distinction between food which is intended to placate the gods and food intended for the ancestors.

The use of food at Rome has very little in common with the above Chinese rituals. Thompson notes that food plays an unusually large role in all Chinese ceremonies.[26] In Rome food appears to play at best a very slight role in the display of the body or during transit to the grave, and no source refers to special foods or offerings expected at this point in the ceremony. Nor do we hear of food at this stage in Greek ritual.

After a burial had taken place, archaic rituals are associated with the purification of the house of death in Roman society.[27] A careful cleansing of the house of death had to be completed, and this can be seen as a parallel to the cleansing of the Greek house with sea-water and hyssop. Much of the terminology associated with the Roman ritual, as outlined above, appears in Festus-Paulus for its curiosity value.

The ritual cleansing fell to the *everriator* who was usually the heir, according to Festus-Paulus.[28] Pontifical law ensured that the responsibility was extended to whoever acquired control of the *sacra*. The term *everriator* derived from *extra verrere*, to sweep out. Serious repercussions (such as death) were thought to ensue if the house was not swept out, or in the event of any inadequacy in the operation. A special type of broom had to be employed for the purging.[29] The right moment for the cleansing was immediately after the removal of the body for burial.

Some aspects of the subsequent chronology are uncertain. The period of mourning known as the feriae *denicales*[30] followed the funeral and was brought to an end by the *novemdial sacrificium*. Cicero has few ideas about the etymology of the term *feriae denicales*, but he situates the mourning in the context of respect for the *sacra* of the individual, and underlines the presence of ritual elements.[31] What is clear is that many types of activity were taboo during this period of mourning[32] and that such matters were closely monitored by the pontiffs.[33] One uncertainty is whether the *novemdial sacrificium* was the same as the *silicernium*, or whether the *silicernium* occurred before the *feriae denicales*. It would make sense if the *silicernium* started the ritual, and the *novemdial* brought it to a conclusion, also at the grave. The sacrifice to the *Lar* appears to be separate, as discussed below.

There seems to be no doubt that the funerary meal known as the *silicernium* occurred at the tomb itself. Festus-Paulus describes it as a kind of sausage, which undoubtedly had some primitive ritual significance.[34] It also appears to be at the tomb that the heir was obliged to sacrifice a sow to Ceres (or possibly to Ceres and Tellus) under a ritual which was to take place in the presence of the deceased (*porca praesentanea*).[35] This sacrifice is an obscurity only recorded by Cicero and Veranius (as reported by Festus-Paulus).[36] Veranius has been identified as Veranius Flaccus, a contemporary of Varro, who had explored pontifical questions in one of his works. We can suspect that the fragment in Festus-Paulus was derived by Verrius Flaccus from this work.[37]

As far as can be ascertained the *porca praesentanea* was an obligatory rite to be performed in the presence of the corpse in every instance of decease. It represents a *piaculum* undertaken to cleanse the pollution of the *familia*, and can be contrasted with the *porca praecidanea* which would only be offered in cases where some omission or error had occurred.[38] Only when a pig had been sacrificed was a grave legally a grave.[39]

Pig sacrifices seem to be very commonly associated with the cleansing of ritual pollution. In relation to the Chinese context Thompson has a detailed discussion and concludes that pig sacrifices mark "the deceased's conversion from (near-) ghost to (near-) ancestor".[40] A direct equivalence is made between the flesh of the pig and the flesh of the deceased. Another emphasis is on the restorative qualities of pig flesh. This is of interest since Roman pig sacrifices are closely related to regeneration, as can be seen from the fact that the sacrifice is to Ceres. Pigs have also been seen as licentious creatures representative of unbridled sexuality and fertility, and this may explain why they are employed in regenerative rituals.[41]

On return from a Roman funeral those who had participated in the interment had to be purified with fire and water. This stage in the cleansing is called the *suffitio*.[42] The ritual involved using a laurel branch to sprinkle water on the participants, after which they were made to pass under the fire. An older term related to this ritual, the precise significance of which is lost, is the word *exfir*.[43] The use of the laurel to purge the pollution of death is also found in association with the Triumph.[44] Festus-Paulus uses the past tense in his description of the *suffitio*, as though it was no longer carried out in his own time (*suffitionibus adhiberi solitum erat*).

The *novemdial sacrificium* consisted of two components, the sacrifice itself and the subsequent banquet. The *Manes* of the deceased were offered unmixed wine as part of the process of settling his soul. Libations of water, milk and blood are also mentioned.[45] The blood would be that of victims offered in sacrifice.[46] There is perhaps here a parallel with the offerings made at a Greek tomb on the 9th day after the funeral. The menu at the banquet was fixed by usage and may be identical to the accompaniments of the purificatory ritual at the *silicernium*: eggs,[47] vegetables,[48] beans,[49] lentils and salt, as well as bread and poultry.[50] The ritual significance of this meal appears no longer to have been fully appreciated in the late Republican and early Imperial period. An heir irritated by the deceased for some reason might abstain from inviting those who assisted at the funeral (admittedly the context is satirical).[51] The occasion could also develop into a debauch despite a provision already found in the Law of the Twelve Tables prohibiting *circumpotatio*.[52] Normally, however, the deceased was not forgotten; food and wine were placed on his tomb. The food offerings provided a temptation for the indigent, who would undergo pollution if they ate this food.[53] Already Plautus talks of them and calls them *bustirapi*.[54]

A sacrifice of wethers to the *Lar* is mentioned by Cicero.[55] Nothing is known about either the location or timing of this event, but it is surely likely to have occurred in the *locus* of the *Lar*, that is at the home of the deceased, and might well be the final stage in the domestic purging. Notice the sacrifice of a sterile animal to the *Lar* in expiation of the death.

Some differences from Chinese practice as well as gaps in our knowledge of Roman ritual can be noted. In China there are constant sacrifices at mealtimes between death and burial. No Roman source suggests this level of observance in the Roman context. Roman practice seems to involve a nine day period, started and concluded with ritual acts, in the course of which the house of death is cleansed of its pollution, and the deceased is settled in his new abode. As in China, Roman superstitions imply that biological death is viewed as "merely a chapter-ending in that individual's more extensive biography".[56] Clearly however it is very problematic to imagine a majority of Romans subscribing to such a view of death in the sceptical world of the late Republic or early Empire.

Occasions for continuing celebrations in honour of the dead

Two major ceremonies were important for the cult of the dead within the Roman calendar. One of these was the *Parentalia* from 13th to 21st February, an occasion when the dead were honoured and appeased by offerings. This incorporated the *Feralia*. The other ceremony, the *Lemuria*, on May 9, 11, 13, was an occasion on which the dead were to be dreaded, and the aim of the occasion was to expel their shades through incantations. This highlights differentiation in categories of the deceased into the beneficient and malicious.[57]

What was critical for the avoidance of the creation of malicious corpses was appropriate burial. This can already be seen in the world of Homer, when Hector in anticipation of his own defeat asks Achilles to cede his corpse to his relatives after his death (*Il.* 22.338-342). A good example from the early Empire can be found in the shade of Caligula, which was said to haunt the Lamian gardens and frighten its custodians (Suet. *Calig.* 59). His burial rites had been truncated and hasty, and the ghost was supposed to have remained restless until his sisters returned from exile and gave him proper burial.[58] It was thought that the *Manes* would refuse to accept into their company the soul of a deceased person who had not been purified by inhumation or incineration under an appropriate Roman ritual. This was why it would wander around on the surface of the earth in the form of an evil ghost.

The *Feralia*[59] was a festival in February in honour of the dead. It is a specialised name for an element of the *Parentalia*, and was applied to the last day, the day when the *Manes* were the object of public hommage. This hommage was offered by the whole city.[60] Ovid places the festival on February 17th, although it is placed on February 21st on the faith of a letter of Cicero.[61] It may be that the discrepancy occurred because the term *Feralia* came to be applied to a segment of the entire February festival.

The complete period of the festival of which this day was the last began on the 13th February with the *parentatio virginis vestalis*. The following days were destined to honour the dead in a private capacity. Their proper name is the *Parentalia* (not the *Feralia* or *ferales dies*). Other days up to and including 22nd February are included. The 22nd itself was the *Caristia*, or *cara cognatio*.[62] The *Parentalia*[63] represent a festival in honour of the cult of parents commemorated by children and close relatives. It would be performed at the tomb side on the anniversary of the decease or funeral, and as a family repast. Tertullian mocks the great expense put out for honouring the dead.[64] Pliny tells us that beans formed part of the menu. Pythagoras had banned these from the standard diet because they formed the soul of the dead.

Early on this familial practice appears to have merged into a public cult under the title *Parentalia*, a festival which was attributed to Numa.[65] It would close with the *Feralia* in February and began near the tomb of Tarpeia with the *parentatio* of the Vestals.[66] Magistrates would participate, but only after abandoning their insignia. Although the festival was common to all the dead of the city the family would profit by it to honour on this day particular dead. Thus both the public and the annual family funerary celebration was called the *Parentalia*.

Numerous inscriptions mention legacies and foundations both private and public providing for the celebration of the *Parentalia*. The best known example here is that in honour of C. Caesar from Pisa. It provides for an annual celebration of the *parentatio*.[67]

The *Lemures*[68] are the spirits of the dead in Roman religion, and are related to the *Manes* and *Laruae*. They are less close to divine nature than the *Manes* and less terrifying than the latter, but share the ability to return to earth on certain days and terrify the living. The etymology of the word is uncertain, and modern scholars have rejected antique attempts to relate it to Remus.

Story has it that the *Lemuria* has nothing in common with the public character of the *Parentalia*, being a feast in honour of the dead for one's own family. The date is fixed as 9, 11, 13 May. Feet would be bare and floating garments would be worn.[69] The father would rise at midnight, would click his thumb against his fingers to prevent the phantoms from appearing to him. Then after purification he would throw black beans behind himself nine times repeating "I throw these beans and through them I bring back me and mine." One imagines that the shades were following without being seen and were gathering the beans. The father purified himself again and hit a vase and again nine times uttered the formula "*Manes* of the family come out". The number nine also emerges in the *novemdiale sacrificium*, the feast ending the nine day period after death during which the house remained soiled by the death. Beans also figure in Greek mortuary lustration. In Rome they are also used during the *Feralia*. As well, the living cast them on tombs to guarantee themselves against the grievous impact of the shades.

In Ovid's Fasti, the old woman who swears to Tacita, the personification of silence, rolls in her mouth seven black beans.[70] Beans were used as a remedy against vampires and their like in the ceremony performed on the Kalends of June in honour of the goddess Carna. The importance of the use of beans led to these Kalends being called *fabariae*. It will be remembered that the *flamen Dialis* was subject to a taboo on touching or naming beans.[71] Commentators note the similarity of Pythagorean views.[72] The three days of the *Lemuria* are *nefasti* like the *Feralia* in February. In consequence temples are shut and marriages are forbidden.[73]

Precisely what connection these public rituals had with domestic worship is less than clear. But it is surely to be expected that all of these rituals, even those celebrated publicly or at the tombside, would be reinforced by ceremonies taking place in the house. Domestic worship was located in the *atrium* of a Roman noble's house. The *Lararium* came to be seen as the resting place of all the divine protectors of the household: the *Lares*, *Penates* and *Manes*. In the famous passage in Polybius (6.53) it is clear that in high status families the *imagines* of the ancestors were not only located in wooden shrines in the *atrium*, but also were subjected to cult on the occasion of public sacrifices.[74] In Pompeian houses the *lararium* often takes the form of a miniature temple; these households are of lower status than the world described by Polybius, and the lararium was used as the focus for domestic worship. The head of the household would honour the *Manes* through libations of honey and milk.[75]

This was palpably the most important place for the continuing veneration of the deceased. Vergil in the *Aeneid* gives us a picture of the rituals performed by Aeneas on return to his father's tomb after 12 months. Aeneas pours on the ground two cups of unmixed wine, two cups of fresh milk, and two cups of sacred blood, as well as spreading flowers (5.77-80).

Low status celebrations

The inscription of the Lanuvium funeral club provides numerous insights into the nature of the organisations which were created for slaves and ex-slaves to ensure that they received decent burial.[76] The function of the club as an organisation for mutual support with reciprocal obligations emerges quite clearly from the constitution of the *collegium*.

Meetings were monthly, and the purpose of the meetings was to contribute the money with which deceased members were to be buried. An initiation fee of 100 sesterces was extracted together with an amphora of good wine. After dealing with the various contingencies under which a club member might die and thus be eligible for the disbursment of funerary costs, as well as the cicumstances under which club members could obtain recompense for expenditures made on behalf of club members, the constitution also dealt with the question of commemorative dinners. Naturally since these are collective celebrations emphasis is on the organsational side of things rather than ritual. These seem to be social gatherings. Chairmen for dinners are selected in turn, four at a time, from the membership list, and are obliged to provide an amphora of good wine, bread and sardines, a room for the dinner, hot water and a waiter. Even the location of the celebration seems to have been removed from the vicinity of the dead. This is a world of commemoration not far removed in spirit from the modern world.

Conclusion

There is no hope of reconstructing all the details of Roman funerary foods and the significance attached to these. There may well have been significant differences between the foods employed by different classes. In any case it is only to be expected that funerary customs will have tended to follow a set pattern over an extended period of time, and the precise signifcance of the rituals can under these circumstances easily be lost. There is something to be gained from the attempt to view Roman practice in relation to other cultural situations, in particular some appreciation of where to expect to find gaps in the picture, although care has to be taken not to build on the results with excessive confidence.

Notes

1. I give here only a summary of the best known practices, and in support have cited a bare minimum of references.
2. Discussed by Alexiou 1974, 5.
3. Details in Alexiou 1974.
4. Alexiou 1974, 7.
5. See Vernant 1982, 45-75.
6. On the prohibition of bull sacrifice, see Plut. *Sol.* 21. Extravagant sacrifices had clearly been the norm in the Mycenaean period. See C. Lecrivain in Daremberg & Saglio s.v. *funus*, col. 1369.
7. This is discussed by Garland 1985, 39ff. See also *RE* s.v. *perdeipnon*.
8. Artem. 5.82T.
9. See van Gennep 1960, 164 on such rituals. Their aim was "to reunite all surviving members of the group with each other, and sometimes also with the deceased, in the same way that a chain which has been broken by the disappearance of one of its links must be rejoined".

10. *Luct.* 24.
11. Briefly summarised in Humphrey 1993, 87-88.
12. This restriction on the length of obsequies may again be a product of the sumptuary legislation of Solon. It has been noticed that the quantity of sacrificial remains on Mycenaean sites testify to a lengthy continuation of the cult. See C. Lecrivain in Daremberg & Saglio s.v. *funus*, col. 1369.
13. There is little literature which deals in any depth with Roman funerary food. I have made greatest use of E. Cuq in Daremberg and Saglio s.v. *funus*. Some additional points have been culled from Toynbee 1971, Hopkins 1983, and Prieur 1984.
14. Festus-Paulus (ed. W.M. Lindsay, 1913).
15. On Verrius Flaccus see Suet. *Gramm.* 17, *RE* s.v. M. Verrius Flaccus (A. Dihle).
16. Suet. *Gramm.* 17, *CIL* 1^2 p. 206.
17. Lindsay, 1996, 271-85.
18. Thompson 1988, 71-108.
19. E.M. Ahern 1973, 91.
20. Thompson 1988, 73.
21. Thompson 1988, 74.
22. On *iustitium* see older discussions in Daremberg & Saglio s.v. *iustitium*, *RE* s.v. *iustitium*. The term was used not merely of a cessation of business on grounds of a death, but was also employed in Republican times for a cessation of business in times of emergency.
23. As E. Cuq maintains in Daremberg & Saglio s.v. *iustitium*. On *iustitium* see Vidmann 1971, 209-12.
24. Notice the very stiff requirements of the *iustitium* for Drusilla (Suet. *Calig.* 24.2 and Lindsay 1993, 109 ad loc).
25. The classic discussion of food as a code is that of Douglas 1971.
26. Douglas 1971, 71.
27. Obsession with ritual pollution is also a feature of Chinese funerary customs. See the illuminating discussion by Watson 1988, 109-34.
28. Festus-Paulus 68L s.v. *everriator*: *everriator vocatur, qui iure accepta hereditate iusta facere defuncto debet; qui si non fecerit, seu quid in ea re turbaverit, suo capite luat.*
29. Festus-Paulus 68L: *id nomen ductum a verrendo. nam exverrae sunt purgatio quaedam domus, ex qua mortuus ad sepulturam ferendus est, quae fit per everriatorem certo genere scoparum adhibito, ab extra verrendo dictarum.*
30. Festus-Paulus 61L s.v. *denicales feriae: colebantur cum hominis mortui causa familia purgabatur.*
31. *Leg.* 2.22.55
32. Gell. *N.A.* 16.4.4.
33. Columella *Rust.* 2.21.
34. On the *silicernium* see Festus-Paulus 377L: *silicernium erat genus farciminis, quo fletu familia purgabatur.* Servius *Ad Aen.* 5.92 thought the word originated from the presentation of the sacrifice on a piece of *silex*, but this may be no better than modern guesses.
35. Le Bonniec 1958, 93ff.
36. Festus-Paulus 296L: *praesen<tanea?> porca dicitur, ut ait Veranius, quae familiae purgandae causa Cereri immolatur, quod pars quaedam eius sacrifici fit in conspectu*

mortui eius cuius funus instituitur. Notice also a vague allusion to a pig sacrifice in Cic. *Leg.* 2.22.55.
37. On Veranius Flaccus see *RE* s.v. Veranius no. 1.
38. On the *porca praecidanea* notice its use before the harvest to satisfy Ceres. See Cato *Agr.* 134. For the use in funeral ritual see Varro *De Vita Populi Romani frag.* 104, Festus-Paulus 218L, Gell. *N.A.* 4.6. Varro and Gellius make it clear that this type of sacrifice is only associated with a situation where an heir has made some omission or error over the funeral. The *porca praecidanea* is discussed by Bonniec 1958, 91-107.
39. Cic. *Leg.* 2.22.55.
40. Thompson, 1988, 96.
41. Thompson 1988, 100.
42. Festus-Paulus 3L s.v. *aqua et igni: funus prosecuti redeuntes ignem supergradiebantur aqua aspersi; quod purgationis genus vocabant suffitionem.*
43. Festus-Paulus 69L s.v. *exfir: purgamentum, unde adhuc manet suffitio.*
44. Festus-Paulus 104L s.v. *laureati: milites sequebantur currum triumphantes, ut quasi purgati a caede humana intrarent urbem. Itaque eandem laurum omnibus suffitionibus adhiberi solitum erat, vel quod medicamento siccissima sit, vel quod omni tempore viret, ut similiter respublica floreat.*
45. Serv. *Ad Aen.* 5.78.
46. Tac. *Ann.* 3.2, *Hist.* 2.95.
47. Juv. 5.85, Lucian *Catapl.* 7, Tac. *Ann.* 6.5.
48. Plut. *Quaest. conv.* 7.
49. Hor. *Sat.* 2.6.63.
50. Plut. *Crass.* 19.
51. Pers. *Sat.* 6.33.
52. Athen. 8.34, Cic. *Leg.* 2.24.
53. Tib. 1.5.53.
54. *Pseudol.* 348.
55. Cic. *Leg.* 2.22.55.
56. Thompson 1988, 80.
57. See Prieur 1984, 14.
58. It is interesting to note that there was a theory that the corpse of a tyrant could not be consumed by fire. See, also Suet. *Tib.* 75.3, commented on by Lindsay 1995.
59. See Daremberg and Saglio s.v. *Feralia*.
60. Ov. *Fasti* 2.553-616.
61. Cicero *Att.* 8.14.
62. Lydus *Mens.* 4.24. On the *De Mensibus* see now Maas 1992, 53-66, especially 61ff.
63. See Daremberg and Saglio s.v. *parentalia, parentatio*.
64. Tert. *De Anim.* 4.
65. Auson. *Parent. praef.*, Ov. *Fasti* 2.543.
66. See Dion. Hal. *Ant. Rom.* 2.40.
67. *ILS* 140 = *EJ*^{2} 69.
68. See Daremberg and Saglio s.v. *Lemures*.
69. Ov. *Fasti* 5.432ff.
70. Ov. *Fasti* 2.571ff.

71. Festus-Paulus 187L.
72. Porph. on *Hor. Sat.* 2.6.63.
73. Ov. *Fasti* 5.485ff.
74. See Lindsay 1996.
75. On domestic worship see Orr 1978, and Harmon, 1978.
76. *CIL* 14.2112 = *ILS* 7212.

Ut Graeco More Biberetur:
Greeks and Romans on the Dining Couch

Katherine M.D. Dunbabin

The quotation in my title comes from one of Cicero's Verrine orations (*Verr.* 2.1.26.66), describing Verres' outrages at the house of the distinguished citizen of Lampsacus, Philodamus. Verres and his cronies have contrived an invitation to a *convivium* at Philodamus' house, and after they have reclined, the proposal is made that they should drink "in the Greek fashion". The host accedes, they call for larger cups, and the party is under way with general conviviality and conversation. Trouble develops when Verres' henchman, Rubrius, asks Philodamus to summon his daughter to the party, and Philodamus replies that "it is not the custom of the Greeks that women should recline at the *convivium* of the men". A brawl breaks out, one of the Romans is killed, and eventually the unfortunate Philodamus and his son are condemned to death.

The episode is located at a crucial stage in the process of mutual acculturation of Greeks and Romans, and of the encounter, and sometimes, as here, the clash, of their practices and expectations. It raises questions not only about the actual differences between Greek and Roman fashions of dining and drinking in the late Republic, but even more about the perception of these differences by the Greeks and Romans themselves.

That there was such a perception is immediately clear in several respects from Cicero's account. We do not know just what was meant by drinking *graeco more*, but it is usually taken to mean either drinking fixed amounts laid down by the master of the feast, or drinking a toast and passing the cup to the person toasted to drain: the passages quoted in support of either interpretation are far from conclusive.[1]

The second obvious distinction is that of the absence of women from the Greek *symposion*, and their presence (implied) at the Roman. This is something of a cliché, though it too might benefit from closer analysis.[2] However the Cicero passage in itself suggests that things were considerably more complex than these two examples suggest. The party, after all, is given in a Greek city, Lampsacus, by a Greek host, to a group of prominent and powerful Romans. Such occasions must have arisen innumerable times in the later centuries of the Republic, as Roman administrators and traders

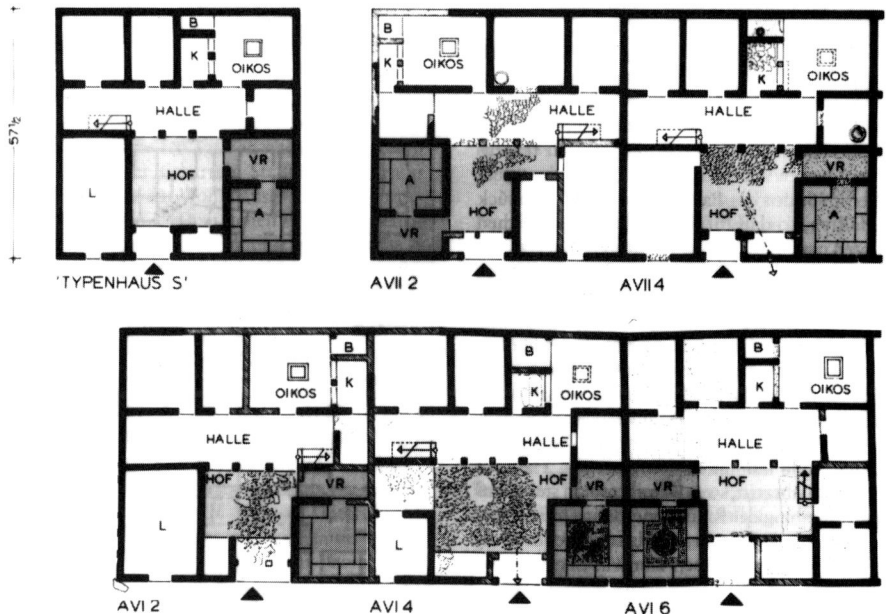

Fig. 1. Olynthus, reconstructed plans of south-facing houses; andrones shaded, and with position of couches indicated. (Hoepfner & Schwandner 1994, fig. 61.)

spread throughout the Greek world; usually, one hopes, the representatives of the two cultures adapted more peacefully to one another's *mores* than on this occasion. But there must have been many respects in which accommodation was needed, and where fashions and conventions differed.

In this paper I propose to examine the nature of the physical spaces within which the two societies were accustomed to dine, in the hope of discovering patterns of behaviour and social climate that these imposed on their users. The archaeological evidence is not sufficient to permit a narrow focus on the late Republic alone; but a wider chronological viewpoint should make possible a picture of changing patterns on a larger scale in the Graeco-Roman world.

The Greek and Hellenistic types of dining rooms

Greek *andrones* of the fifth and fourth centuries BC have a classic form of remarkable homogeneity in lay-out and scale, at least for rooms designed for private dining. A Greek could go from Olynthus to Eretria, from Athens to Kassope, and find himself in familiar surroundings when invited to a *symposion* (Fig. 1).[3] The characteristic features are well known: a near-square room with off-centre door, and a trottoir (or *kline*-band) for the couches around the edge of three-and-a-half sides. In addition the sizes too are standard. In the majority of domestic buildings the rooms are designed to hold seven couches of more or less standard dimensions, about 1.80 to 1.90 m long and 0.80 to 0.90 m wide. Rooms of the same shape holding eleven couches are common in buildings for civic and ritual dining, and in some grander private houses. Other numbers of couches such as five or nine necessitate a rectangular shape; nine is quite common at Olynthus, often as a result of later alterations to the original plan.[4] Rooms for three couches are rare; a richly decorated example occurs in the House of the Mosaics at Eretria alongside seven- and eleven-couch rooms in the same house.[5] Other shapes and sizes are current in civic and ritual contexts, and I return to some of them below; but it is the typical domestic form that principally concerns me here.

From such an arrangement follow certain consequences for social behaviour. Assuming that each *kline* could hold either one or two guests, a characteristic Greek private dinner or *symposion* would offer space for up to fourteen guests without a squeeze in a seven-*kline* room, up to twenty-two in one with eleven. Each guest, or pair of guests, has his own table; the servants must bustle about in the centre to serve them. An eleven-couch room measures about 6.50-6.80 m square, a seven-couch one about 4.50-4.80.[6] These are therefore quite substantial rooms; communication between guests on opposite sides is possible only if strict order is maintained. Intimate discussion between the assembled guests is therefore hardly the norm in such rooms; they are well adapted for more formal performances, the guests entertaining one another with singing or the lyre, or speaking in strict order of seating. Otherwise there will be a tendency to break up into smaller groups, or for discussion to deteriorate into shouting across the room.

The physical arrangement had other consequences too. The lay-out of the couches around the four walls of the room gives little opportunity for any difference in status between them. It is true that the sources distinguish a place for the guest of honour on the first couch to the right of the door, while the host has the bottom place on the last couch on the left; but there is no sign of any strict hierarchical arrangement, and the couches are equidistant from the service and entertainment in the centre.[7] The lay-out lends itself to the same sort of ethos as the practice of communal mixing and of drinking in turn: a circle meeting on equal terms and united by common behaviour.

Dining rooms of this type continue to be found, and certainly continued to be used, in the Hellenistic period. One at Arta, for example, appears to have a *terminus post quem* of 168 BC: it is rectangular, designed to hold nine couches, and otherwise of traditional form.[8] In general, however, other forms appear to have predominated at this time, insofar as can be judged

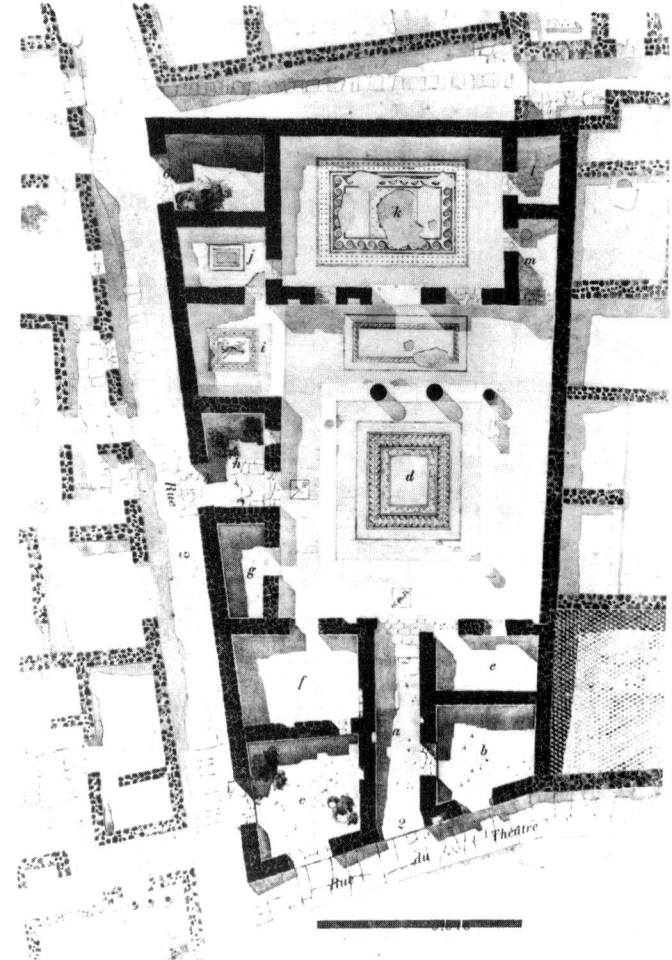

Fig. 2. Delos, Maison du Trident. (Chamonard 1922, pl. 13.)

from the notoriously limited evidence for Hellenistic domestic architecture. Birgitta Bergquist has distinguished two common types, the broad-room and the long-room; both go back to the classical and even the archaic periods, when they are more frequent in public and religious than in domestic architecture.[9] By the Hellenistic period, the broad-room has become the dominant form for the main dining and reception room of the house, at least if we may judge by the evidence from Delos. Here the typical main room is the so-called *oecus maior* or Broad-Room. It is usually on the central axis, is broader than it is long, and the door is normally central. Rooms of this type were evidently multi-functional, and in smaller houses served as the main living quarters of the household. In the grander houses, however, they are identified as reception and dining rooms.[10] Their

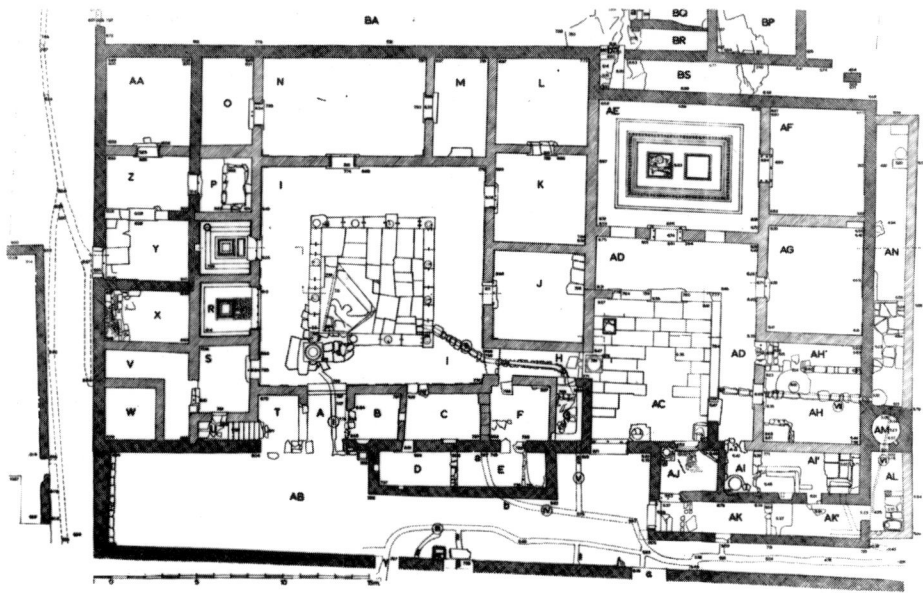

Fig. 3. Delos, Maison des Comédiens (left) and Maison des Tritons (right), plan. (Bruneau & Vatin 1970, pl. A.)

use for dining is often indicated by the lay-out of the pavement. A regular band on all four sides marks the space for the couches; the centre is usually distinguished from this band by a change in texture or quality, for instance from one pavement-type to another, as well as by its richer ornamentation. Such an arrangement is found, for instance, in the Maison du Trident (Fig. 2) and the Maison des Tritons (Fig. 3, right).[11] Occasionally too the outer band is raised above the rest of the surface with a marble frame at its edge, as in the Ilot des Bijoux at Delos, and in a Hellenistic building with mosaics at Samos.[12]

The plan and design of these rooms at Delos raise various questions about their use. The room is no longer designed specifically to fit the lay-out of the couches; if the couches were laid around the room in succession starting from the right of the door, a space would be left empty at the foot of the last couch to the left, since the door is usually no longer off-centre. Nor does it appear to be possible now to calculate a standard size of couch which will fit neatly into the available space in almost all rooms; we have to assume either that furniture of varying sizes was specially designed, or else that it no longer exactly fitted the space.

One suggestion is that couches were placed on three sides only, by analogy, supposedly, with Roman practice: that is, to form a Pi-shape.[13] The design of the pavements, with a band on all four sides, argues against this; nor would it in fact conform to normal Roman practice in the late Republic:

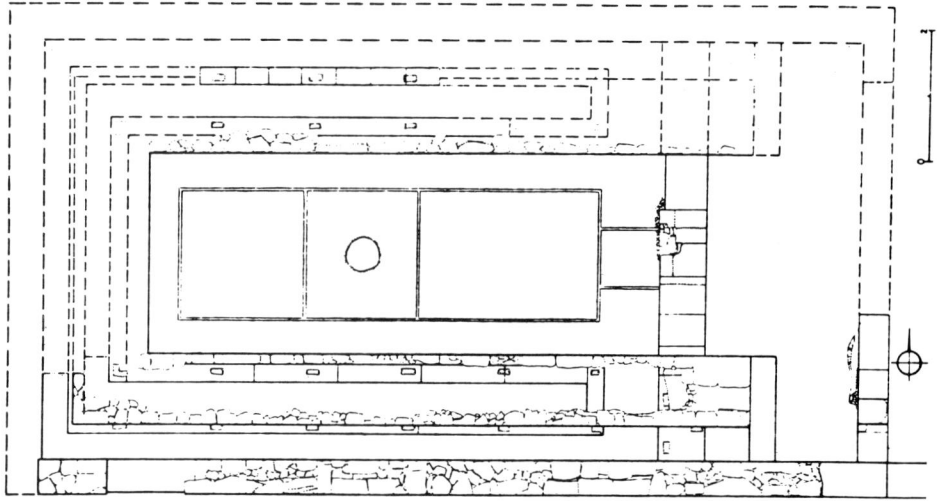

Fig. 4. Cyrene, northern Hestiatorion, plan showing structures of first and second phases. (Baldassarre 1976, fig. 12.)

I return to this question below. Another possibility might be that these rooms held two Pi-shaped sets of couches, one at either side of the room: that is, in the arrangement that Vitruvius describes as that of a Cyzicene *oikos*, with two *triclinia* facing one another (*duo triclinia inter se spectantia*).[14] However we have no other evidence to confirm this, and the proportions are sometimes strange. It seems, in any case, as if the rooms were no longer intended exclusively for use as a dining room; there is a new interest in the overall appearance of the room when not laid out with dining furniture, a requirement that it should be symmetrical and impressive when empty.

An alternative pattern is the longitudinal lay-out, with the room entered on its short side. This is fairly frequent in civic and religious dining rooms, where it can be traced back to the archaic period.[15] It can be seen, for instance, in the Hellenistic *Hestiatoria* at Cyrene, probably dating from the first half of the second century BC.[16] In the better preserved, the northern, the remains from the first phase show a Pi-shaped band marked off by limestone blocks, in which were cuttings for the supports of the couches, at a regular distance of 1.85 m. Corridors, barely wide enough for circulation, are left around the outer edges. The *klinai*, evidently of wood, which fitted into this strip, must have joined together in a continuous row. In a second phase, a masonry structure forming a continuous (rather longer) bench was substituted, though the rest of the lay-out was unchanged (Fig. 4).

In a room like this it seems likely that social behaviour would be subtly different from that in the square *andron*. It is difficult to imagine, for instance, that the traditional place of honour on the first couch to the right

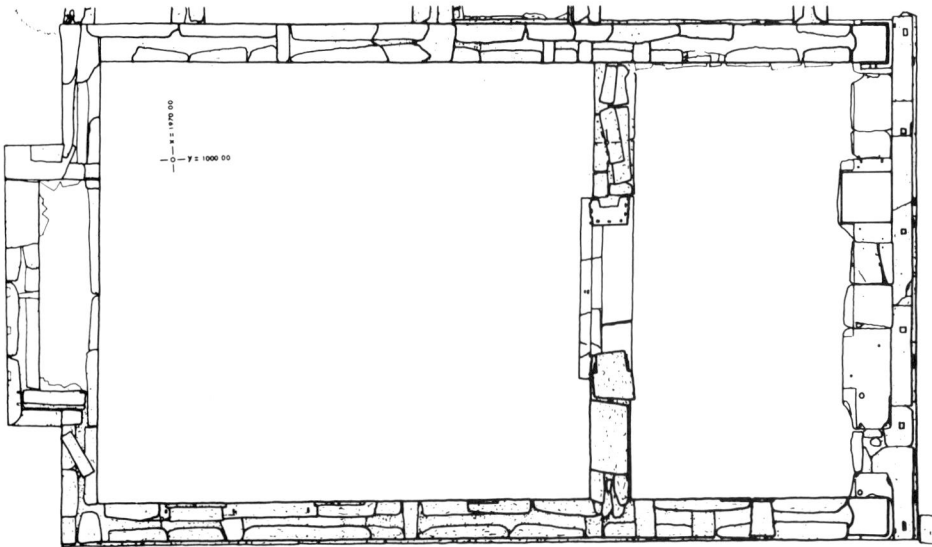

Fig. 5. Labraunda, Andron B, plan. (Hellström 1990, 247, fig. 2b.)

of the door was retained here, and one would guess that the bench or couches across the inner end were more prestigious. There is inevitably a separation between the guests in the inner part of the room and those at the ends of the couches, which makes communication between them, in a room some 11 m long, impossible. On the other hand, the continuous bench allowed much greater flexibility in the numbers of those partaking than was possible with separate couches.

Similar characteristics have been well brought out by Pontus Hellström in his account of the *andrones* at Labraunda, whose use for ritual dining he demonstrates.[17] These too have a longitudinal lay-out, and the place of honour must have been in the middle of the back wall (Fig. 5). As he says, this creates a "completely new banqueting type" from the traditional *andron*: one better suited to use in a royal — and ritual — context than to a normal Greek *symposion*. A literary reference to the same type, from approximately the same date, may be seen in the passage of Athenaeus (7.289e) describing how Philip II of Macedon entertained the megalomaniac Menecrates of Syracuse who called himself Zeus. Menecrates and his band of fellow-gods (evidently several of them, though we are not told how many) were made by Philip to recline on the middle couch (*epi tes meses klines*), which was raised very high and decked out ceremoniously: there they were fed with libations and incense while the rest of the company dined. This can only, I think, be imagined in a room shaped like the Labraunda buildings, which allowed special emphasis to be given to the middle couch. It would certainly not work in a traditional square *andron*, however large: the huge *androni* of Pella and Vergina, for instance, could not have been used in the way this implies.[18]

These characteristics may have made the longitudinal room more suitable for a royal or cult banquet than for a private dinner and *symposion*; I know of no examples of its use in large format in Greek private domestic architecture. On the other hand, the Pi-shaped lay-out could also be used on a very small scale, to provide rooms for more intimate dining. Delos provides some examples of small rooms which look as though they are designed to hold three couches. In the Maison des Comédiens, for instance, there are two rooms (R and Q) on the west side of the peristyle; Q measures 3.95 x 3 m, the dimensions of R are not given, but it appears to be about the same size (Fig. 3, left). In both, the pavement is divided into a plain surround on three sides and an ornamented central area; in R this had a frame of white marble and was slightly depressed.[19] It does not seem possible in these rooms to calculate a standard size of *kline*; the dimensions do not fit. Instead we have to assume, either couches of varying size, or continuous benches. Despite their small size, they belong to the representative section of the house: they are not meant simply for the family meals.[20]

The vocabulary used for dining rooms in the late Classical and Hellenistic periods complicates the issue further. Often it indicates that the design of the room to fit a specific number of couches was seen as its determining feature. Athenaeus (2.47f), writing in the second century AD, speaks of *triklinoi oikoi kai tetraklinoi kai heptaklinoi kai enneaklinoi*, rooms with three, four, seven, nine couches and so on, as being in use among the ancients, quoting sources predominantly from the fourth century BC. The Egyptian papyri of the third century BC from the Zenon archive which give the contracts for the decoration of the house of Diotimos at Philadelphia in the Fayoum show that it contained one *heptaklinon* (with a vaulted ceiling) and at least two *pentaklina*.[21] Other sources tell of the gigantic rooms for thirty, *triakontaklinoi*, and one hundred couches associated with the Hellenistic dynasts or the notoriously wealthy.[22] The terms came to be used at times simply as a unit of measurement, for rooms that were never meant to hold couches.[23]

On the other hand *triklinos*, which should mean a three-couch room, is attested as a term more often than we might expect from the rather scanty archaeological evidence for rooms suited for only three couches; though it is far from being the standard term at this period, it does seem to have a wider use.[24] It looks as though *triklinos* was used simply for a dining-area, regardless of size; at least when it occurs in a civic or ritual context, it seems likely that it refers not to three individual couches, but to the Pi-shaped arrangement. For instance, in the second-century inscription from Amorgos which I shall discuss shortly, the word is used to describe the dining arrangements for the locals — evidently the whole city — and visiting Greeks: the food, for instance, is distributed *kata triklinon*.[25] Since they appear to be spread out in the gymnasium, this can mean little more than "at table", presumably with a temporary structure of planks or benches.

The Roman type of dining room

The typical Roman *triclinium*, as we find it attested in the late Republic or early Empire, is also marked by a Pi-shaped lay-out of the couches. Occasionally this is demonstrated by real couches in masonry, for instance in the summer *triclinium* of the Casa del Moralista at Pompeii (III.4.2-3) (Figs. 6-7); more often the lay-out is indicated by markings on the floor.[26] What needs to be stressed, however, is the difference between Greek customs, even in their later Hellenistic manifestations, and Roman. The Romans took their name for a dining room from the Greek, but in a very specific form; there is no mention of the various seven-couch rooms or eleven-couch rooms, but only of three. The word *triclinium* came to be used of a dining room regardless of size, and in the later empire regardless of shape; but our earlier sources make it clear that in the late Republic it meant indeed three couches.

Traditional protocol laid down rules for the disposition of the guests: up to three per couch, with a strict hierarchy dictating their positions; the place of honour the *locus consularis*, no. 3 on the middle couch, the host next at the top of the lowest, and so on. Nothing about these arrangements corresponds to Greek antecedents; they reflect very clearly the Roman social *mores* of the Republic. The couches were broader than the normal Greek form, to allow for a more diagonal position of the guests.[27] Different too is the way in which they were packed close together around the single table, from which the guests ate communally; they were brought thereby much closer together as a group than in the Greek arrangement. This too surely has social consequences. The Roman *triclinium*, in its original form, seems designed to enforce a group solidarity, a very close contact between the diners, and to encourage discussion between all the participants. Attendants and slaves were kept largely outside the group, at least while they were eating; and in this early arrangement there was virtually no room for entertainers. John D'Arms has well shown that behind the ideals of equality and of the breaking down of social barriers at the Roman dinner table, which many of our sources express, lurk discrimination and the complex social structures of *clientela* and *amicitia*.[28] The physical setting encourages and reinforces, both the illusion of community, and the hierarchical order that lies behind that illusion (see Bradley in this volume).

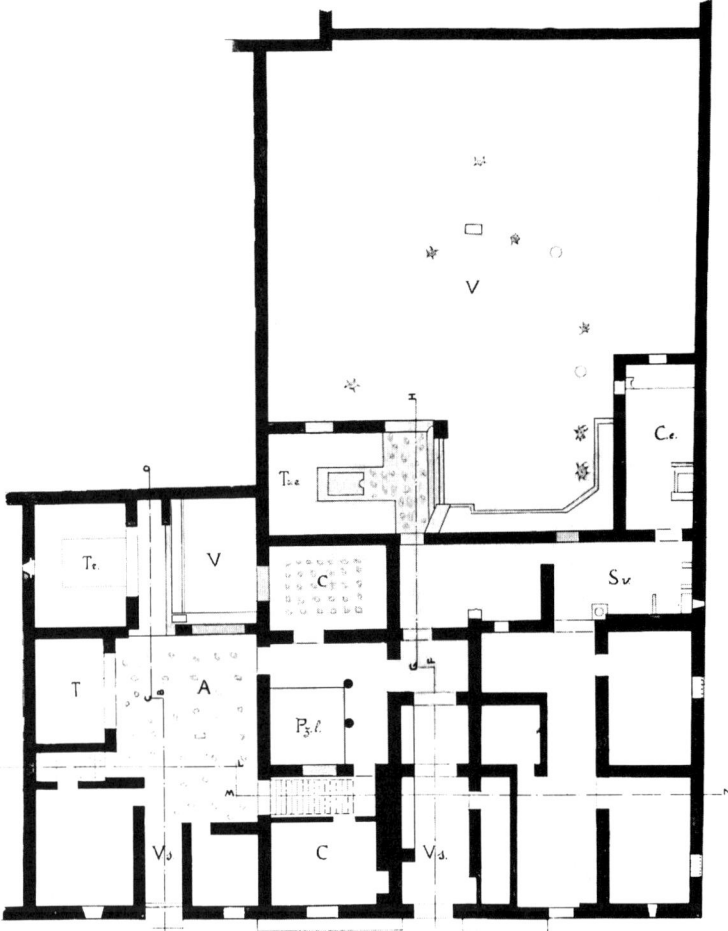

Fig. 6. Pompeii, Casa del Moralista (III.4.2-3), plan with triclinium *(Tr) and summer* triclinium *(Tr.e) marked. (Spinazzola 1953, vol. 2, fig. 699.)*

Greek *andron* or Roman *triclinium*? The clash of two cultures

Given that the Greek and Roman patterns were so different, and conveyed such different social messages, what happened when the two met? For wealthy Greeks in the Hellenistic East, the need to entertain visiting Roman dignitaries or rich Italian merchants must have arisen fairly frequently. One can imagine that for those who possessed an old-fashioned, *andron*-type dining room, this raised problems: an eminent Roman might well take offence if he was expected to recline in the more egalitarian atmosphere that such rooms were designed to encourage. The Hellenistic broad-room, as seen on Delos, might seem more suitable, but it was not what the Romans would be used to, and it also raises questions (which we do not

Fig. 7. Pompeii, Casa del Moralista (III.4.2-3), summer triclinium *with masonry couches and table. (Spinazzola 1953, vol. 2, fig. 730.)*

have the evidence to resolve) as to how it could convey the sort of hierarchical values that they would expect: it is not at all clear, to us at least, where the place of honour would be. When Philodamus entertained Verres and his company, it was surely desirable that Verres' superior position be in some way acknowledged.

Another story of the clash of the two cultures, a generation later in dramatic date, makes the point clear. The elder Seneca (*Suas.* 7.13) describes an occasion when Cicero's son Marcus was governor of Asia, and the rhetorician Cestius Pius from Smyrna dined with him. The drunken Marcus keeps asking the name of the man on the lowest couch, and being reminded of Cestius' name in vain by the slave. The phrase is characteristic of the Roman custom — *quid ille vocaretur qui in imo recumberet* — as indeed is the whole scene: the arrogant drunken Roman host, the slave whispering the name in his ear. The outcome also reminds us how far we are in such a context from the Greek ideal: the slave at last tries to make Marcus remember the name by telling him that Cestius had spoken scathingly of the elder Cicero, whereupon Marcus instantly orders Cestius to be flogged — evidently in the middle of dinner.

The situation would be more complicated still in a place like Delos, where large numbers of Romans and Italians were settled, including a substantial number of somewhat questionable social position such as freedmen; we may wonder to what extent the houses here are really representative of contemporary Greek forms, or whether they permitted some sort of a compromise, where the two traditions could mix.[29] Greek awareness of the distinctness of Roman custom, and of the need to provide for it, appears clearly on an inscription from Amorgos of the end of the second century BC, recording the public banquet given in the gymnasium by a certain Kritolaos (*IG* XII 7.515).[30] After listing the arrangements for locals and strangers, evidently Greek, it specifies that the Romans and their sons are to recline separately *kata ennea*, in groups of nine: i.e. in the traditional Roman *triclinium* format. It is striking both that there are enough Romans (presumably merchants) expected to be present to justify special arrangements, and that there is a consciousness that they should not be expected to recline in the same manner as the rest of the populace.

From the Roman viewpoint, adaptation to Greek customs might be appropriate in certain circumstances. The philhellene Roman, consciously relaxing in a setting designed for *otium*, could of course adopt Greek ways of behaviour, and this might on occasion extend to the lay-out of the space used for dining; for instance Octavian's notorious *dodekatheos* banquet can hardly have been suited to a regular Roman *triclinium*.[31] Awareness of the distinction undoubtedly existed, though Roman reaction may have been ambivalent. At all events, nothing in any Roman town house or villa known to me suggests the adoption of any recognisable form of the Greek domestic dining room, square or broad, as we have seen it so far.

However the typical Roman *triclinium* did change substantially under the Empire. There is a tendency for the rooms to grow larger; the couches move further apart, and are able to accommodate a larger number than the traditional nine, the space in the centre takes on more importance. The emphasis remains, as in the Republican *triclinium*, on the longitudinal dimension, and the head is very clearly at the short end. The pattern, most easily identified by the characteristic T+U design of the mosaics which mark the lay-out of the couches, developed in Italy in the 1st century AD, and then spread widely.[32] In the western provinces rooms of this sort were used as the characteristic main reception room, usually on the main axis of the peristyle and dominating it, in innumerable wealthy houses all around the Mediterranean, from at least the early second century till the fourth. We have no clear evidence for the nature of the furniture used in such rooms; a plausible reconstruction in many of them would be a continuous bench supporting a mattress along each side.[33]

More important for my present topic is that the pattern prevailed also in the Greek world of the Empire, eliminating all trace of the traditions of

Fig. 8. Antioch, Atrium House, mosaics of triclinium. *(Levi 1947, fig. 2.)*

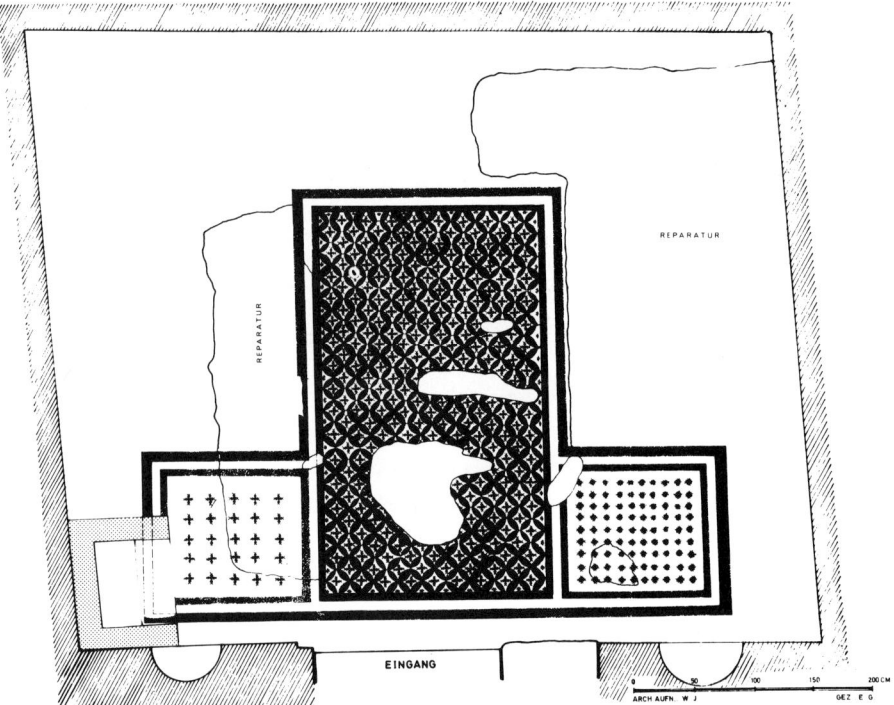

Fig. 9. Ephesus, Hanghaus 2/SR 24, plan of triclinium. *(Jobst 1977, fig. 154.)*

earlier Greek domestic architecture. We lack, notoriously, evidence for domestic architecture in the Greek East from the late first century BC and the first AD. When we meet examples again from about the beginning of the second century onwards, for instance at Antioch (Fig. 8) or Corinth, we are confronted by rooms unmistakably marked out for dining by the design of the mosaics: the pattern invariably is that of the fully developed Roman *triclinium* of the Empire, with the T+U design.[34] The Greek form has entirely disappeared, not only the classical *andron* but also the Hellenistic broad-room; only the longitudinal form suitable for the elongated Pi-shaped arrangement remains. And it is no longer confined to small rooms with space for three or four couches, as at Delos; the form is adapted to rooms of any size. The pattern recurs throughout the Eastern Mediterranean through the second, third, and even the fourth centuries, though at least by the fourth it was giving way to the fashion for the curving *sigma*-couch.[35] Among numerous examples, I may quote the house with the splendid Dionysiac pavement at Sepphoris in Israel, or a floor in one of the Hanghäuser at Ephesus dated by Jobst to the last quarter of the 4th century (Fig. 9).[36]

Again it is the social implications of the change that interest me. It implies a wholesale adoption by the Greeks of the Empire of their erstwhile

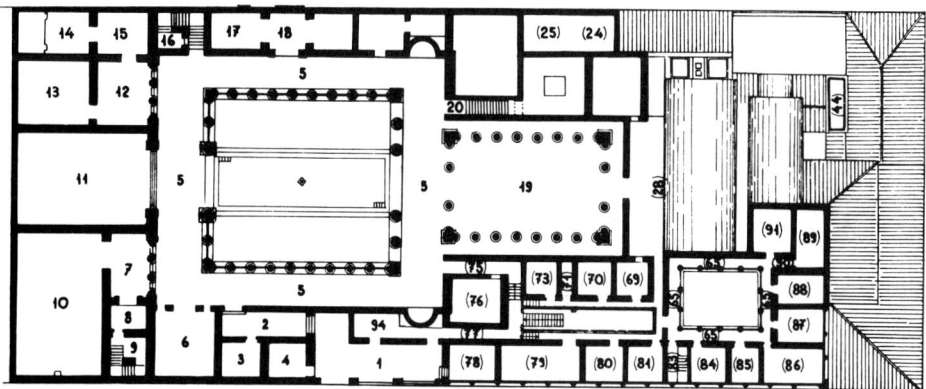

Fig. 10. Ptolemais, Palazzo delle Colonne, plan. (Pesce 1950, pl. 11.)

conquerors' fashions. The changes may seem small, and some had probably been anticipated already in the Greek world: continuous furniture instead of separate couches, emphasis on the long axis instead of the broad. But some are significant. They imply the adoption of the Roman hierarchical arrangement, with the places of honour on the top couch, not the first by the door: literary sources such as Plutarch confirm the change.[37] With a large party, the Roman design separates the guests and makes communication difficult between all except those on or adjacent to the central couch: those at the ends are clearly in an inferior position. It establishes the whole party as more of a spectacle of social order to be admired from outside, less of a coherent group, than the traditional Greek system, or indeed the Roman one of the Republic. At the same time it opens up the room in a way which allows much more space for formal entertainment: if the guests can no longer communicate easily with any but their immediate neighbours, they are much better able to be the passive spectators of entertainment provided in the central part of the room.[38]

Yet there is a further dimension to the change. I have described rooms such as these as Roman-style *triclinia*, and that is undoubtedly correct. The pattern can be seen emerging at Pompeii in the first century AD, undoubtedly copying the fashions of the capital. Plutarch later gives an indication how in his day fashions might be introduced in Rome and expected to spread widely.[39] Yet the form, as we have seen, was no longer that of the traditional Roman *triclinium* of the Republic with its three couches and nine places. The Romans themselves had abandoned this under the Empire, at least for formal, representational dining, in favour of big rooms with a longitudinal arrangement of couches, capable of holding twice or three times the traditional number. These rooms in turn recall the lay-out used in the Hellenistic world for civic and ritual banquets, and in the royal or near-royal sphere, as at Labraunda.[40]

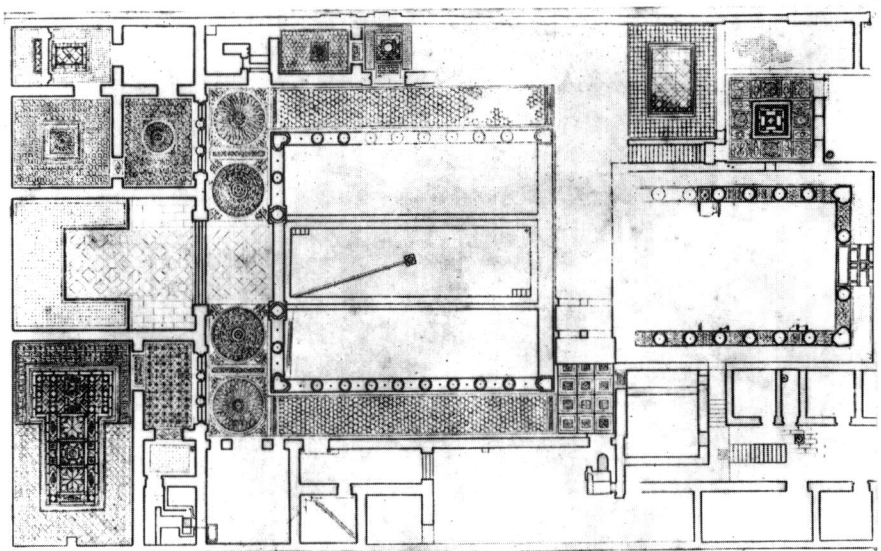

Fig. 11. Ptolemais, Palazzo delle Colonne, plan of structures around great peristyle, with mosaics probably of Flavian period. (Pesce 1950, pl. 15.)

The chain of influences may therefore be more complicated. The big Roman halls in their turn have surely come under Hellenistic influence: not so much the rather *ad hoc* arrangements that might be adopted for public banquets, but the great halls of the Hellenistic palaces or near-palaces (see Nielsen in this volume). The Palazzo delle Colonne at Ptolemais, probably the governor's palace, whose original phase Lauter has shown to be late Hellenistic, has two such long halls (nos. 11, 19) facing each other on the main axis across the peristyle (Fig. 10).[41] The larger (19) has columns around all four sides, and should perhaps be identified as an *oecus aegyptius* of the type described by Vitruvius (6.3.9) The smaller, though still substantial, room 11 and the long inner room (10) adjacent to it were paved in a later phase, probably Flavian, with T+U pavements of *opus sectile* and mosaic, indicating that at that time their function was that of *triclinium* (Fig. 11); it is likely that they had served a similar function previously. Room 19 may have been used for other official functions, but surely also for grandiose reception and dining.[42]

Immense long halls columned around three sides were found also in the first and third Winter Palaces of Herod at Jericho (Fig. 12). Although some features of Herod's buildings show the influence of Roman architecture, these halls surely belong in the tradition of the royal architecture of the Hellenistic East.[43] The earlier Hasmonean palace on the same site contains at least one similar long hall (though without columns) that probably served a similar function.[44]

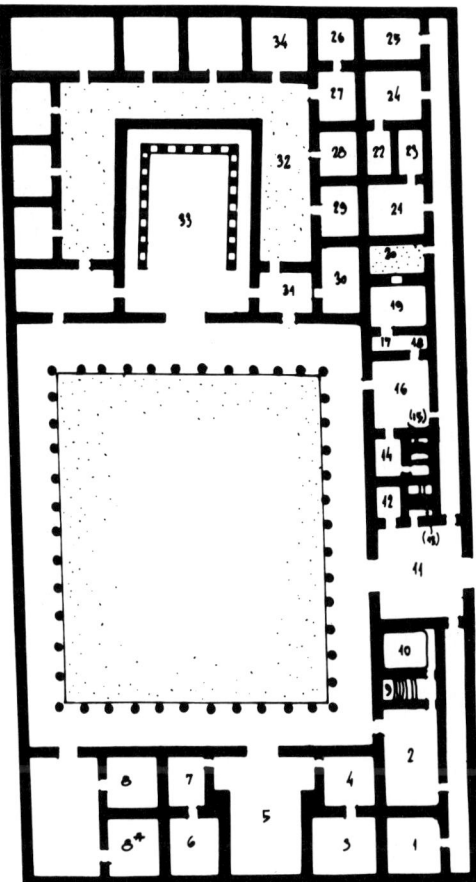

Fig. 12. Jericho, Herod's first Winter Palace, reconstructed plan. (Netzer 1990, 44, fig. 9.)

The connection would seem to run that the Roman aristocracy adopted the fashions set by Hellenistic royalty, and in turn were copied, less grandly and on a smaller scale, by the wealthy of a town like Pompeii, and doubtless elsewhere in Italy. In time, these same fashions came back to the Greek world, to the circles of men like Plutarch or whoever owned the Atrium House at Antioch, but now as a way of adopting Roman manners. Regrettably, though, it must be admitted that the paucity of examples, either of really grand Hellenistic domestic architecture or of the domestic architecture of the Greek world in the first century AD, makes it impossible to confirm this development for certain; the mutual influences between the late Hellenistic and Roman worlds remain inextricably interwoven.[45]

But the complications are hardly surprising. Modern discussions that speak of "the Greek" or "the Roman" dining patterns simplify an infinitely more varied picture. We must allow, not only for fashions which changed over centuries, but also for the extraordinary complexities that can arise from the meeting of cultures and the demands of acculturation. Needless to say, the pattern will have been even more complicated in regions where other ingredients and other cultural traditions entered into the Greek/Roman mix.

In conclusion, I want to stress that both the traditional Greek *andron* of the classical period and the Roman *triclinium* of the Republic were peculiar forms inseparable from the social structures that gave them birth. I drew attention at the start of this paper to the wide distribution and standardised form of the Greek *andron*, but it must also be recognised that it is a very artificial form. Only a strong sense of the ethos that such rooms were supposed to inculcate could justify the design of such specialised rooms, not only in innumerable private houses, but in groups in civic or religious settings, where larger rooms accommodating greater numbers might seem on the face of it more practical. For a society that wished to stress above all the civic identity of the citizen, and his membership of a coherent and integrated group, such rooms were ideal; but once that ethos declined, they became inappropriate. Equally confined to a specific social context is the Republican *triclinium*, with its small group closely packed together. The pattern of the Empire was more flexible in terms of numbers, and was designed to express hierarchical ranking more visibly. Formal dining, it makes clear, was no longer seen primarily as a means of achieving group solidarity, but rather as conveying a message of status.

Notes

1. E.g. Marquardt 1886, 331, who quotes Cic. *Tusc.* 5.41.118, referring to *illa lex, quae in Graecorum conviviis obtinetur: aut bibat, inquit, aut abeat,* which seems a different thing from drinking *graeco more*. H. de la Ville de Mirmont in the Budé edition of *Verr.* II.1 (1921), *ad loc.,* quotes the same passage and Gell. *N.A.* 15.2.4-8, which has even less relevance. T. Mitchell *ad loc.* (1986) thinks that "the likeliest explanation" is that suggested by Cic. *Tusc.* 1.40, 96, where Theramenes drinks the health of Critias in hemlock: *Graeci enim in conviviis solent nominari cui poculum tradituri sint*; but the fact that a custom is ascribed to the Greeks does not necessarily mean that it constituted "the Greek way of drinking".
2. References in Marquardt 1886, 339, Mau 1901, 1203. The practices governing the appearance and behaviour of women at dinner or drinking parties in both the Hellenistic Greek and the Republican Roman worlds were evidently more complex than such generalisations suggest, and need more careful analysis. See also Bradley in this volume.
3. For the Greek *andron*, see references in Bergquist 1990, especially 44 on private

dining rooms; Dunbabin 1991, 121-22, Hoepfner & Schwandner 1994, 98-99, 108-10, 146, 327-28, Hoepfner 1996, 2-6.

4. Bergquist 1990, *loc.cit.*; Heermann 1986, 336-45.
5. Ducrey, Metzger & Reber 1993, 46-47, rm. 6. Cf. Heermann 1986, 341, n. 1007, quoting two possible examples of rooms for three couches from Olynthus (A vi 5; B vii 7). Hoepfner & Schwandner 1994, 216-17, reconstruct *andrones* for three couches (sometimes longer than usual) in the basic house-type at Priene, but this use is not demonstrable.
6. For typical sizes of rooms and couches, see the tables of Miller 1978, 219-24; Bergquist 1990, 37-39; both are based on examples of civic and ritual dining rooms.
7. Plato, *Symp.* 175c and 177d, are regularly quoted for the "first" and "last" positions: see A. Hug, *Platons Symposion* (2nd ed., 1884), *ad loc.*
8. Chrysostomou 1988, 307-9, pl. 152.
9. Bergquist 1990, 37-65. For hellenistic dining rooms see also Hoepfner 1996, 17-36.
10. Cf. Chamonard 1922, 169-74, Hoepfner & Schwandner 1994, 296-97, Raeder 1988, 326-46.
11. Maison du Trident: Chamonard 1922, 27-29, 139-52, Bruneau 1972, 268, no. 236, fig. 221: a white outer border surrounds a decorated central area. Maison des Tritons, where a band of white marble chips about 1 m. wide surrounds the central rectangular area: Bruneau & Vatin 1970, 94-96, 143-47, Bruneau 1972, 174-78, no. 75, figs. 88-91.
12. Ilot des Bijoux, room AL: Bruneau & Siebert 1969, especially 268-70, Bruneau 1972, 156-69, no. 68. Samos, mosaic of Griffins: Giannouli & Guimier-Sorbets 1988, especially 559.
13. Heermann 1986, 507, n. 1024.
14. Vitr. 6.3.10; suggested by Raeder 1988, 338, n. 53. Ginouvès 1977, 106, makes the same suggestion to explain the curious lay-out of Room AL in the Ilot des Bijoux on Delos (above, n. 12). It might also account for the orientation of the surviving central panel in the Maison des Tritons (above, n. 11), facing one short side, with its lost companion piece presumably facing the other, giving two privileged viewing points, one at each side of the room. Most other recent studies have equated the term with a type of large longitudinal hall found in Roman buildings, despite Vitruvius' reference to *non italicae consuetudinis oeci*: e.g. Rakob 1987, 17.
15. Bergquist 1990, 40-41.
16. Baldassarre 1976, 201-9.
17. Hellström 1990, 243-52, Hellström 1989, 99-104, Hellström 1996, 164-68.
18. Recently Hoepfner (1996, 29-31) has identified the room on the central axis of the East Peristyle of Palace II on the Acropolis at Pella as a Broad-Room used for ceremonial dining. Here the row of couches along the (long) back wall must evidently be taken as more honorific than the rest, with the king's couch presumably in the centre. Although substantially later in date than Athenaeus' story (Hoepfner accepts the reign of Philip V), it too illustrates a suitable setting where such a scene could be imagined.

19. Bruneau & Vatin 1970, 34-36, 141-43, Bruneau 1972, 172-74, nos. 72-73. Two more rooms that may be ascribed to this type are Room EE in the Ilot des Bronzes: Bruneau 1972, 151-52, no. 54; and Room G in the Maison de l'Hermès: Bruneau 1972, 205-6, no. 152, fig. 122. For the identification as dining rooms, see Ginouvès 1977, 106.
20. For a comparable three-couch room at Eretria, see above, n. 5.
21. *PCairZen* 59445 (= *Sel. Pap.* I, no. 171), and cf. *PMichZen* 37. Cf. Nowicka 1969, 140-41, Husson, 1983, 223-24.
22. E.g. Ath. 12.541c, on Dionysius the Younger of Syracuse; Plut. *Quest. conv.* 5.5, 679b; or the *skene hekatontaklinos* and *oikos hekatontaklinos* of Alexander, though these were not permanent structures (Diod.Sic. 17.16.4, Ath. 12.538c). See also the descriptions of the Nile boat of Ptolemy Philopator, with a range of cabins whose size is given in couch-numbers (Ath. 5.204d-206c; Casparri 1916, 43 n. 3), and of the pavilion *hekaton triakonta klinas epidekhomenon kukloi* of Ptolemy Philadelphus (Ath. 5.196b, on which most recently Winter & Christie 1985, Salza Prina Ricotti 1988-89).
23. Pollux 1.79; McCartney 1934, 30-35. Cf. also Heermann 1986, 339-41 on these terms.
24. See references in Gauthier 1980, 215 n. 55. Several of the sources quoted in Ath. 2.47-8 also appear to use *triklinos* in a generic sense, with no necessary reference to the number of couches.
25. Cf. Gauthier 1980, 210-20. He concludes that *triklinos* must mean "salle de repas"; but given that the banquet takes place in the gymnasium, we should probably think of temporary structures set up in the porticoes and other available space, rather than actual rooms.
26. Spinazzola 1953, vol. 2, 750-56. For fuller discussion cf. Dunbabin 1991, 123-24, with references.
27. Mau 1885, 69-70, calculated on the basis of the cuttings for the insertion of couches in the walls of Pompeian *triclinia* that the length of couches varied between ca. 2.25 to 2.80 m, the breadth between ca. 1.20 to 1.50 m. The reconstructed *lectus* in the Museo Nazionale at Naples measures 2.33 x 1.20 m. (Pozzi *et al.* 1986, 186 no. 97). If three diners are to be fitted onto one couch, clearly it is necessary for them to lie diagonally across it, with their feet towards the outer edge.
28. D'Arms 1990.
29. For Romans and Italians owning or inhabiting houses at Delos, see Rauh 1993, 193-249.
30. Cf. Gauthier 1980, 210-20.
31. Suet. *Aug.* 70.1.
32. For this whole section see my discussion in Dunbabin 1991, 125-28, with references.
33. Amedick 1994, 112-15, argues that such rooms should be seen as a transfer indoors of the type of arrangement used for outdoor dining, to which the term *stibadium* rather than *triclinium* should be applied. Although I agree that the rooms are more suitable for continuous bench-like couches than for the traditional sofa-like *lecti* or *klinai*, I do not think this proves the influence of outdoor dining; it is a natural consequence of the desire for larger numbers. As seen

elsewhere in this paper, there are grounds for supposing the existence of this "elongated Pi" arrangement indoors at an earlier date in the Hellenistic world. Here and in a previous article (Amedick 1993, 179) Amedick argues that the distinction between *kline*-dining and *stibadia* lay in the fact that on the *kline* one always reclined parallel to the edge of the furniture, on the *stibadium* diagonally in towards the middle, and hence that any arrangements in which the guests reclined with their heads pointing in towards the centre must be called *stibadia* regardless of their shape. This takes no account of the fact that even in the traditional Roman three-couch arrangement, the guests must always have reclined at such an angle, in order to reach the communal table; nor could three be fitted onto a couch in any other way (cf. n. 27). The representations in funerary sculpture that she quotes of the dead reclining on sofa-type couches as if at table do not represent normal convivial behaviour.

34. Antioch: Stillwell 1961, 47-57; probably the earliest is the Atrium House, of the early or mid-2nd century, Levi 1947, 15-25, pls. 1-2. Corinth: Miller 1972, 332-54, with a *terminus post quem* of the 3rd quarter of the 1st century AD.
35. See my references in Dunbabin 1991, 128-31, 142-44, especially Duval 1984, 457-64, Balty 1984, 473-78; add Sodini 1984, 375-83.
36. Sepphoris: Netzer & Weiss 1994, 30-39. Ephesus: Jobst 1977, 84-86, H 2/SR24, pls. 92, 152-57.
37. Cf. Plut. *Quest. conv.* 1.3, 619b-f, a discussion of the *hypatikos topos*, comparing it with the former Greek practice where the first place was the most honoured. Plut. *Quest. conv.* 1.2, 615d ff. also deals with the placing of guests, making clear both how important a matter this was, and also that several diferent positions could be seen as honorific.
38. See Dunbabin 1996, 72-74.
39. Plut. *Quest. conv.* 7.8, 711b-d.
40. Above, nn. 16-17.
41. Pesce 1950, 37-39, 43-46, Lauter 1971, 149-78, McKenzie 1990, 75-77, Nielsen 1994b, 146-52. For a construction date ca. 145-40 BC, see Lauter-Bufe 1987, 62-63.
42. Lauter 1971, 176-78, suggests that rooms 10 and 11 may have had light vaults over their back section, like numerous examples in Pompeii, and raises the question of the direction in which influence flowed; but the main source for the architecture at Ptolemais was surely, as he argues, Alexandria. The measurements are: Room 19, 17.60 x 12.90 m. (central area within the columns 15.20 x 10.65); Room 11, 12.60 x 9 m; Room 10, 14.10 x 8.25 m.
43. Netzer 1990, 44-46, Nielsen 1994b, 193-200.
44. Nielsen 1994b, 155-60: the room in question is the *"oecus"* built by Queen Alexandra; Netzer 1996, 203-8.
45. The possibility cannot be entirely ruled out that the Graeco-Roman forms found in the eastern Empire in the second century AD and later may also have been inspired directly from late Hellenistic royal palaces (see Nielsen in this volume). However this seems to me much less likely, in the absence of intermediate examples, and given the development that can be seen taking place in Italy.

Royal Banquets:
The Development of Royal Banquets and Banqueting Halls from Alexander to the Tetrarchs

Inge Nielsen

Monarchs have always used the banquet as one of the main tools for creating contact with their subjects. Such banquets were closely related to the audience ceremony, and the way in which both ceremonies took place is revealing for the kind of relationship existing between the king and his subjects.

As for the direct predecessors of the Hellenistic kings, the Persian kings and the old Macedonian kings, their dining habits differed greatly. While at the Persian official banquets, which were very solemn, ceremonial and luxurious, the king dined alone, behind a curtain, a sign of his elevated status in relation to his guests, the Macedonian kings dined together with their guests at rather rustic feasts, which often developed into heavy drinking parties.[1] These two dining models were, together with the traditional Greek *symposion*, influential when the new Hellenistic kings were to create their way of banqueting and its setting. We know that both the Hellenistic kings and the Roman emperors always took part personally in the official banquets like the Macedonian kings, but also that their banquets were often highly ceremonial and lavish, a loan from the Persian kings. But again, there were graduations between the various monarchs and emperors, a fact which also had great influence on the setting for these official banquets in the various palaces.

In general, one might distinguish between two kinds of royal banquets: 1. the private banquets, for the royal family and close friends, taking place in the private section of the palace; 2. the official banquets, held by the king according to his status as the highest power in society, and involving entertaining both his own officials, such as in the Hellenistic period his "friends", in the Roman period his senators, and also foreign ambassadors, guests, audience seekers, etc. These banquets took place in the official banqueting halls of the royal palace. In both cases the dinner parties were held in the afternoon and early evening.

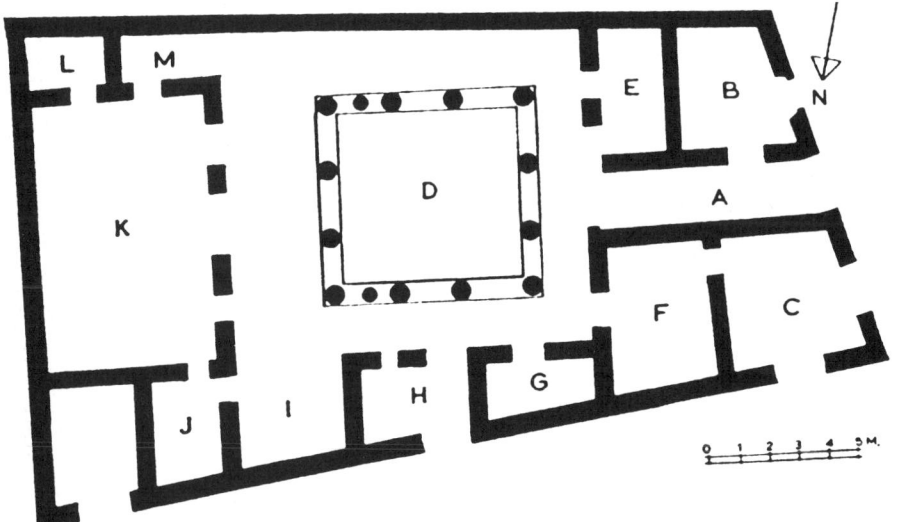

Fig. 1. Delos. Maison du Trident, Room K. (Guide Archéologique de Delos, p. 251.)

In the following I shall concentrate on the second type, since the first type does not differ perceptibly from family parties held by the élite. Also public or state banquets will be left out, since they were for a great crowd, even for the whole people, and normally took place outside the palace, in public or religious places. The same is the case with the large banquets in connection with religious feasts, although the king might be the giver of such a banquet.

Before looking at the setting for such official banquets in the palaces I shall very briefly mention the terminology involved since it may sometimes be revealing for the function and setting of the banquets. In the Hellenistic period, the words used for such a banquet in the written sources are *deipnon* and *symposion*. Already during Alexander's reign we have certain information on how a formal banquet (*symposion*) was structured. It began with sacrifices, since the religious element was always in evidence, then came the dinner (*deipnon*), and finally the drinking party, and entertainment formed an integral part of the proceedings.[2] Shortly after Alexander's death we hear of the *deipna* of Demetrius of Phaleron (or Poliorketes), which overshadowed the Macedonian ones and could rival those held in Cyprus and Phoenicia, which were probably in Oriental style.[3] Thus *deipnon* and *symposion* could both be used for such banquets as a whole, and for the single elements, that is, *deipnon* for the dinner, *symposion*, or *potos* for the drinking party.

The halls, in which such banquets took place in the Hellenistic palaces, are usually called *symposia* and *andrones*, both words being used also for the Greek dining rooms in private houses. Also the broader designation, *oikos*,

Fig. 2. The Nile mosaic from Praeneste. Scene with stibadia. *(Amedick 1993, pl. XLV.)*

is used to designate such a hall, for example for the tent used by Alexander the Great for his wedding banquet (see n. 2). Because of the many different types of banquet, there must have been many forms and sizes of halls reserved for this purpose in the palaces. Thus the audience hall could apparently be used for large banquets, as is clear from the Letter of Aristeas (180-300), which tells us about the fictive banquets held by Ptolemy II for the 72 Jewish scholars, whom he had invited to Alexandria to furnish him with a Greek translation of the Torah for his famous Library: since a banquet often followed upon the audience, movable *klinai* could be placed in the audience hall, thus transforming this, the largest and most sumptuous hall in the palace, into a banqueting hall (Aristeas 183). Perhaps this was the hall in which Cleopatra held a banquet in Caesar's honour during his visit to the Alexandrian court, for the hall was called *aula* and compared to a temple: it had marble walls, a wooden ceiling overlaid with gold leaf, a floor of alabaster, and decorations executed in precious stones and ivory. The dining hall used by this queen to impress Mark Antony in Cilicia is called a *basilikon symposion*,[4] while Josephus gives the name *andrones megistoi* to the opulent banqueting halls in the palace of their contemporary, Herod the Great, in Jerusalem.[5] Of special structures for banquets one may mention the dining-pavilion set up by Ptolemy II in the palace of Alexandria during the feast for Dionysus, called *skene*, tent, and also the dining rooms, called *symposia* and *oikoi*, aboard Ptolemy IV's Nile barge, the Thalamegos.[6]

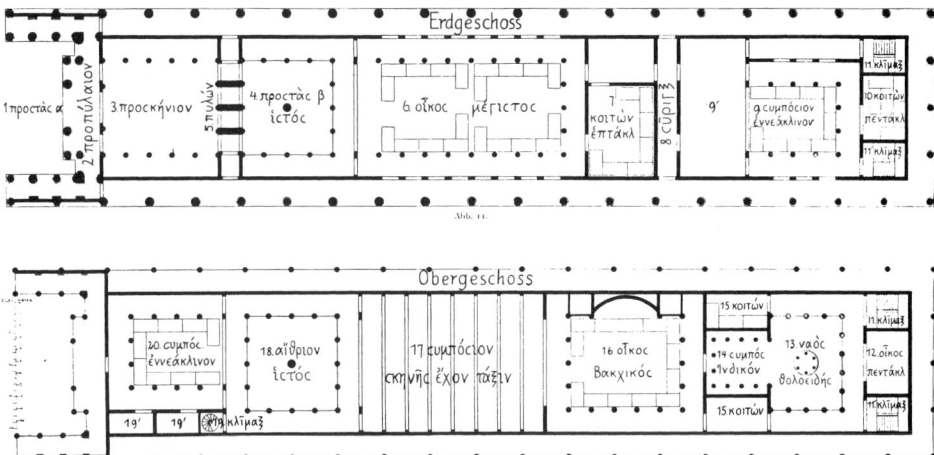

Fig. 3. *The Thalamegos, plans of the two storeys. The temple of Aphrodite is on the first floor, no. 13. (Nielsen 1994, fig. 71 below.)*

In the latin terminology, a banquet is designated *cenatio* and *cena*, and also *convivium* and *epulum*. The two latter designations were used only for banquets outside the family circle, and *epulum* normally for public banquets, *epulae publicae*.[7] It is characteristic that terms specifically for drinking are not used so frequently as in the Hellenistic period, probably a general reflection of the different attitude to eating and drinking of the Greeks and Romans, the Romans preferring to drink during the meals instead of only afterwards.[8]

The dining halls in the palaces of the Roman emperors were, like those of the houses of the élite, called by various names. *Triclinium*, which is the most common term at all times, is a latinization of the Greek *triklinon*,[9] and first used as a designation for a room by Varro (*Ling.* 8); at the same time preserved *triclinia* have been ascertained archaeologically, in private houses in Pompeii. Each *kline*, or couch, could house three diners. But the custom of reclining at a table was known much earlier in Italy; *symposia*, Greek style, had long been in use in the Greek colonies of South Italy, and in Etruria we see representations of banquets with guests reclining on couches from the late 7th century BC (at Murlo) and into the 3rd century BC (in tomb paintings).[10] In all cases, however, only two persons reclined together on each *kline*, i.e. after Greek custom. In Rome, reclining at banquets were at least known by Plautus, who probably refers to local, rather than Greek customs,[11] but we do not know which room was used for that purpose and how many guests dined on each couch. As mentioned (n. 9), Polybius used the word *triklina* to designate the way people dined at a great feast in Antioch, arranged by the likewise Romanophile Antiochos IV, which might indicate that the custom of dining on three *klinai* was already in evidence in

Fig. 4. The circular dining (?) pavilion in the Northern Palace of Masada, seen from above. (Author's photo.)

Rome at that time (i.e. 1st half of 2nd century BC). Then, the word *triklina* probably referred to the arrangements of *klinai* around three sides of the table (cf. Varro *Rust*. 3.13.2) rather than to dining rooms.

The word *triclinium* was later used also for other kinds of official halls, as was the *oecus*, which according to Vitruvius could have many forms, i.e. tetrastyle, Corinthian, Egyptian, Cyzicene; I shall return to these types later.[12] *Cenatio* came after the time of Augustus to designate the dining hall as well as the dinner itself; thus Suetonius uses it for banqueting halls in the Domus Aurea, and Seneca mentions various elements in *cenationes*, such as *nymphaea*, hypocausts, draperies (*vela*), and large windows (*specularia*).[13] Thus in Silver latin is seems that while *triclinium* was used for all kinds of dining rooms, *cenatio* was mostly used for large halls, often with columns and gables, *fastigia*; the same elements are known for the audience hall, which was undoubtedly, as in Alexandria, often used for banqueting.[14]

The setting

In the following I shall concentrate on the preserved banqueting halls of the Hellenistic and Roman palaces and related buildings, and, together with what we know from the written sources, try to elucidate the appearance of such halls. Some elements are the same for all kinds of dining rooms, including private ones, others are characteristic of only royal or at least aristocratic and official dining halls.[15]

Let us begin with the size and form of the rooms in question: Large rooms were a necessity for official banquets, which demanded room for many guests reclining on *klinai*. Thus we hear of halls able to house 100 *klinai* at Alexandria and Jerusalem, and Agathocles of Syracuse had a famous hall for 60 couches.[16] Of halls with preserved *kline* bands the three large ones in the western wing of the palace of Vergina each had room for 35 *klinai*.[17] It is in this connection to be remembered that while the Greek style *kline* could carry only one or two persons and generally measured c. 1.8 x 1 m, the Roman ones, used in the *triclinia*, each accomodated three guests and measured normally 2-4 x 1.5 m. A special kind of dining couch, designated *stibadium*, was hemicyclical, with room for 5-12 persons and was often placed in apses with a diameter of c. 6 m.

While the typical private Greek *andron* was normally square, and the Roman *triclinium* mostly rectangular, since there was a free area in front of the couches, the royal banqueting halls could have all forms: square, rectangular, sometimes formed as a broad-room, and, at least in Roman times, polygonal, round, or apsidal. The broad-room is of un-Greek origin, and is undoubtedly a loan from the Orient where this room-form was often used for audience halls and other important rooms, including dining halls.[18] This form was taken over also in the Delian houses, for the main *oecus*, and

Fig. 5A & B. Villa Adriana. Palazzo imperiale with apsidal summer triclinium *in the form of a* stibadium *facing the garden. A: seen from the garden; B: detail of the stibadium. (Author's photo.)*

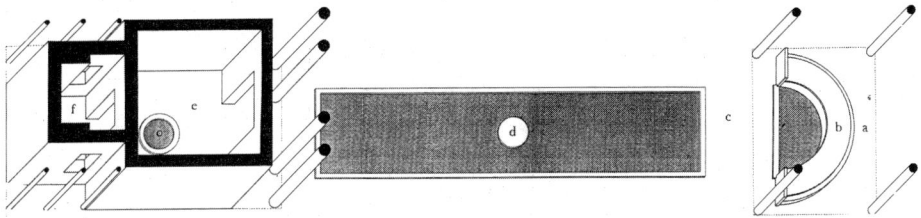

Fig. 6. The stibadium of Pliny the younger, reconstruction by E. Salza Prina Ricotti. (Salza Prina Ricotti 1987, fig. 1.)

placed as in the palaces, that is, centrally and axially to the entrance, in contrast to the Greek houses, where the *andrones* were generally tucked away (Fig. 1).[19]

Apsidal and rounded rooms were often combined with a *stibadium* couch, which, as Katherine Dunbabin (1991) has shown, might well have been used for dining already in the garden pavilions of the late Republican villas, and which, as the word says, originally designated the way in which the worshippers feasted in the open air in the Greek sanctuaries. This mode may also have been propagated to Italy through Ptolemaic Egypt, for such *stibadia* in garden settings are represented both in the famous Nile mosaic of Praeneste from the late 2nd century BC, where there are two *stibadia* groups flanking a Nile arm, perhaps at Canopus, as well as in mostly 4th style Egyptianizing wall-paintings in Pompeii, often featuring pygmies at dinner (Fig. 2).[20] Also *stibadia* placed in rooms or pavilions might well have been known already in Ptolemaic Egypt. At least rounded buildings were not unknown, as indicated by the Kashneh facade of neighbouring Petra and the facades of Palazzo delle Colonne, a Ptolemaic governor's palace (see Fig. 13).[21] The round temple of Aphrodite on the Nile Boat of Ptolemy IV, mentioned by Callixenus, might, in fact, have been used also for dining (Fig. 3); at least the wooden temple for the same goddess on the huge ship called the Syracusia built by Hieron II could house three *klinai* and was furnished with drinking vessels.[22] One might imagine similar rounded pavilions situated in the palace gardens of Alexandria. Thus Herod's round pavilions in his palaces of Masada, Jericho, and Herodium, which were probably used for dining, may well have been inspired from Alexandria, although an influence from Italy directly is also possible,[23] since already Varro had a tholos-shaped aviary used also for dining in his villa at Casinum.[24] But all in all a common Hellenistic model is perhaps more likely (Fig. 4).

This Hellenistic and late Republican use of *stibadia* in a garden setting was continued in the first two centuries of the Roman Empire and they are first mentioned in the written sources by Martial and Pliny the younger (Fig. 6).[25] The latter had one in his Tuscan villa, (*Ep.* 5.6.36-40) connected to

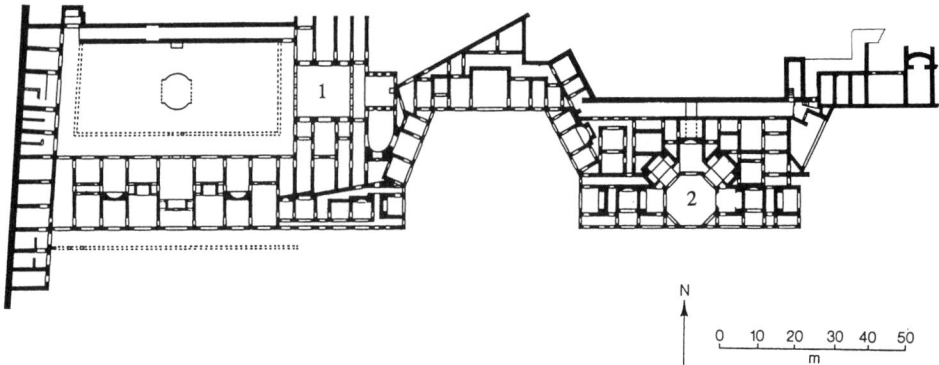

Fig. 7. Domus Aurea. Plan of the main palace, with the proposed dining rooms 1 and 2. (Coarelli 1976, 198.)

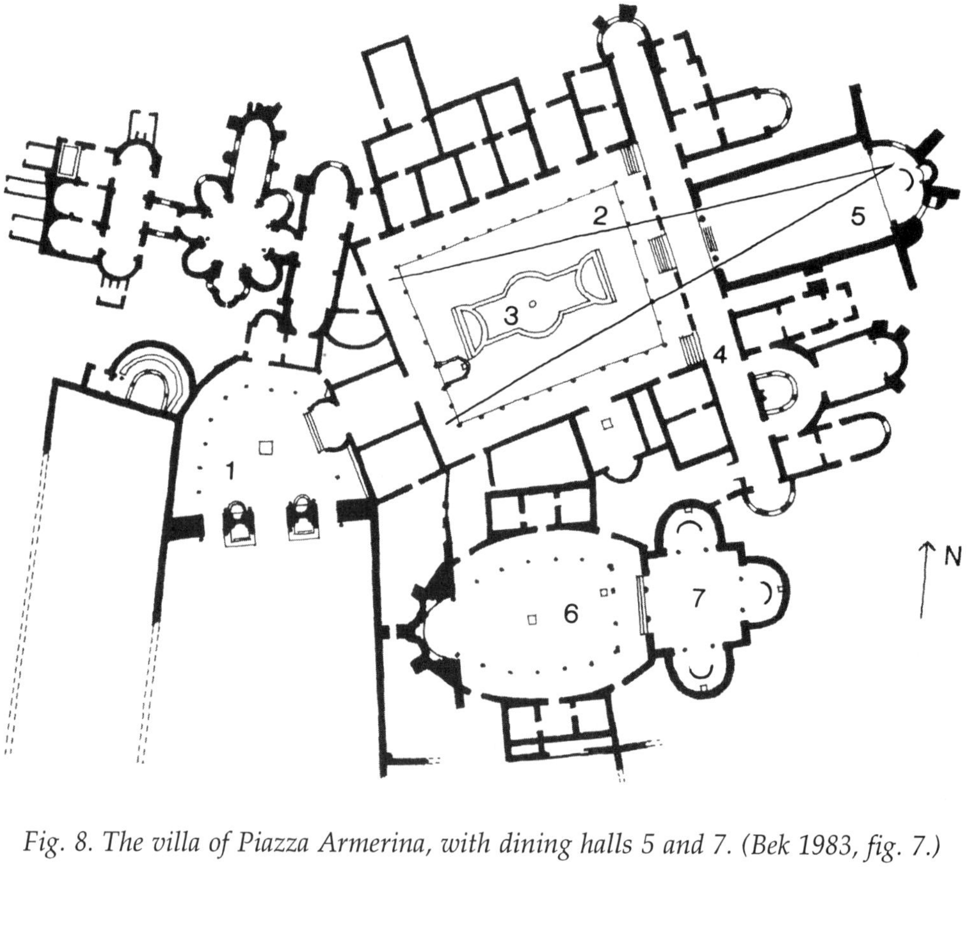

Fig. 8. The villa of Piazza Armerina, with dining halls 5 and 7. (Bek 1983, fig. 7.)

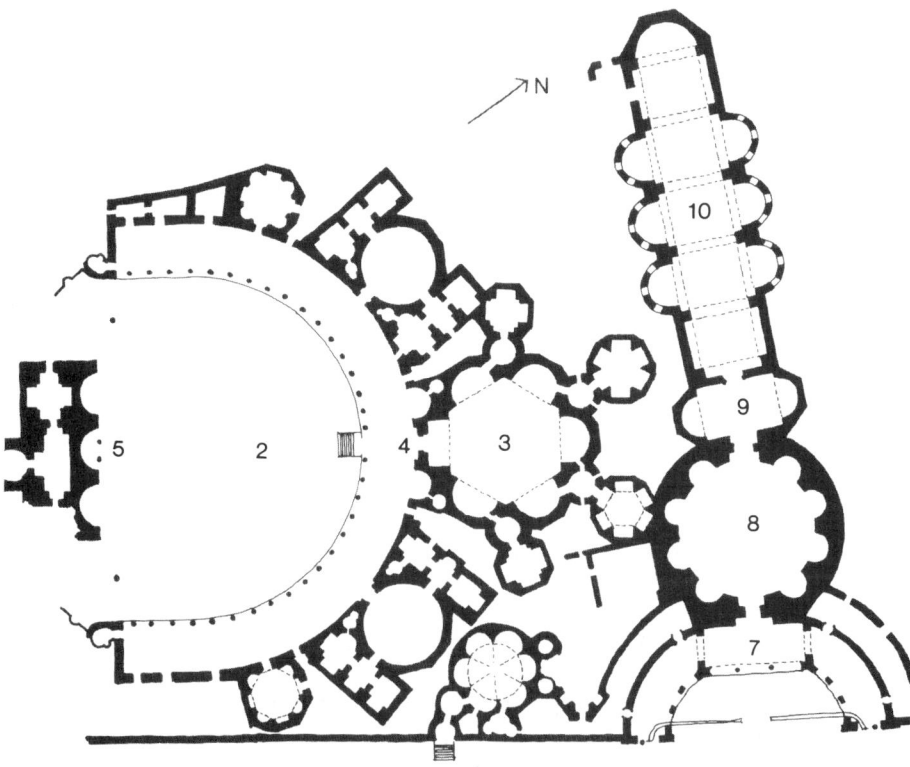

Fig. 9. The palace of Constantinople, with dining halls 3 and 10. (Bek 1983, fig. 9.)

Fig. 10 Vergina. One of the dining rooms in the southern wing, with kline *bands. (Author's photo.)*

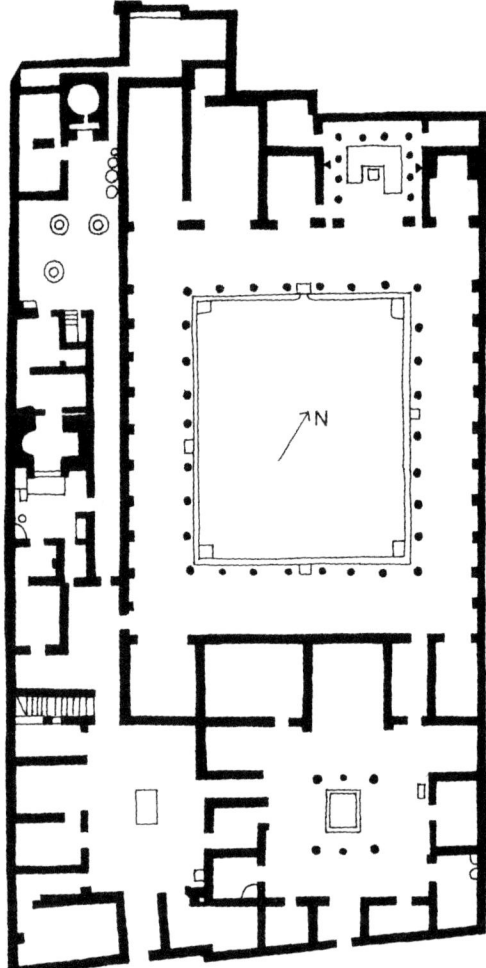

Fig. 11. House of the Labyrinth in Pompeii, with triclinium. *(Bek 1983, fig. 1.)*

gardens and with a small pool with floating plates for table. In the Villa Adriana such *stibadia* were numerous, but still used only for the summer dining rooms (Fig. 5 A, B).[26]

For indoor use, in the main dining halls, *stibadia* became widespread only in late Antiquity, when they dominated over the old *triclinium* type. However, as suggested by Dunbabin, the first example of an indoor *stibadium* might well have been Nero's *cenatio rotunda* in the Domus Aurea (Fig. 7, no. 2).[27] The continuous popularity of this *sigma* couch is revealed by the expanded use of the tri- or multi-conch rooms in the palaces of late Antiquity, for example in the Villa of Piazza Armerina and the palace of Constan-

Fig. 12. The Pavilion of Ptolemy II. Reconstruction by Studniczka. (Nielsen 1994, fig. 70.)

tinople; the placement of the guests in apses on *stibadia* gave room for a greater number of people, all facing the central area (Fig. 8-9).[28] Of course, a combination of *stibadia* and normal *klinai* should probably be envisaged as well.

Like the *klinai* themselves, their inner arrangement in the royal dining halls may well differ according to which period we are dealing with. Although in Roman times permanent couches in masonry are sometimes seen, the *klinai* of both periods were normally movable, and their presence cannot always be ascertained. The decoration of the floor may sometimes reveal the presence of *klinai*, since there could be bands, sometimes slightly raised, along the walls in a simpler decoration for them (Fig. 10); but in the cases where multi-functional halls are concerned, for example the audience hall, such bands are, of course, absent. Another indication of the presence of *klinai* is only valid for the Hellenistic period, namely the asymmetrical doors, since they depended on the Greek custom of placing *klinai* along all four walls of the room. In Roman times, when the *triclinium* system was introduced, couches were placed only along three walls, with the fourth wall housing the entrance. The door could now be placed in the centre, or the room could open entirely to the outside, which is the most frequent solution. Thus double doors, *valvae*, are often mentioned in relation to such dining halls (Fig. 11). This planning made serving and entertainment easier to

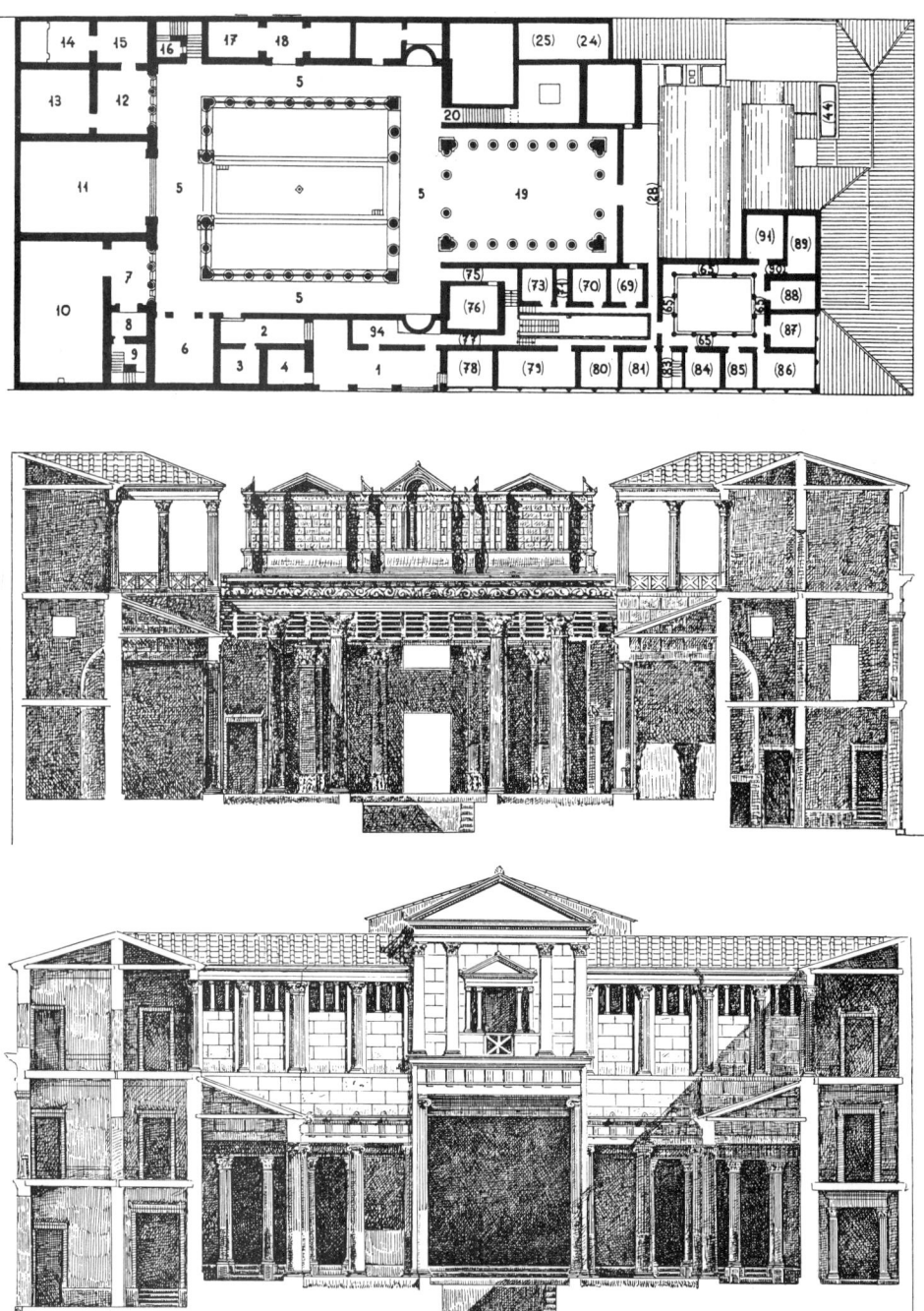

Fig. 13. The palace of Ptolemais, plan with dining halls 11 and 19 with a reconstruction of the facades facing the garden. (Nielsen 1994, figs 78 and 80.)

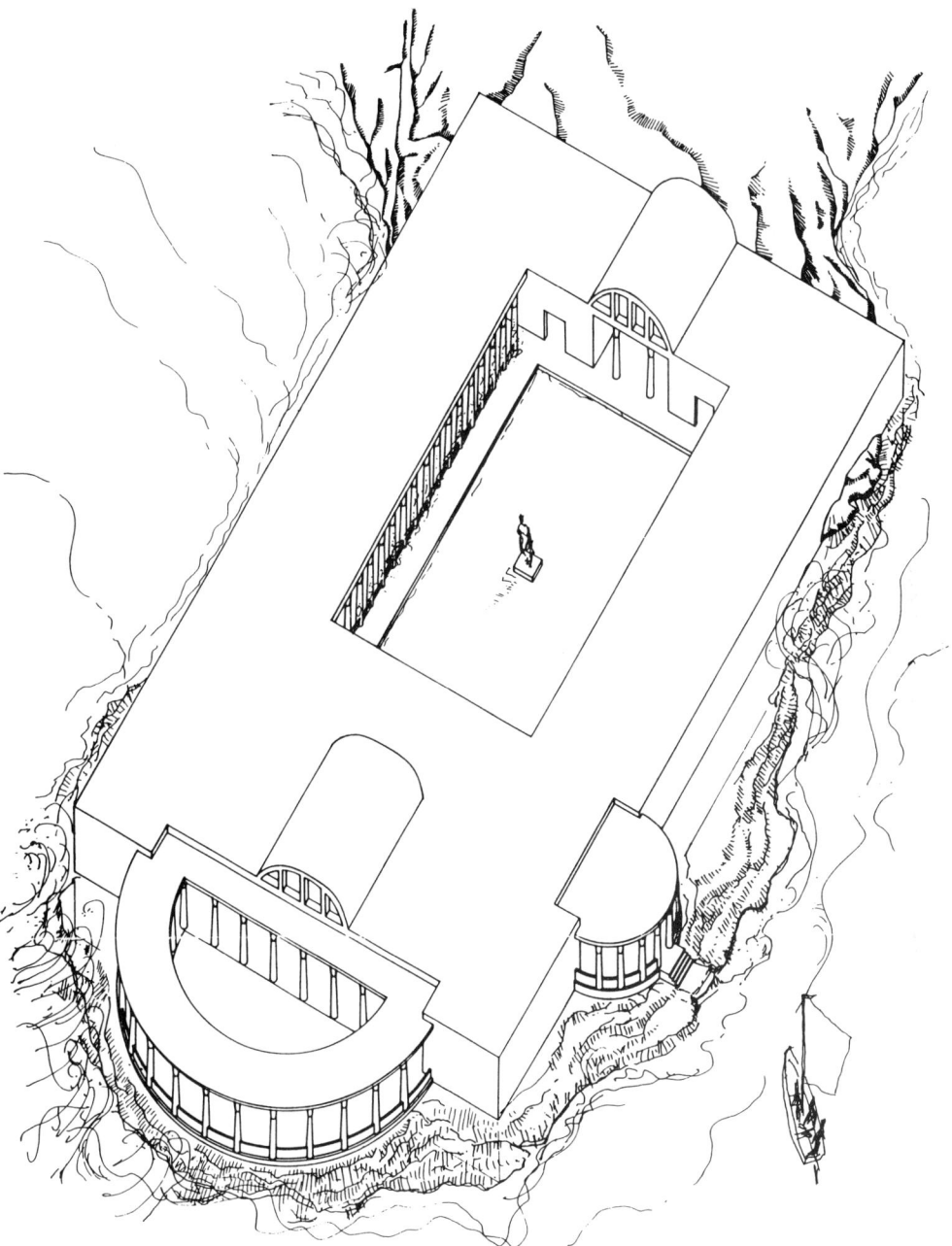

Fig. 14. The royal Herodian palace of Caesarea, Palestine. A reconstruction by E. Netzer of the dining hall facing the swimming pool and surrounding garden. (Nielsen 1994, fig. 95.)

Fig. 15. The Corinthian oecus *in the House of Meleager in Pompeii. (Author's photo.)*

arrange, and the number of guests could be augmented by placing more or longer *klinai* along the lateral walls, as was often done in dining halls in the rich houses from the 2nd-3rd century AD.[29].

There are, however, some indications that this open form of dining hall was already known in the Hellenistic royal palaces. Although the traditional square and closed Greek *symposion* with *klinai* around all walls was, at the beginning, apparently taken over by the Macedonian kings, as is evident from the palace of Vergina (Fig. 10), and was the type of dining hall used in the palace of Pergamon too, the situation was different in the new kingdoms in the East.[30] Already the Pavilion of Ptolemy II in the Alexandrian palace had one side open to the garden (Fig. 12), and also some of the many *symposia* recorded in the Nile boat seem to have been open, since views are mentioned (see Fig. 3). No doubt, the same was the case with other dining halls in Alexandria. Also the dining halls in the Ptolemaic governor's palace in Ptolemais, the Palazzo delle Colonne (Fig. 13), and those of the Hasmonean and Herodian palaces, undoubtedly inspired from the palace of Alexandria, were open on one side (Figs. 14 and 17). In this connection it is worth remarking that already before the earthquake of 115 AD in Antioch, the *triclinium* system seems to have been used in the rich houses there.[31] Perhaps the reason for this is that the Greek style *andron* with its inherent social pattern never became very popular in the East, so that these Antioch-

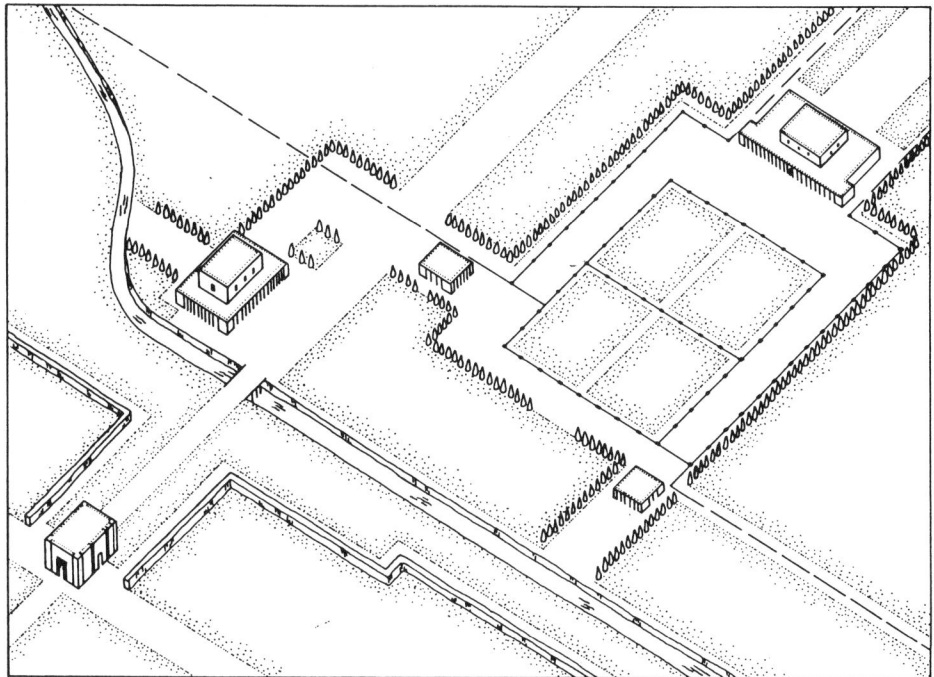

Fig. 16. The palace of Pasargadae with its gardens, built by Cyrus the Great. Reconstruction by Stronach. (Nielsen 1994, fig. 12.)

ene houses rather reflected the royal mode of dining in the Hellenistic period. The Greek *andron* type was not used in the Hellenistic governor's palaces in the East, either.[32]

As is clear from both written sources and the archaeological remains the official royal dining halls were always lavishly embellished. Mosaic or marble floors, marbled walls, panelled golden ceilings, hangings of fine materials (*aulaiai*), and rich coverings for the couches are often mentioned, as is the use of gold and silver, and precious stones. Rich baldachins seem to have covered some of these halls as well. These could sometimes be carried by columns, which were often present in the larger halls. There is no doubt that the different types of columnar *oeci* recorded by Vitruvius for the fine houses of Italy were modelled on palatial halls in the Hellenistic East as well as probably on airy garden pavilions. The names for some of them, the Egyptian and Corinthian *oeci* as well as the special Cyzicene *oecus*, a non-Italian type, are indications of this (Fig. 15). Thus the Egyptian *oecus* with columns in two storeys was, according to Vitruvius, akin to the *basilica*, a word with a royal connotation indicating a loan from one of the large halls of the palace of Alexandria, probably the combined audience and dining hall. In these columnar dining halls the diners reclined on couches along the inner side of the columns; thus Vitruvius (6.3.8) states that in the private

Fig. 17. The view from the northern palace of Masada, from the upper terrace. Below, the rectangular dining hall is seen. (Author's photo.)

triclinia, the area inside the columns should have the same size as a normal *triclinium*. The area behind the columns could accomodate the slaves and followers of the diners.

With the opening up of the dining room its orientation and the view from it became important: in general such halls faced north or south, according to the season.[33] While the summer rooms, facing north, are sometimes very experimental in form, the winter rooms, facing south, which could in the Roman period sometimes be heated, seem to be more traditional in form, and mostly rectangular. Both opened normally to gardens and views. This idea that a view was important for the diners and an enjoyment in itself was probably an inheritance from the Orient. Thus in the Achaemenid palaces, gardens, *paradeisoi*, played a very important part in architecture and also formed the setting for ceremonies (Fig. 16). In addition, the earliest preserved scene with the king and queen dining on couches, from Assurbanipal's palace of Niniveh, in fact took place in a garden pavilion. Dining in tents was undoubtedly at the bottom of it all.[34] Thus in connection with Alexander's campaign, we hear of *klinai* and a throne placed in a *paradeisos*.[35]

Views are often referred to in the sources, and in some of the preserved palaces it is obvious that great care has been taken to create the best view possible. One should not forget that the Seleucids took over some of the Persian palaces directly, and in addition to the garden views mentioned in

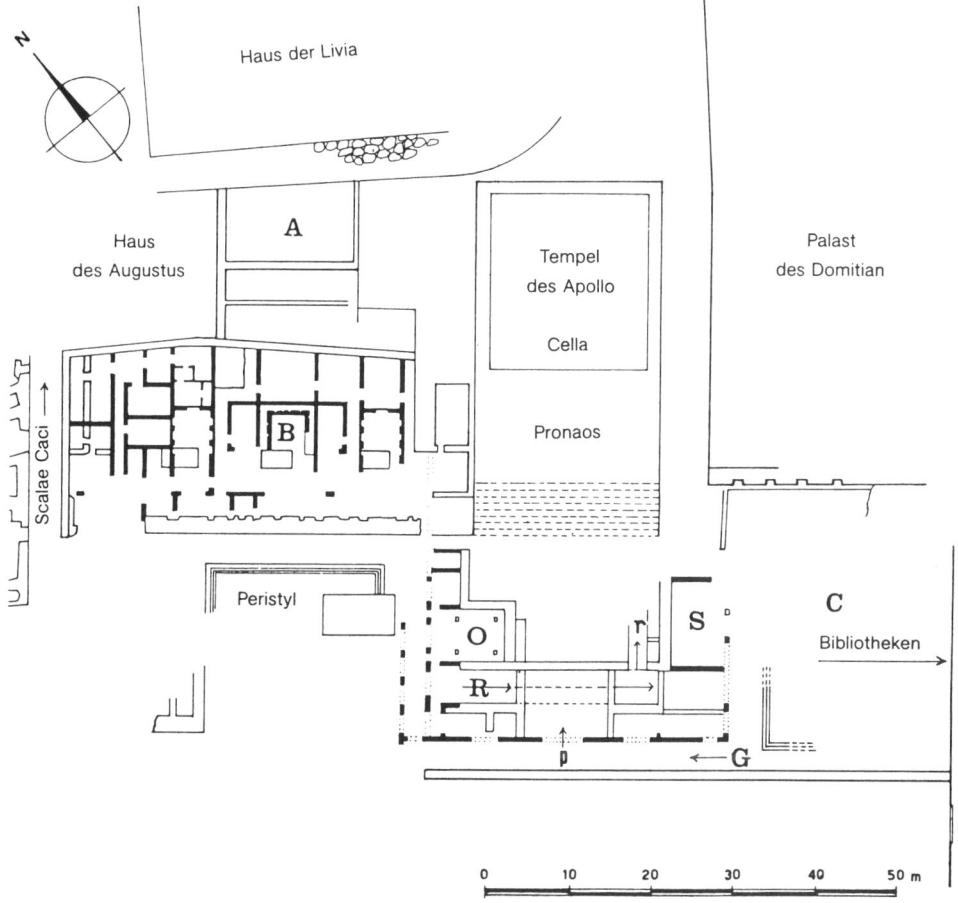

Fig. 18. Casa di Augusto on the Palatine, with dining rooms O and probably S. (Nielsen 1994, fig. 92.)

connection with the Pavilion of Alexandria and evident from Palazzo delle Colonne, one needs only mention the stunning view from the dining halls of Herod the Great's northern palace of Masada (Figs. 4 and 17). The blasphemic view from the Hasmonean palace of Jerusalem to the Temple platform, mentioned by Josephus, was undoubtedly enjoyed from the dining room.[36]

There is a direct line from these Hellenistic royal dining halls with a view to those of the late Republican villas and houses in Campania and eventually to those of the Roman palaces. From the late Republican period we have several descriptions of sumptuous banquets held by generals back from the East, where they had seen and participated in the royal banquets of the Hellenistic kings.[37] These dinner parties and the rooms used to house them became in their turn highly influential on the way the Roman

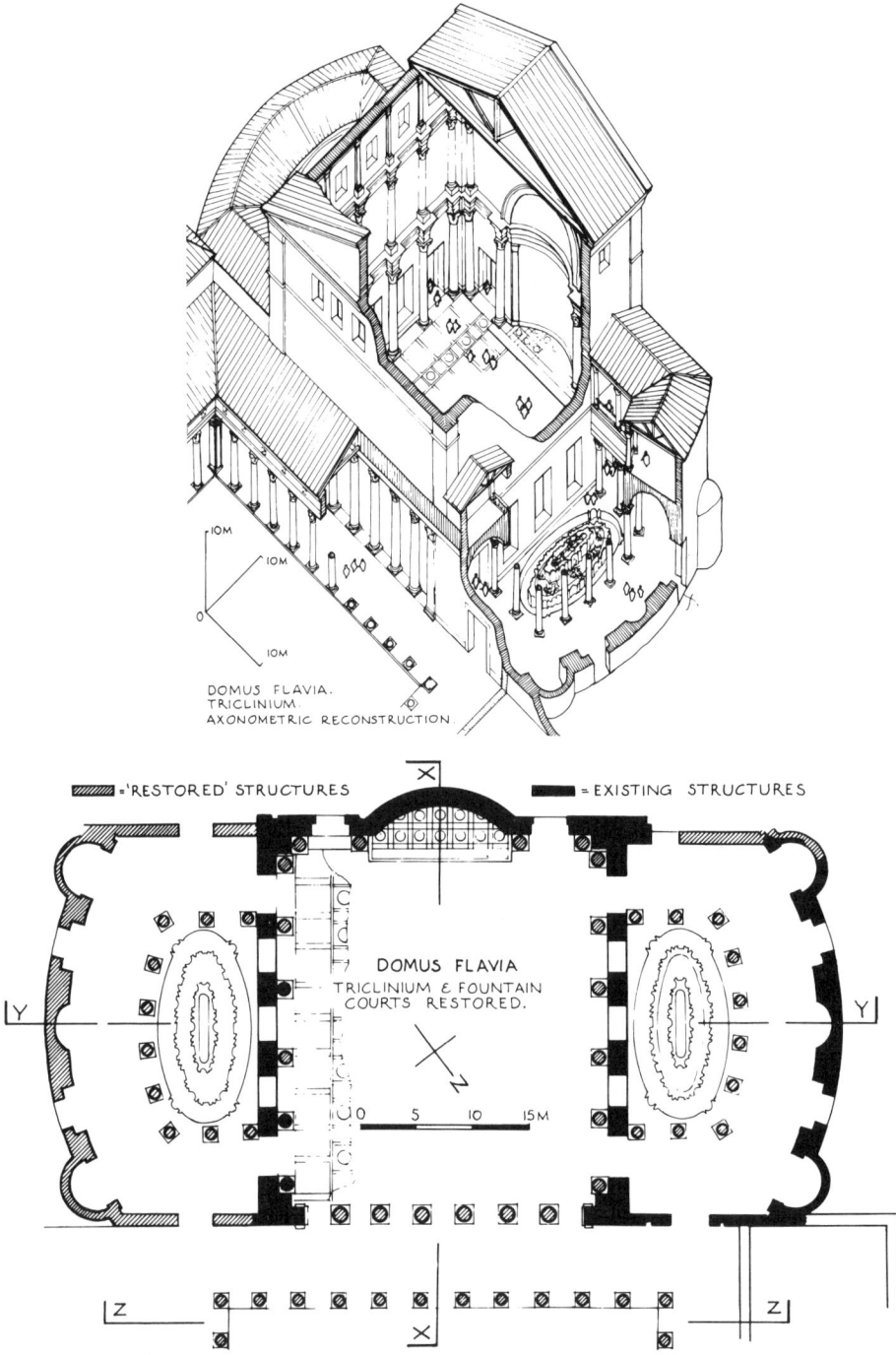

Fig. 19. Domus Flavia. The triclinium, *reconstruction and plan. (Gibson et al. 1994, figs. 9 and 29.)*

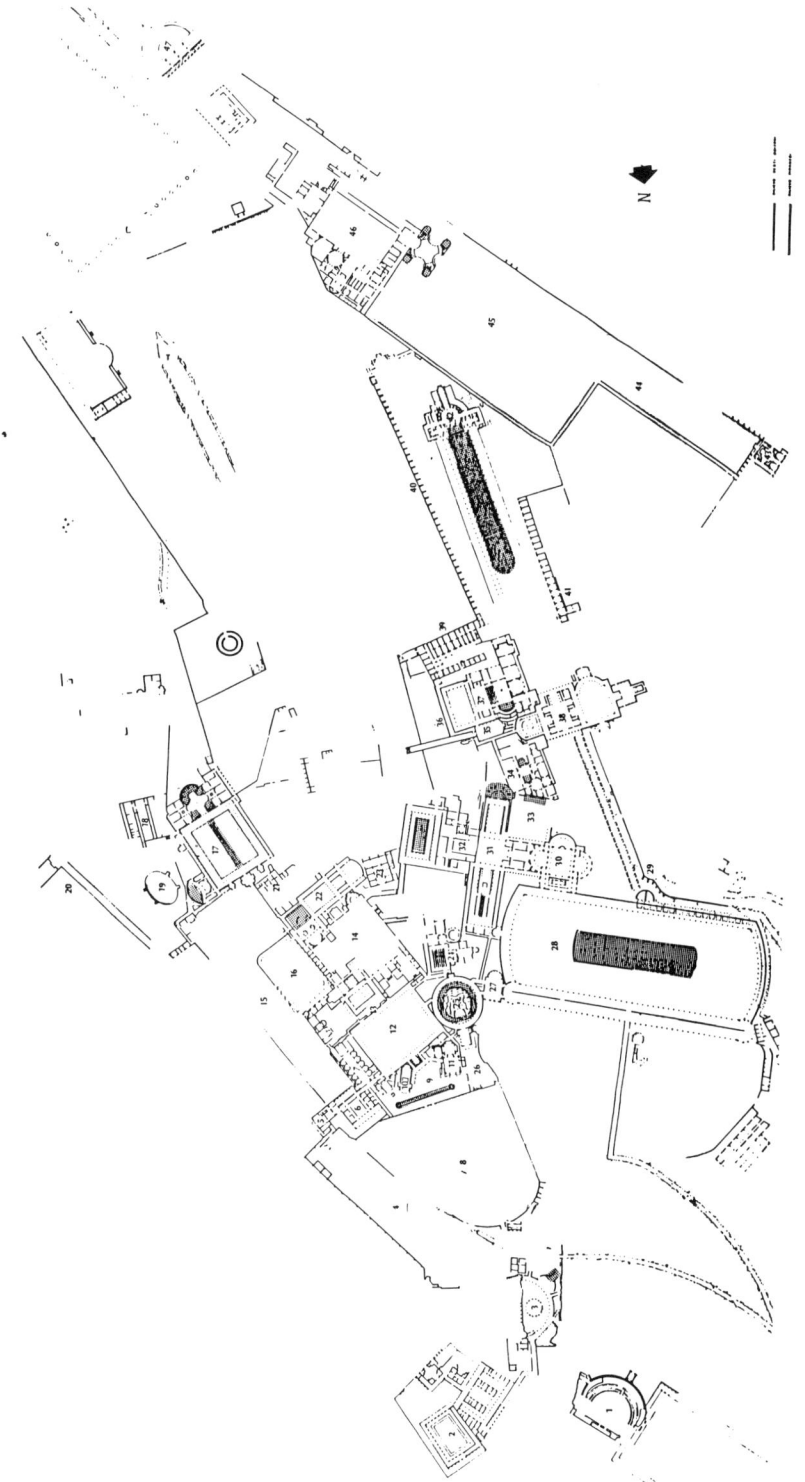

Fig. 20. General plan of Villa Adriana, with the fountains hatched in. (Franceschini 1991, pl. 97.)

Fig. 21. The early garden triclinium from the Hasmonean palace of Jericho. (Author's photo.)

emperors banqueted officially as well as in private.[38] As mentioned, the Roman way of dining was based on an opening of the room on one side. Also, windows are often referred to, for example in Vitruvius' Cyzicene *oecus*; his remark that this was not an Italian custom gives credit to the theory that this idea might have been taken over from the Hellenistic palaces of the East.

As far as the imperial palaces are concerned, already the Casa di Augusto on the Palatine had a tetrastyle *oecus* facing a peristylar garden, and perhaps the marble-clad hall facing the Portico of the Danaids in this palatial complex could be used for official banquets as well (Fig. 18).[39] A direct parallel to the story of the view to the temple platform i Jerusalem is available from Rome too, where we are told that Caligula watched his grandmother Antonia's funeral in the Forum from his *triclinium* in his palace on the Palatine, and of Vitellius we hear that he could see a fire and fighting on the Capitol from there.[40] Undoubtedly the Neronian Domus Tiberiana on the Germalus was the location for this latter dining room.[41] Nero's *cenationes* in the Domus Aurea faced, if the proposed identifications are the true ones (Fig. 7),[42] partly a peristylar garden, and partly the lake in the Colosseum valley, while the huge banqueting hall on the Palatine, which was built by Domitian and was flanked by two gardens with fountains, faced a garden with fountain as well (Fig. 19).[43] Of course such views were especially well

Fig. 22. Domus Flavia on the Palatine. The apse of the triclinium. *(Author's photo.)*

suited for villas, and in that context dining room views had been exploited from late Republican times; of the imperial villas one may mention Tiberius' on Capri and at Sperlonga, the latter built into a grotto, as were the ones in the imperial villas of Punta dell'Epitaffio at Baia, Domitian's villa at Albano, and of course Villa Adriana (Figs. 20 and 25).[44]

That views were important is clear also from the fact that, if they were not present, they could be painted on the walls. This is sometimes done in *triclinia* in Pompeii and Herculaneum, especially in the summer *triclinia*.[45] Even more interesting in this connection is the presence of such illusionist paintings in the so-called Auditorium Maecenatis, situated in the Esquiline gardens belonging to the emperor. This subterranean room with a large stepped *nymphaeum* which had niches with garden paintings, was at least in Tiberian times used as a dining hall. The *triclinium* proper faced the *nymphaeum* and the "garden" illusioned in the niches.[46]

It is thus evident that, together with gardens, fountains were very frequently used as view-points for those dining in the dining rooms. Both gave an illusion of dining in a garden. In addition such fountains could, at least in Roman times, be placed in the hall proper, for example behind the main seat, thus forming an impressive backdrop for the host. Water was associated especially with the summer *triclinia*, as illustrated in the Villa Adriana, but could also be used in the main *triclinia* of the palaces, as seen in the two

Fig. 23. Piazza Armerina. One of the apses for stibadia *in the triconch of the imperial villa. (Author's photo.)*

dining halls of the Domus Aurea, and in Domitian's great *triclinium* on the Palatine (cf. Fig. 21).[47]

The function

Turning now from the appearance of the royal dining halls to their function, the question is how the official dinner parties were organized. One of the problems which has been much discussed is the placement of the *klinai* in the large dining halls.[48] In the Hellenistic period, the smaller royal halls, as seen for example at Vergina and Pergamon, generally had *klinai* along all the walls, facing the central area with the tables (Fig. 10). Thus they mirrored the normal Greek *andron*, where this was a practical arrangement, since one of the aims of the Greek *symposia* was conversation. If the same placement of the *klinai* was used in large halls, however, conversation became impossible. It has been argued, latest by Birgitta Bergquist (1990), that instead of one large group of diners several smaller *symposion* groups could be spread in such a banqueting hall. Studniczka used this principle in his reconstruction of the huge Pavilion of Ptolemy II, where he placed the 100 couches for 200 guests in nine separate *symposia* (Fig. 12). At a smaller scale, this is the way things were done in Vitruvius' Cyzicene *oecus*, where two *triclinia* were placed facing each other.[49]

While this system would be appropriate both for private houses and at public or religious feasts, its weakness in a royal setting is that some of the guests would then turn their back to the king. Also the entertainment, which we know formed an integral part of royal dinner parties, would demand a large free area, which could be overseen by all the guests.[50] This would be difficult to create if small groups of *symposia* were used. In fact some of the preserved larger royal dining halls show a different arrangement from the Greek one. Thus in one of the *andrones* of king Mausolus in the sanctuary of Labraunda, where *kline* bands are preserved, the main couch was undoubtedly placed beneath a large niche probably with dynastic statues, and the other couches, 19-22 all in all, were placed along the walls.[51] In the aforementioned large rooms for max. 35 *klinai* in the west wing of the palace of Vergina there were *kline* bands along the walls as well. The written sources give a similar impression. Thus already at the mass wedding at Babylon we are told that Alexander's golden couch, as well as the 100 couches for the other couples, together faced special couches for Alexander's foreign friends, which gives the impression of one large dining group.[52] Also the use of the audience hall for banquets, mentioned in the Letter of Aristeas, might indicate that the king stayed at the same central place at the back wall, while the guests were placed surrounding him.

In fact nothing indicates that the primary concern of the royal banquets at least of the personal monarchs was, indeed, conversation. Rather one gets the impression that the focus of the royal dinner was the king, and that the important thing for the guests was not to enjoy themselves with conversation in small groups, but to behold the king and show their respect to him. With the introduction of the *stibadium* into the larger dining halls in late Antiquity it became possible to host even more diners, since in contrast to the *symposia* and the *triclinia*, these couches opened in a semicircle and could thus be placed in such a way that all had an identical focus (Fig. 8-9). In general, the royal banquets were ceremonial rather than social, both in the Hellenistic and the Roman period.

There is no doubt, in my opinion, that the disposition of the dining hall reflected the position of the king. In contrast to the Persian king, who, as mentioned, dined behind a curtain, the likewise autocratic Hellenistic kings and Roman emperors dined in the company of their guests, and the visibility of the sovereign became the primary concern. This meant that a special couch must have been placed centrally and visible for all guests and therefore undoubtedly raised above them, as was also the case with couches for the gods.[53] One must envisage a placement at the centre of the back wall, as was probably the case with the throne during audiences, and as was the custom in Oriental palaces. The position of the royal couch could undoubtedly be marked by a special kind of floor decoration which faced his way.[54]

A niche with statues behind and above the king could also be used, as was done in Mausolus' *andron*, and probably also in the Nile Boat of Ptolemy IV, where the grotto with dynastic statues in the Bacchic *oecus* would certainly have served as an effective backdrop for the king's couch (Fig. 3).

In the Roman period, it seems that already Augustus used the later canonical apse for this purpose, as is evident from the tetrastyle *oecus* of the Casa di Augusto (Fig. 18). He might not have reclined in this later walled up apse, but it would create an effective backdrop, as did later the fine fountains at the back of the Neronian *triclinia* in the Domus Aurea and in the Hadrianic ones in the Villa Adriana (Fig. 26).

But the absolute emperor Domitian dined, indeed, on a raised couch placed in the large apse in the huge banqueting hall on the Palatine, and from that high place we are informed that he looked intimidating down on his guests (Fig. 19, 22).[55] Apses became canonical both in the audience halls and the official dining halls of late Antiquity (Fig. 23). The round form, including the apse, gave an aura of something sacred and had cosmic associations. In general one should not underestimate the influence of these royal apses and gables on the Christian basilicas, which did not only borrow the form of these royal halls, but also the function; thus Christ could, from His elevated position in the apse, survey the Eucharist taking place in front of him.

Conclusion

During the long period which has been in focus here, the dining halls of the royal palaces developed in many ways. There are certain indications that the kind of monarchy housed in the various palaces was reflected to some extent not only in the audience halls, which I have tried to show earlier,[56] but also in the dining halls (Fig. 24). The size of these halls may thus illuminate what kind of monarchy we are dealing with, and what kind of ambition the monarch in question harboured. The same is the case with the marking of the seat of the king in these halls.

In the Hellenistic period the palaces of the "constitutional" kings, or kings inspired from the Greek notion of monarchy, that is, the kings of Macedonia and Pergamon, seemingly took over the Greek-style dining room, *andron*, with its square form and closed aspect, as is evident from the palaces of Vergina and Pergamon. The new palaces of the personal kings in the East, on the other hand, which included the Seleucids, Ptolemies and also the Hasmoneans and the client king Herod the Great, used different models. Both the size and the internal arrangement were different; the great halls with *klinai* along the walls excluded conversation and reflected the omnipotent and semi-divine status of the monarchies, which were Oriental in style rather than Greek. Thus the Seleucids took over some of the palaces of the Persian kings including their large and sumptuous ceremonial halls,

Palaces	national	personal
Persepolis, Achaemenid		900 m²
Labraunda, Hecatomnid		200 m²
Vergina, Macedonian	296/100 m²	
Pella, Macedonian		400 m²
Pergamon, Attalid	133/73 m²	
Babylon, Main palace, Seleucid		?884 m²
Susa, Main palace, Seleucid		364 m²
Alexandria, Pavilion, Ptolemaic		?3735 m²
Ptolemais, governors' Palace, Ptolemaic	227/113 m²	
Jericho, Hasmonean	70 m²	
Jerusalem, late Herodian		?2500 m²
Masada, West, early Herodian	36 m²	
Masada, North, late Herodian		289 m²
Jericho, first Herodian Palace	234/163 m²	
Jericho, third Herodian Palace		551 m²
Rome, Augustus' House	66/55 m²	
Rome, Domus Aurea		217/284 m²
Rome, Domus Flavia		914 m²
Villa Adriana, "Serapeum"		220 m²
Piazza Armerina, Triconch		625 m²
Spalato, Diocletianic		384/121 m²
Constantinople, early byzantine		1218/729 m²

Fig. 24. Table showing the size of the royal banqueting halls in the palaces of the constitutional (national) and autocratic (personal) kings/emperors, respectively.

Fig. 25. Villa Adriana. View from the stibadium *of the "Serapeum" by the Canopus. (Author's photo.)*

without any change. Also the Pavilion and the banqueting halls in Alexandria and Jerusalem, which we know only from descriptions, give an impression of dining halls which could accomodate a large number of guests and which were richly furnished.

In Italy, it was this kind of banqueting hall, which had already been used by the Syracusian kings for a long time before Sicily became a Roman province,[57] that attracted the new élite and conquerors in the two last centuries BC. Also, it was this kind of dining room, which eventually became the model also for the Roman emperors who were by no means unaccustomed to this kind of *luxuria*, since they took over many of the palaces of the Hellenistic kings. The introduction of the *triclinium* system, with one side open to the surroundings, instead of the Greek *andron* type, undoubtedly reflects the importance of having a view from the dining room. The placement of the three couches around the three walls of the rooms may mirror the placement of the *klinai* of some royal dining halls. Thus the Roman *triclinium* was probably an adaptation partly of the royal dining hall plan, and partly of the Greek notion of conversation, now called *convivium*, making a party of only nine people desirable.[58]

As was the case at the courts of the personal Hellenistic kings, it soon became the Roman emperor, not conversation, that was in focus at the

Fig. 26. Villa Adriana. The raised dais behind the stibadium, *perhaps for the emperor. (Author's photo.)*

banquets of the Roman court, and the *convivium* of the Roman élite became ceremonalized to a royal banquet with sacred undertones.[59] The placement of the emperor in an apse, raising him above his guests, is a clear sign that "democracy" and *convivium* was not in the centre of the proceedings, and although Pliny in his Panegyrics to Trajan contrasts the social behaviour of this idealized emperor to the autocratic one of the hated Domitian, Trajan still used the same apsed dining hall, and there was also a raised platform for the emperor at the back of the official summer-*stibadium*, the so-called Serapeum, of the villa which his adopted son Hadrian built in Tivoli (Figs. 25-26). The same elevated position was used in the second official banqueting area there, the stadio-nymfeo. Eugenia Salza Prina Ricotti (1987, 177) aptly formulates the role of the emperor like this: "A large part of the awe inspired by a man, who was deemed to be a god and surely would become a god on his death, depended on the way people saw him during his public appearances." In late Antiquity this tendency was developed further, making the emperor divine and removed from the sphere of the living, who as guests at his banquets and placed on their many *stibadia* looked only up to him, and did not discuss freely between them. The *convivium* had become a sacred ceremony, and could therefore easily be taken over by the Christians for their own use.[60]

Notes

1. See for the Persian banquets, e.g. Ath. 4.145-46 (cit. Heracleides), cf. Lewis 1987; for the Macedonian banquets, Borza 1983 with references.
2. I.e. in connection with the mass wedding of Babylon: Ath. 12.538cff (cit. Chares); Aelian, *VH* 8.7. For the entertainment: e.g. 5.211aff.
3. Ath. 12.542c (cit. Duris), Aelian *VH* 9.9.
4. See Lucan 10.111-21 for Caesar's banquet; Ath. 4.147f-148b (cit. Socrates of Rhodes), for Marc Antony's banquet.
5. Joseph. *BJ* 5.4.4 (177-78).
6. Ptolemy IIs Pavilion: Ath. 5.196-97 (cit. Callixenus); The Thalamegos: Ath. 5.204ff (cit. Callixenus).
7. For the latin terminology of both the function and the setting, see Tamm 1963, 189ff.
8. See Dunbabin 1995.
9. The designations of Greek dining rooms were based on the number of *klinai*, thus e.g. rooms called *pentaklinos* (*oikos*), *enneaklinos* (*oikos*), never transcribed into latin, are known in addition to *triklinos*, which could also be used as a substantive: *to triklinon*. In the description of the Nile boat belonging to Ptolemy IV, the word *triklinos* is used in connection with a *thalamos*, i.e. a bedroom, since it ought to be a small room (Ath. 5.207c (cit. Moschion)). More interesting is the use of the word *triklinon* by Polybius (30.26, cf. Ath. 5.195d) in his description of the feast held by Antiochos IV in Daphne in 168 BC. Figures of 1000 and 1500 *triklina* are mentioned, indicating a participation of a large amount of guests. Here, the use of the word is unusual, and might have something to do with Antiochos IV having lived in Rome for many years. In this case, the *triclinium* form may have existed there already at this time (v.i.). It is thought-provoking that according to Plutarch (*Aem.* 28) the feast was designed to rival that held in Macedonia by Aemilius Paullus after the victory at Pydna in the same year. See also Dunbabin in this volume.
10. For Murlo, see latest Rathje 1995; for the late period, especially the painted chamber tombs found south of Orvieto, the Tombe Golini I-II (probably 2nd half of 4th cent. BC) and the Tomba degli Hescanas (late 4th-early 3rd cent. BC), see *Pittura Etrusca à Orvieto*. Exhibition Catalogue, Rome 1982.
11. E.g. *Miles Gloriosus* 642ff, 652ff; cf. Salza Prina Ricotti 1983 passim. In the same period, Cato Censorius probably dined seated in his rustic villa (*Rust.* 14.1-2), however.
12. Vitr. 6.5.8-9.
13. For the Domus Aurea, Suet. *Ner.* 31.2. Seneca uses *cenatio* for banqueting halls in general: *Ep.* 78.23, 90.9, 90.15; he mentions a *cenatio* with rich columns which could hold the whole people: *Ep.* 115.8. Heating: *Prov.* 4.9; *vela* and *specularia*: *QNat.* 4.13.7.
14. See Nielsen 1994, 21 n. 50.

15. For these royal palaces and their dining halls, see in general Nielsen 1994 for the Hellenistic and early Roman period, Bek 1983 for the Roman and Byzantine period.
16. In Alexandria we hear that the Pavilion of Ptolemy II could accomodate 130 *klinai*, but that only 100, for 200 guests, were placed there (Ath. 5.195-96). Cf. Studniczka 1914 and, with an alternative reconstruction, Salza Prina Ricotti 1988-89. For the banqueting halls of Herod the Great in Jerusalem, *hekatontaklinos andrones*, see Joseph. BJ 5.4.4 (176-78); for Agathocles' hall called *hexakontaklinos*, see Diod. 16.83.2. One may compare with the tent of Alexander the Great, which could hold 100 *klinai* (Diod. 17.16.4).
17. See for this palace, Heermann 1986, 239ff, cf. Nielsen 1994, cat. no. 11.
18. Such a broad-room constituted the main hall in the palace of Pella in Macedonia; see Nielsen 1994, 88ff, cat. no. 12, with earlier literature.
19. For broad-rooms, see in general Hoepfner & Schwandner 1994, who compare the Delian houses with those of Dura Europos and Babylon. Cf. Nielsen 1994, passim, and Dunbabin in this volume.
20. For example, this is the case in the Nile scene with *stibadium* decorating the *triclinium* of the Casa dell' Efebeo and which could be viewed by the diners. In the *praedium* of Julia Felix the dining grotto is decorated with Nile scenes, and in the Casa di Loreio Tiburtino the channel is flanked by egyptianizing sculpture. Cf. Mayboom 1995, 80ff, who has treated the Praeneste mosaic, where *i.a.* a group of diners are depicted on a *stibadium*. One may also introduce a coptic textile with a *stibadium* motif, see Dunbabin 1991, 134f, figs. 28, 33-35. Cf. Lembke 1994, 59ff.
21. For this palace, see Pesce 1950, Lauter 1971. Cf. Nielsen 1994, 146ff, cat. no. 22.
22. Ath. 5.207 (cit. Moschion). Temples of Aphrodite were often round, an imitation of the famous Knidian temple.
23. For these Herodian palaces, see for Masada Netzer 1991; for Jericho and Herodium, latest Netzer 1990. Cf. Nielsen 1994, cat. nos. 27, 30, and 31.
24. Varro *Rust.* 3.5.9-17.
25. Pliny *Ep.* 5.6.36. Martial's epigram on *stibadia* (Ep. 14.87) runs like this: *accipe lunata scriptum testudine sigma. octo capit; veniat quisquis amicus erit*. I.e. room for eight.
26. See Salza Prina Ricotti 1987, Franceschini 1991, passim.
27. Suet. *Ner.* 31.2, Dunbabin 1991, 135.
28. For these rooms from late Antiquity, see Lavin 1962, Bek 1983, Dunbabin 1991 and latest 1996, Rossiter 1991. But already in the palace of the Dux Ripae in Dura Europos there might have been a triconch in addition to the apsidal hall, facing the Euphrat. See *Dura Europos Report*, 9th Season, 1935-36.
29. Dunbabin 1991 and latest 1996.
30. For the palace of Vergina, see e.g. Andronicos 1984, 38ff, cf. Nielsen 1994, 81ff, Cat. no. 10. For the palace of Pergamon, see Kawerau & Wiegand 1930, Radt 1988, 83-105, cf. Nielsen 1994, 102ff, cat. no. 14.
31. Dunbabin 1991 and her article in this volume.
32. For these governors' palaces in general, see Nielsen 1994, passim.
33. Cf. Vitruvius' suggestions how to place dining rooms according to the four seasons (6.4.1-2).
34. See Nielsen, 1994, 35ff and passim, and Salza Prina Ricotti 1988-89.

35. Ath. 12.537d (cit. Ephippus).
36. Joseph. *AJ* 20.190, cf. *BJ* 2.344. Cf. Nielsen 1994a.
37. Polybius 31.25 links the rapid spread of drinking parties among young nobles with the extravagance learned during the war against the last Macedonian king Perseus. One may mention also the banquet held by Metellus Pius in 75 BC in Spain. It took place in a hall decorated to resemble a temple and may thus be compared with Cleopatra's dining hall, see Plut. *Sert.* 22.2-3 and Val. Max. 9.1.5. What Valerius Maximus finds particularly objectionable was that this did not take place in Greece or Asia, where such extravagance was only to be expected, but in provincial Spain. Cf. the feast of Mithridates held in the theatre of Pergamon in 88 BC (Plut. *Sull.* 11.1-2).
38. For this development and the various forms of rooms for dining in the Greek and Roman period, see latest Dunbabin 1991 with earlier literature, and in this volume.
39. For the Casa di Augusto, see latest the article in *LTUR* II, 1995, 46-48 by Jacobi. Cf. Nielsen 1994, 171ff, cat. no. 25.
40. See Suet. *Cal.* 23.2, and *Vit.* 15.3.
41. In the new excavations of this palace, a presumably private dining hall from the Vespasianic rebuilding of Nero's palace can be gleaned from the foundations. It was placed in the centre of the northern wing and faced the Forum. It was presumably an apsidal broad-room surrounded by gardens on three sides. According to the excavators it measured 28 x 35 Roman feet, and including the apses the width was 60 feet (see Krause 1995; the publication, Krause, C., *Domus Tiberiana. Gli scavi 1981-1987*, is forthcoming).
42. The octagonal one may well be identical with the round dining hall with rotating ceiling described by Suetonius (*Ner.* 31.2, cf. Petron. *Sat.* 60). The ceilings of other dining halls in this palace could open and flowers and scent be scattered over the diners. One may compare with Elegabal, who by means of a reversible ceiling brought a flower garden into his banqueting hall and suffocated his guests, some of them to death, with violets (*SHA Heliogab.* 21.5).
43. For Domus Aurea, see latest the article in *LTUR*, vol. 2, 1995, 49-64 by various authors. Cf. Bek 1983. For Domus Flavia, see Tamm 1963, Finsen 1969, Bek 1983 and latest the article by L. Sasso D'Elia in *LTUR*, vol. 2, 1995, 40-45, and, specifically for the *triclinium*, with a new reconstruction, Gibson *et al.* 1994, where the *triclinium* is compared with an outsized Cyzicene *oecus*. For the Vespasianic *cenatio* of Domus Tiberiana flanked by gardens as well, see n. 41.
44. See Tac. *Ann.* 4.59.1-2, Suet. *Tib.* 39; cf. Strabo 5.3.6. Cf. Salza Prina Ricotti 1987. For that of Baia, see Giangrotta 1983.
45. For example, in the *triclinium* of the House of the Labyrinth, see Bek 1983, and for summer *triclinia*, Amedick 1993.
46. See La Rocca 1986, 24f, and Franceschini 1991, 509f.
47. See Salza Prina Ricotti 1987. Dining in the open in gardens was popular in both the Hellenistic and Roman period. In this connection one should not underestimate the significance of the presence already in the first half of the 1st century BC of a permanent open-air *triclinium* in the garden of one of the Twin Palaces of the Hasmonaean palace in Jericho (Fig. 21). This palace was clearly inspired from the palace of Alexandria where, as mentioned above in connection with

stibadia, such garden dining had presumably been popular for a long time. From Italy we have several descriptions of such open-air dining with views to gardens and nature belonging to the villas of the late Republican élite. L. Licinius Lucullus had several in his villa near Tusculum (Plut. *Luc.* 39.4-5; Varro *Rust.* 3.4.3), and he combined installations for dining with an aviary, as did Varro in his villa at Casinum. Open-air dining installations could even be placed outside the villa proper, in woods, the most extreme example being the banquet set up by Q. Hortensius the orator in a walled forest belonging to his villa near Laurentum, with wild animals as spectators (Varro *Rust.* 3.13). One may compare with the emperor Elegabal who had lions and leopards trained to participate in his dinner parties to frighten his guests (*SHA Heliogab.* 21.1). The Roman emperors soon followed suit; Tiberius' *triclinium* at Sperlonga was placed outside the grotto proper, in the middle of a fish-pool, and Caligula had a dining room, which could house 15 guests with servants, built into a plane tree in his villa at Velitrae! (Pliny *HN* 12.5.10). In Villa Adriana, great banquets were undoubtedly often laid out in the open in the garden, as suggested by Salza Prina Ricotti (1987) in several persuasive reconstructions. See in general for the pertinent written sources, Littlewood 1987.

48. See latest Bergquist 1990, with earlier literature.
49. Also, Bergquist has argued for a division into two separate groups placed in a horseshoe in the rectangular Greek and Hellenistic dining halls, as for example the broad-rooms of Delos, and Joachim Raeder (1988) in fact compares these Delian rooms with Vitruvius' Cyzicene *oecus*. See also Dunbabin's article in this volume.
50. For entertainment at banquets in general, see Jones 1991.
51. See Hellström 1989 and latest 1996. Cf. Nielsen 1994, 65f.
52. Ath. 12.538b-c (cit. Chares).
53. Ath. 4.148b-d (cit. Socrates of Rhodes), on Antony; 152f-153c (cit. Posidonius), on the Parthian kings.
54. A reflection of this may be seen later in the rich Roman houses for example at Antioch, where the central motif normally faced the *kline* at the back wall (See Dunbabin 1991).
55. Pliny *Pan.* 49.6-8.
56. Nielsen 1994, 209ff, fig. 114.
57. In the palace built by his father, Dionysius II had a banqueting hall with 30 *klinai* (Ath. 12.541c), and a hall with 60 *klinai* is attributed to the restoration of this palace by Agathocles. The palace was reused by the Roman governors, including the notorious Verres (Cic. *Verr.* 2.4.54).
58. It is interesting that already in the 2nd-1st century BC the newly excavated palatial house near the Acropolis of Rhodes had an oblong *triclinium*-type dining hall covering 80 m² in the official part of the house. See Dreliossi-Herakleidou 1996.
59. As Lise Bek formulates it (1983, 95): "The display of social interrelation has become an official show or state ceremony."
60. Lavin 1962, Bek 1983.

The Sixth Hour is the Mealtime for Scholars: Jewish Meals in the Roman World

David Noy

Many aspects of the lives of Diaspora Jews are illuminated by finds from the Jewish catacombs of Rome, but unfortunately not their dining practices. The only possible source of such information is a 4th century CE gold-glass which may originally have depicted some sort of meal.[1] Slightly less than half survives of what was originally probably the base of a bowl, about 10 cm in diameter. The glass could have been pressed into the plaster sealing a grave in a catacomb as a means of identification. The surviving, upper part depicts the usual symbols found on such objects: a torah-shrine, with to the left a *menorah* and a scroll and to the right a *menorah*, a *shofar* and a circle which may be a *matzah*. All that survives of the lower part is the head of a fish, lying on a plate or table, along with something which has been variously identified as a cushion or a couch. There was a Latin inscription around the outside. The surviving part reads: [- -]*ci bibas cum Eulogia conp[are (?) - -]*

Eulogia may be a personal name ("may you drink with Eulogia, your spouse (?)") or a Greek word in the Latin alphabet ("may you drink with a blessing").

The presence of a fish is a reminder of the one pagan description of a Jewish meal, presumably imagined as taking place at Rome. This was written by Persius in the mid-1st century CE and forms part of a section illustrating that "superstitions make demands on men". Persius is typical of pagan writers in looking at the content of a Jewish meal and saying little about who was eating it.

> But when Herod's days arrive, and lamps entwined with violets
> are placed on the greasy window-sills spewing out heavy clouds
> of smoke, and when the tunny's tail swims around, encircling
> the cheap red dish, and the white jar is bloated with wine,
> you move your lips in silence and blanch at the circumcised sabbath.[2]

There are a number of difficulties in interpreting this passage. Herod's days are taken to be the sabbath by Stern (1976) and Harvey (1981), with a reference to lighting the lamp on the sabbath eve, which was a Jewish practice familiar to non-Jews.[3] The prominence of the lamp might instead be a reference to Hanukkah (Festival of Lights). These explanations assume that "Herod" represents the Jews as a whole, as Harvey believes he does when Horace refers to "Herod's rich palm-groves" as a contrast to an Italian farm.[4] Horbury (1991), however, thinks that Horace means Herod personally, and that Persius is discussing the observance of Herod's accession day (and perhaps celebrations for other members of the Herodian family too, to explain the plural). Fish would be an appropriate meal either on the sabbath (see below) or a festival. The general tone of the passage is that the Jews are having a poor meal, even if it is on a festive occasion. According to Harvey's analysis, the tuna's tail is the inferior cut; the red dish is Arretine earthenware, used by the poor; the fact that the tail encircles the dish indicates the largeness of the fish or more probably the smallness of the plate.

There are also rabbinic references to one particular dining practice of 2nd century CE Jews at Rome, concerning the arrangements made by R. Theodosius or Theudas (Hebrew Todos) about eating a lamb or kid at Passover. One version is part of a discussion about the lenient rulings of Rabban Gamaliel, with which "the sages" disagreed. Theodosius "introduced among the community of Rome the practice of eating a helmeted kid on Passover night". Gamaliel approved, but others said that people should not be eating consecrated animals outside Jerusalem.[5] A "helmeted kid" was roasted whole, with the legs and entrails hanging over the head.[6] The alternative version is identical except that the animals eaten are lambs roasted whole.[7] The reason for the dispute is that the practice at Rome is, according to some, too similar to what should only be done in the Temple. The implication is that Roman Jews held large gatherings at Passover, since the cooking of whole animals would hardly be viable otherwise. Julius Caesar issued a decree in which he complained that the Jews of Delos were not allowed to carry out various of their customs including "bringing in contributions for common meals (*syndeipna*) and holy rites", whereas at Rome they could do so;[8] Passover meals may have been the issue there too.

Pagans tended to regard Jews as exclusive diners. Tacitus takes as evidence of Jewish misanthropy that "they sit apart at meals and they sleep apart", and Philostratus makes Euphrates the Stoic describe the Jews as "a race that has made its own a life apart and irreconcilable, that cannot share with the rest of mankind in the pleasures of the table nor join in their libations or prayers or sacrifices".[9] There was a fascination with the taboo on eating pork, regarded as particularly eccentric by Greeks and Romans, but little interest in the other dietary laws (although Plutarch discusses not eating hare).[10] Jewish separateness at mealtimes may, if true and not just a symbol of misanthropy, have been due more to practical considerations (the difficulty of complying with dietary laws in a non-Jewish house) than to any deliberate policy of separate eating. However, the problems of Jews dining at pagan houses were addressed in the Mishnah and Talmud, and R. Judah the Prince supposedly dined with the emperor.[11] In fact, at least in late Antiquity, there was some Christian concern that Jews were not separate enough. The issues involved are explained in *Concilium Veneticum*, canon 12 (dated 461-491):

All clergy should avoid dining with Jews, nor should anyone receive them to dine. Since at Christian houses they do not take the general food, it is unworthy and sacrilegious that their food should be eaten by Christians. Since things which we eat with the apostle's permission are judged by them to be unclean, the clergy would start to be inferior to the Jews if we take what is served by them but they scorn what is offered by us.

This canon echoes canon 50 of the Council of Elvira (early 4th century), and was repeated almost word for word at the Council of Agde (canon 40) in 506, suggesting that the "problem" was a continuing one.[12]

Rabbinic sources on meals

For Jewish evidence about practices and beliefs concerning meals, reliance on rabbinic texts is unavoidable. These are of course very problematic in terms of how far they reflect real practices rather than ideal ones, how closely they reflect the period they purport to describe rather than the time at which they were redacted,[13] and how significant rabbinic Judaism was for most Jews in the Roman Empire. The passages cited below may therefore be of limited value as historical evidence. However, the incidental details about practice for which they are cited here are usually subordinate to the main issues involved in the texts, and are therefore perhaps less likely to have been distorted or to show rabbinic behaviour which differed from that of other Jews.

The time at which you ate could be related to moral worth or to your social role. Rabbis advised people that eating breakfast early was good for them,[14] and the time at which you ate your main meal was particularly significant:

Our rabbis taught: The first hour is the mealtime for gladiators; the second for robbers; the third for heirs; the fourth for labourers; the fifth for all [other] people. But that is not so, for R. Papa said: The fourth [hour] is the mealtime for all people? – Rather the fourth hour is the mealtime for all [other] people, the fifth for [agricultural] labourers and the sixth for scholars. After that it is like throwing a stone into a barrel. Abaye said: That was said only if nothing at all is eaten in the morning; but if something is eaten in the morning, there is no objection [to having the main meal later].[15]

It is difficult to be certain if this list is simply one of increasing moral value, or if it reflects real practices. All the mealtimes are earlier than what was usual for wealthy Romans (the eighth or ninth hour). Agricultural workers in Mediterranean society might well work early, then dine and rest when it became too hot to work. The Essenes worked until the fifth hour, then washed and ate; they resumed work later and had another meal in the evening.[16] The gladiators' final meal, the *cena libera*, was traditionally eaten the night before they performed, but if they were to have anything to eat on the day of performance, it would have to be early in the day. Why robbers and heirs should have special dining hours is less clear; "heirs" could mean *captatores* who have to attend their potential benefactors and therefore eat at home before they go out.

As far as scholars are concerned, their dining later than others presumably shows some sort of moral or social superiority. If they had been at work since an early breakfast, they would have a longer working day than anyone else, extended by the after-dinner discussions in which some rabbis evidently indulged (see below). Alternatively, dining later might be seen as a more "civilized" practice. The most romanized Jews were thought to follow Roman custom: "King Agrippa" dined at the ninth hour.[17]

In general, the rabbinic texts show no great disapproval for eating well and spending money on good food, although gluttony was condemned and some rabbis praised basic foods like eggs and cabbage.[18] R. Judah the Prince was able to serve out-of-season (but not particularly luxurious) foods.[19] The ability to put on a good meal was seen very positively, as shown by the story of a butcher of Laodicea who was rewarded for his piety by being given the means to provide a lavish meal served on a golden table carried by sixteen men.[20] There are many anecdotes about rabbis dining out, and although the quality and quantity of the food and tableware is not usually mentioned, a certain amount of refinement seems to be assumed.

Dining involved rituals which also reveal something of what was taken for granted. For example, diners were encouraged to wash their hands before eating, or at least the right hand, with which they were expected to eat as they would be reclining on the left elbow, showing the assumption that people would eat with their fingers and not with cutlery; washing the hands after a meal is also recommended. The desirability of washing, which is mentioned in the New Testament as a custom of "all the Jews" but not as a specifically Jewish habit, probably had as much to do with general cleanliness as with fear of impurity, but an additional ingenious reason was given: it was meritorious to obey the sages who recommended it.[21]

Anything to be eaten should first be blessed.[22] This led to much debate over whether separate blessings were required for individual items of a meal or for separate courses, over what happened if the meal was interrupted, and over whether the blessing needed to be spoken aloud.[23] The general rule seems to have been that the meal began with breaking bread, which was blessed first, and that the wine was blessed separately.[24] After that, no more separate blessings were needed. Wine before meals was treated differently from wine with meals, and there was a different ritual for those who were going to drink and not eat.[25] Considerations of etiquette arose: the host must not break bread until the guests have finished saying Amen to the blessing; the guests must not begin eating until the one who breaks bread has tasted.[26]

A blessing was needed for the group of diners as well as for individuals. The host should be blessed too.[27] This indicates that the sort of meal which is the context for rabbinic discussions is not usually a family meal (although it is sometimes possible to have a child present)[28] but one where a group of rabbis gather at the house of one of them. Rabbis are regularly shown giving dinner invitations to each other,[29] and dining with "ignorant persons" was discouraged.[30] When rabbis dined together, their wives were not expected to be present; to this extent they were behaving in a "Greek" rather than a "Roman" way, but perhaps from their own motives (the assumption that women would not be able to take part in learned discussion) rather than through imitation of anyone else. When R. `Ulla dined at the house of R. Nahman, Nahman's wife was in another room (the kitchen?); when `Ulla refused to send the cup of benediction (for the grace after meals) to her, she wrecked the wine store.[31] R. Papa's wife apparently did the cooking for her family.[32] Some texts seem to assume that it was exceptional for scholars and their wives to dine together at all, even for everyday meals.[33]

It is assumed that diners will recline for their meal after sitting for their aperitif,[34] and reclining is a synonym for dining.[35] Servants are expected to be present,[36] although the host might serve the guests himself — thus, when a rabbi is mentioned as serving the others, it may mean that he is the host.[37] Several courses were usually served.[38] The meal should probably be imagined as taking place in a *triclinium*, since much etiquette is involved in who reclines first if there are two or three couches.[39] The host reclined at the middle of the middle couch, with the place of honour to his right — this is somewhat different from Roman practice, where the host took the innermost place on the *lectus imus* with the place of honour to his left. The setting for such a meal could just as well be pagan as Jewish, but rabbis sometimes objected to Graeco-Roman habits such as giving wreaths to guests.[40] At the conclusion of a meal, the grace after meals should be said; some rabbis decided that saying it mentally was sufficient,[41] perhaps having in mind a situation where a Jew was dining with non-Jews. After the meal, it was normal to go and bathe: there is a discussion about whether it is also acceptable to do this after the last meal before the fast of 9th Ab.[42]

There was a duty to be hospitable to equals. A 4th-century text explains how the destruction of the Temple was the final stage of a series of events which began with an inhospitable act by a man of Jerusalem. He sent out a servant (evidently a sort of *vocator*) to invite his friend Kamza, but instead the invitation went to his enemy Bar Kamza, who arrived for his dinner but was refused admittance despite increasingly desperate pleas ("I will pay the cost of the whole meal"). This text also describes an elaborate system of dining out in pre-70 Jerusalem, no doubt fictitious but perhaps based on later practices.[43] The invitee was informed who the other guests would be and was given a menu. He changed his buckle from his left to his right shoulder to indicate that he had accepted an invitation. A cloth was spread over the house door while the meal was in progress. The food was provided by a caterer, and "if he spoilt anything connected with the meal, they fined him in accordance with the status of the hosts and his guests".[44]

The meals in the background of the rabbinic texts do not usually seem to be taken on special occasions. However, meals taken at certain significant times entailed different practices. Many pagans formed the impression that the sabbath was a fast,[45] although Juvenal knew of the "sabbath haybox" for keeping food warm, and Plutarch referred to Jews inviting each other to drink wine on the sabbath.[46] The misunderstanding may have arisen from Jews who were willing to dine with non-Jews on other days but not on the sabbath.[47] The sabbath meal was in fact the focus of considerable rabbinic discussion, and was expected to be a better meal than was eaten on other days. The main concern was that eating would interfere with other sabbath duties: the practice of taking the sabbath meal "at the hour when the discourse is given in the *beth-midrash*" could even be cited as a reason for the destruction of Jerusalem, and eating after the service was the recommended way.[48]

Communal meals for groups of *haberim*, men who co-operated in strict observance of purity regulations,[49] could take place on Friday (starting late so that it could last into the sabbath) or Saturday evening. They would include the study of Torah as well as the actual dining. The establishment of an *erub* enabled food to be carried from house to house for communal meals on the sabbath, at least within a restricted area.[50] It was customary in Palestine to eat fish on the sabbath; in the case of the poor, this would be an addition to a basically vegetarian regular diet.[51] Hence the suggestion that the gold-glass from Rome shows a Sabbath meal.

The communal meal on the night before 15th Nisan (*seder*) was an important part of the celebration of Passover, initially at Jerusalem (where large groups might eat together in a courtyard or on a rooftop)[52] and later elsewhere. At Jerusalem, the paschal lamb was taken to the Temple to be sacrificed and then brought home to be cooked and eaten. After the destruction of the Temple, and even before it for those who could not be at Jerusalem on the appropriate date, the meal and the associated rituals were still very significant. The meal must not begin before nightfall.[53] There were prescriptions for what should be eaten (including bitter herbs and *haroset*, a mixture of apples, nuts and wine) and drunk, and what should be discussed: the story of the Exodus was told, and sons asked their fathers ritualized questions about various customs and traditions.[54]

Some of the rituals of the Passover meal, including the element of formal discussion, had at least superficial similarities to a symposium.[55] Reclining for the meal was particularly important at Passover. "Even the poorest Israelite should not eat until he reclines at his table".[56] Bokser suggests that the Mishnah consciously attempts to distinguish the meal from a symposium.[57] The Passover practice of eating a whole lamb (or kid; see above) was probably the source of the misunderstanding that some Jews still carried out sacrifices after the destruction of the Temple.[58] The importance of a meal in which everyone participated, with a set of procedures which, theoretically, all Jews would be following at the same time can be seen as a way of preserving identity and community without the Temple, although too close an imitation of Temple practices was not approved.[59]

Passover was not necessarily the only festival observed with a communal meal. In Augustus' time, there was legislation against people who stole Jewish communal funds from "a sabbath-house (synagogue) or dining-room".[60] A 1st century BCE ostrakon from Apollinopolis Magna gives details of contributions to common feasts (*poseis*) on the 15th and 16th of an unknown month; "Josepos *hiereus*" is named on both days, and the feasts may be Passover meals or some other Jewish festival.[61] In a 2nd/3rd-century CE letter explaining to a strategos about discrepancies in the numbers of some sheep and goats, there is a reference to animals being "[sold?] to the Jews for a contributory feast (*Ioudaiois eis symbole[n]*)" - this could be Passover, or another festival such as Tabernacles.[62] A 2nd century CE account from an estate, probably at Edfu, lists a payment of 100 *drachmae* "by Amarantos, on the *pannychis* of the Feast of Tabernacles (*dia Amarantou tei panny[khi]d(i) tes skenopegias*)".[63] At least in the 3rd century CE, meals were taken in the synagogue at the sanctification of the new moon, and this may explain the existence of a *triclinium* at the Stobi synagogue (see White in this volume). R. Yohanan was able to gather leftover scraps in the morning after one such meal.[64]

Food was also consumed at funerals, and the meals provided were one of the reasons for concern over excessive expenditure on funerals.[65] Contributions of food were brought by those who came to console the bereaved; mourners should not eat their own food on the day after the funeral.[66] The first meal after the funeral, se`udat havra'ah ("meal of comfort") was perhaps a family occasion in most cases, but for a sage everyone should take part in it, in the public square.[67] The chief mourner reclined in the place of honour.[68] Overturning the couches in the house was a ritual of mourning, and the question of whether they should be replaced for the meal was debated.⁶⁹ Ten cups of wine were drunk before, during and after the meal; this increased to thirteen at the death of Rabban Gamaliel, but there was a return to the previous practice because of the resulting drunkenness.⁷⁰

Whereas pagan epitaphs sometimes mention meals to be held in commemoration of the deceased, Jewish epitaphs never do so. Pagan tombs sometimes had adjacent *triclinia*, and stone benches and tables which could be used for dining have been found in Christian catacombs,⁷¹ but the surviving Jewish catacombs of Italy have no such provision. The general absence of dates in Jewish epitaphs may also indicate that a commemorative meal on the anniversary of the death was not a Jewish practice.

Dining was part of family celebrations too. According to Josephus, it was acceptable to hold a feast to celebrate a circumcision but not a birthday.⁷² The wedding feast is the main family feast mentioned in rabbinic writings. It was provided by the bridegroom's father and held in his house, and it could last for seven days.⁷³ Whole animals might need to be cooked: R. Aqiba met Rabban Gamaliel and R. Joshua in the meat-market of Emmaus, "where they had gone to buy a beast for the banquet of Rabban Gamaliel's son ...".⁷⁴ The bridegroom reclined in the place of honour and received the good wishes of the other guests.⁷⁵

There is no evidence that the Jews in general had any developed belief in the importance of table-fellowship.⁷⁶ Sanders shows that the Pharisees did not regard eating together as a means of salvation, and only tended to have common meals when they lived in the same alley or courtyard.⁷⁷ It was a good thing for scholars to dine together, and for important rites of passage to be marked by a meal, but the only time at which the meal in itself acquired much ideological value was at Passover. Some of the dining practices described in rabbinic texts would have been quite familiar to well-to-do non-Jews, and in some respects non-Jews would have felt quite at home dining with Rabban Gamaliel. However, there would also have been very unfamiliar elements such as the blessing of the food and drink, the absence of women, and of course the nature of the food being eaten.

Notes

* This paper has benefited from discussion at the conference at Fuglsang and with colleagues at Lampeter; I am especially grateful to Carol Déry for her help and advice.
1. *CIJ* I 518, *JIWE* II 591, giving full bibliography. It is now in the Metropolitan Museum, New York. The original findspot is not known.
2. Persius, *Sat.* 5.179-184; the translation is slightly altered from that of N. Rudd in the Penguin edition. The Latin text is:
    ... at cum

> *Herodis venere dies unctaque fenestra*
> *dispositae pinguem nebulam vomuere lucernae*
> *portantes violas rubrumque amplexa catinum*
> *cauda natat thynni, tumet alba fidelia vino,*
> *labra moves tacitus recutitaque sabbata palles.*

Rudd translates "*Herodis dies*" as "Herod's birthday".
3. Sen. *Ep.* 95.47, Tert. *Ad Nat.* 13, Safrai 1976, 807.
4. Hor. *Epist.* 2.2.184.
5. Bab. Talmud, *Bezah* 23a.
6. M. Ginsberg, *Bezah* (Soncino Press translation of the Babylonian Talmud, 1938), 116 n. 9, P. Blackman, *Mishnayoth* vol. 2 (Judaica Press, 1990), 361-62 n. 7.
7. Tosefta, *Yom Tov* 2.15. This passage comes immediately after a definition of what constitutes a "kid roasted whole". The texts are discussed by Bokser 1990.
8. Joseph. *AJ* 14.214.
9. Tac. *Hist.* 5.5.1, Philostr. *Ap.T.* 5.33.
10. Philo, *Leg.* 361, Plut. *Quaest.conv.* 4.4.4-5.3.
11. Mishnah, `*Abodah Zarah* 5.5, Bab. Talmud `*Abodah Zarah* 8a, *Shabbath* 122a, Midrash Esther Rabbah 1.16.
12. Texts in *CCSL* 148 (Concilia Galliae 314-506).
13. The redaction was done c. 200 for the Mishnah, and probably in the 5th century for the Palestinian Talmud and the 6th century for the Babylonian Talmud. However, the majority of rabbis cited in the Talmud lived in the 2nd and 3rd centuries.
14. Bab. Talmud, *Baba Kamma* 92b, *Baba Mezi`a* 107b.
15. Bab. Talmud, *Shabbath* 10a, translation by H. Freedman, Soncino Press, 1938.
16. Joseph. *BJ* 2.125-132. However, Bab. Talmud, *Berakoth* 2a-b seems to envisage a poor man coming home "to eat his bread with salt", presumably after a day of manual labour, towards evening — but he would have to finish eating before dark, as he would not be able to afford artificial light. See also Bilde in this volume.
17. Bab. Talmud, *Pesahim* 107b: Agrippa I or II could be meant.
18. Bab. Talmud, *Hullin* 105b, *Berakoth* 44b.
19. Bab. Talmud, *Berakoth* 57b, `*Abodah Zarah* 11a.
20. Bab. Talmud, *Shabbath* 119a.
21. Bab. Talmud, *Hullin* 106a, *Berakoth* 47a, Mark 7.3, Safrai 1976, 743, 802, Sanders 1992, 437-8.
22. Bab. Talmud, *Berakoth* 35a.
23. E.g. Bab. Talmud, *Berakoth* 15b.
24. Safrai 1976, 802.
25. Elaborate procedures are described in Bab. Talmud, *Berakoth* 43a.
26. Bab. Talmud, *Berakoth* 47a.
27. Bab. Talmud, *Berakoth* 46a.
28. Bab. Talmud, *Baba Bathra* 57b.
29. E.g. Bab. Talmud, *Berakoth* 46a, *Hullin* 86b and 104b.
30. Bab. Talmud, *Berakoth* 43b.
31. Bab. Talmud, *Berakoth* 51b.
32. Bab. Talmud, *Berakoth* 44b.

33. E.g. Mishnah, *Ketuboth* 5.9, where it only happens on the sabbath, Bab. Talmud, *Shabbath* 13b.
34. Bab. Talmud, *Berakoth* 43a.
35. E.g. Bab. Talmud, *Pesahim* 100a. Cf. *discumbo* in Latin, *kataklino* in Greek.
36. Bab. Talmud, *Baba Bathra* 57b, *Hullin* 107b.
37. E.g. Bab. Talmud, *Hullin* 86b.
38. Bab. Talmud, *Berakoth* 42b, *Hullin* 104b. Midrash Lamentations Rabbah 3.17.6 describes the Exilarch at Babylon serving a meal of eighty courses, and a Palestinian rabbi serving twenty-four courses for an ordinary meal and twice as many on the Sabbath.
39. Bab. Talmud, *Berakoth* 46b.
40. Rops 1962, 208. Mishnah, *Abodah Zarah* 4.2, objects to wreaths of corn because of their association with idolatry; cf. *Encyclopedia Judaica* vol. 5 cols. 1132-33. Wearing wreaths at weddings was abolished after the destruction of the Temple: Bab. Talmud, *Sotah* 49a; Midrash Lamentations Rabbah 5.16.1.
41. Bab. Talmud, *Berakoth* 15b.
42. Bab. Talmud, *Ta`anith* 30a.
43. Midrash Lamentations Rabbah 4.2.3-4.
44. Some of these details are also given in Bab. Talmud, *Baba Bathra* 93b.
45. E.g. Suet. *Aug.* 76; Petron. *Fr.* 37; Mart. *Ep.* 4.4.
46. Juv. *Sat.* 3.14 and 6.542 (with scholion), Plut. *Quaest.conv.* 6.2.
47. Fasting on the sabbath is explicitly rejected: Midrash Lamentations Rabbah 1.16.51.
48. Bab. Talmud, *Gittin* 38b, Safrai 1976, 806.
49. *Encyclopedia Judaica*, vol. 7 cols. 1489-92.
50. Safrai 1976, 803-6, Sanders 1992, 425.
51. Safrai 1976, 747, Sanders 1992, 129.
52. Safrai 1976, 730, 732.
53. Mishnah, *Pesahim* 10.1, Bab. Talmud, *Pesahim* 107b. It was a common practice to begin the sabbath eve meal late as well. At Passover, if the lamb sacrificed between the ninth and eleventh hours was then to be cooked for the meal (Sanders 1992, 135-37), very late dining would be inevitable.
54. Safrai 1976, 808-9, Sanders 1992, 137-8.
55. Safrai 1976, 810, Bokser 1984, 52.
56. Mishnah, *Pesahim* 10.1. Waiters are expected to be present, however (Tosefta, *Pesahim* 10.4), so the Passover meals of the poorest Israelites were not what really interested the rabbis.
57. Bokser 1984, 49-66.
58. This is the interpretation of Julian, *Con.Gal.* 305E ("the Jews do sacrifice in their own houses...") offered by Horbury, quoted by Millar 1992, 107. The Christian martyr Phileas (died c. 304 CE) said that Jews were allowed to sacrifice only in Jerusalem and sinned by carrying out their rites elsewhere: Musurillo 1972, 330-31, 344-45, Sanders (1992, 134) suggests that there were some Passover "sacrifices" outside Jerusalem before the destruction. There are also some Jewish texts which could be interpreted as showing that sacrifice really did continue after 70: Bokser 1984, App. A.
59. Bokser 1984, 83.

60. Joseph. *AJ* 16.164, reading *andronos*; the alternative reading *aaronos* would be a graecized form of the Hebrew word for "ark" which may only have come into use later in the sense of something in a synagogue.
61. *CPJ* I 139.
62. *CPJ* III 467.
63. *CPJ* III 452a. The term *pannychis* generally signifies a night-time festival. It is used several times by Philo: in *de Cherubim* 92 it is part of a list of forms of self-indulgence; similarly in *Legatio* 12, but used more positively; in *de Vita Contemplativa* it is a sacred rite observed after the evening meal.
64. Pal. Talmud, *Sanhedrin* VIII 2.26b; Levine 1979, 670.
65. Safrai 1976, 777, 783.
66. Bab. Talmud, *Mo`ed Katan* 27a-b.
67. Bab. Talmud, *Shabbath* 105b.
68. Bab. Talmud, *Mo`ed Katan* 28b.
69. Bab. Talmud, *Mo`ed Katan* 26b.
70. Pal. Talmud, *Berakoth* III 6a.
71. Stevenson 1978, 96-97.
72. Joseph. *Ap.* 2.204; Safrai 1976, 767.
73. Bab. Talmud, *Berakoth* 30b, 42a, 47a, *Ketuboth* 8a; Midrash Ecclesiastes Rabbah 1.3.1, 2.2.4; Safrai 1976, 759.
74. Mishnah, *Kerithoth* 3.7; Safrai 1976, 760.
75. Bab. Talmud, *Mo`ed Katan* 28b, *Berakoth* 6b.
76. Although it was very important for the Essenes: e.g. 1QS 6. See also Bilde in this volume.
77. Sanders 1992, 441-43; contra Bokser 1984, 11.

The Common Meal in the Qumran-Essene Communities

Per Bilde

Introduction

It is well-known that a common meal is a fundamental social act loaded with feelings, values and meaning.[1] A meal is more than just eating and drinking. Obviously, it matters *what* you eat and drink, but a meal is also *how* you eat, *where* you eat, *with whom* you eat, and under *which circumstances*. In other words: *a meal is eating and drinking plus something else*. We might paraphrase the "something else" as the admittedly vague — and today often misused — notion "culture" in the sense of a) *material culture*; b) *tradition and history*; c) *social context and function*; d) *feelings, values and expectations* invested in the actual meal.

a) Naturally, a meal implies a great deal of *material culture*. What kind of food and drink? What kind of recipes and cookery? What kind of furniture and tableware?
b) With these material elements of the meal we have already moved far into *tradition and history*. The means of supplying food — hunting, fishing and nearly all forms of agriculture and animal husbandry — have been inherited from our ancestors and marked by their culture. The same applies to recipes, cookery, the way meals are served and, of course, how you eat and drink.
c) By definition, a common meal is also a *social phenomenon*. Who are invited, and who take part? How are the participants dressed? How are they placed at the table? Which table manners and rituals are followed? In addition, meals generally play an important role in connection with social or political events, such as childbirths, anniversaries, weddings, funerals, initiations, sacrifices, gatherings, associations, military and non-military victories, enthronisations, and other public festivals. In other words: how is the common meal related to its social context, to status, influence and power in the society? Meals have different functions in different social contexts but, apparently, a meal always seems to play an important role in connection with all kinds of social events.
d) Considerations of these social aspects of meals inevitably lead to their *symbolic meaning*. The various sorts of food and drink are more than

means for saturation. Water, juice, beer and wine; bread; salt; vegetables; and, not least, the various sorts of animal flesh have different connotations, and therefore they are subject to specific rules regarding their suitability as food.[2] Fasting, on the other hand, is never unimportant, but usually loaded with as much symbolic meaning as eating, as we shall have the opportunity to see in Philo. Eating and drinking is thus related to all kinds of strong feelings, values and expectations.

We may summarize these four points by stating that, undoubtedly, the *identity* of human beings is closely bound up with the way they eat and drink — or abstain from it.[3]

In this essay it is my intention to describe and analyse the available sources on meals in the Qumran-Essene communities with regard to their social function and symbolic meaning, as outlined above.

In the discussion of this subject a great deal of energy has been expended on two partly related questions. First, do we have to consider and categorize the meals of the Qumran-Essene communities as "holy," "sacred" or even "sacramental"?[4] Secondly, do these meals replace, in a spiritualising way, the sacrificial cult in the Temple of Jerusalem?[5]

I shall begin by giving a brief presentation of Qumran, the Dead Sea Scrolls and the Essenes and continue with a short reading and interpretation of the relevant sources: two texts from the Dead Sea Scrolls, three from Philo and one from Josephus. An overall analysis leads to my conclusions accompanied by a few general remarks on the social function and the symbolic meaning of the Qumran-Essene meals.

Qumran, the Qumran-Essenes and our Sources

Khirbet Qumran is the Arabic name of an ancient ruin near the North Western shore of the Dead Sea. The neighbouring mountains of the Judean Desert are rich in caves, and in the years 1947-56 more than 20,000 fragments of about 800-900 different Jewish writings were found in eleven of these caves (see the map of "The Caves of Qumran", p. 147, and Figs. 1-3).[6] As seven caves out of these eleven are situated a few hundred metres from Khirbet Qumran, a connection between this place and the caves was immediately suspected. In the years 1951-58 the ruin was excavated under the direction of Roland de Vaux, who discovered an ancient building complex which he interpreted as the centre of the same religious group that had produced the writings (See Figs. 4-9).[7]

Roland de Vaux — and several other scholars with him — soon identified this group with the Essenes, whom we know from Philo and, in particular, from Josephus.[8] The basic argument for this identification is a

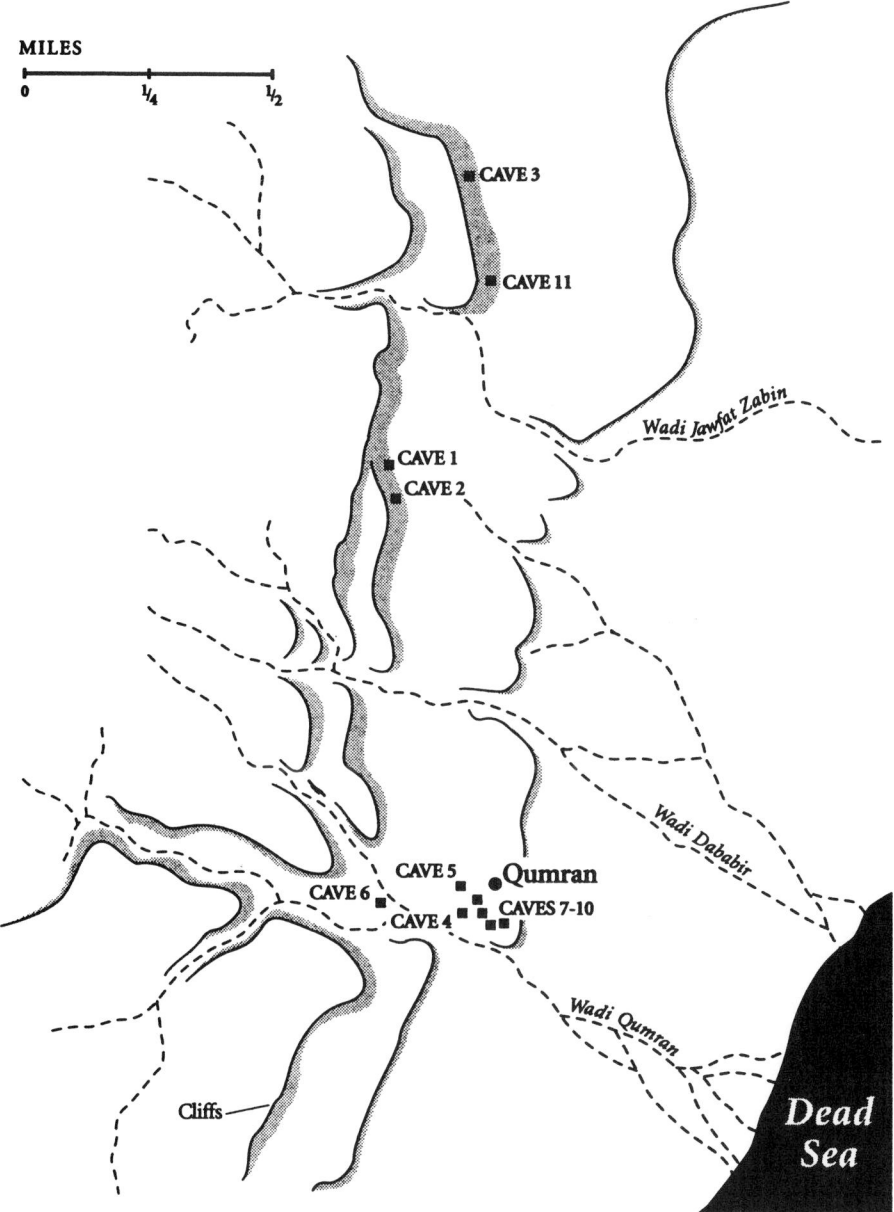

The Caves of Qumran

paragraph in the *Historia Naturalis* of Pliny (23-79 CE) where he presents the Essenes as follows:

On the west side of the Dead Sea, but out of range of the noxious exhalations of the coast, is the solitary tribe of the Essenes, which is remarkable beyond all other tribes

Fig. 1. Qumran. Plateau with cave no. 4. (Photo: Palestine Archaeological Museum.)

in the whole world, as it has no women and has renounced all sexual desire, has no money, and has only palm-trees for company. Day by day the throng of refugees is recruited to an equal number by numerous accessions of persons tired of life, and driven thither by the waves of fortune to adopt their manners. Thus through thousands of ages (incredible to relate) a race in which no one is born lives on for ever; so prolific for their advantage is other men's weariness of life!

Lying below the Essenes was formerly the town of Engedi, second only to Jerusalem in the fertility of its land and in its groves of palm-trees, but now like Jerusalem a heap of ashes. Next comes Masada, a fortress on a rock, itself also not far from the Dead Sea. This is the limit of Judaea.[9]

Pliny's geographical placing of the Essenes corresponds exactly to the position of Khirbet Qumran. A second argument supports the first one, namely the relatively high degree of similarity between, on the one hand, the contents of the Dead Sea Scrolls and, on the other hand, the descriptions in Philo, Josephus (and Pliny) of the Essenes.[10] Impressed by the weight of these two arguments most scholars accept that the community behind the Dead Sea Scrolls is identical with the Essenes, as known from the classical sources. So do I, and this is the reason for the terminology chosen in this paper: the *Qumran-Essenes*.[11]

More or less in conformity with Pliny's picture, Philo and Josephus

Fig. 2. Qumran. One of the scrolls. (Photo: Palestine Archaeological Museum.)

describe the Essenes as an admirable voluntary association of pious and extremely virtuous men, living a simple, disciplined and healthy common life.[12] The Essenes are portrayed as a peculiar social group, clearly distinguished by a high degree of fellowship, common economy and common meals, and by hard labour of their hands in agriculture and crafts. Their piety is characterized by intensive study of the Jewish Holy Scriptures, by a spiritualised interpretation of traditional Jewish religious values such as Scripture and Temple, further by prayer, severe ethical demands, frugality and a certain degree of asceticism. It should be noted, however, that the accounts in Philo and Josephus differ at several points, in particular concerning the geographical location of the group and its attitude to sexual love and marriage.[13]

As already mentioned, there is a remarkable correspondence between the accounts of Philo, Josephus, Pliny and the Dead Sea Scrolls. This fact, however, should not prevent us from noting the important differences. First and foremost, the Dead Sea Scrolls are characterized by a strong eschatological and messianic expectation[14] and a corresponding eschatological and actualizing reinterpretation of the Jewish Holy Scriptures. These features are virtually absent in Philo, (Pliny) and Josephus.

This observation should lead us to an adequate understanding of the different natures of these two groups of sources. The Dead Sea Scrolls are

Fig. 3. Qumran. "The copper scroll". (Photo: Palestine Archaeological Museum.)

the community's own writings, written by insiders and meant for internal religious consumption. Philo, Josephus and Pliny are outsiders, certainly admiring outsiders, but still outsiders who address themselves to a Hellenistic-Roman public, in general. Therefore, they tend to Hellenize their accounts and adapt their picture of the Essenes to well-known analogies such as the Hellenistic-Roman philosophical schools and other voluntary religious associations. In addition, Philo and Josephus are influenced by Jewish apologetic interests, and they present the Essenes as the finest example of the ancient, wise, virtuous and highly valuable religion of the Jewish people, as the Jewish élite *par exellance*.[15]

The Dead Sea Scrolls

In the Dead Sea Scrolls there are only two direct references to meals, one in *The Community Rule* (or *The Manual of Discipline*): 1QS 6.2-6 (cf. 6.16-17. 24-25) and one in *The Messianic Rule* (or *The Rule of the Congregation*): 1QSa 2.17-22. 1QS 6.2-6 reads as follows:
(2) These are the ways in which all of them shall walk, each man with his companion, wherever they dwell. The man of lesser rank shall obey the greater in matters of work and money. *They shall eat in common* and (3) bless in common and deliberate in common. Wherever there are ten[16] men of the Council of the Community *there shall not*

Fig. 4. Qumran. Aerial view of the excavations (Photo: Palestine Archaeological Museum.)

lack a Priest among them. (4) And they shall sit before him according to their rank and shall be asked their counsel in all things in that order. *And when the table has been prepared for eating, and the new wine (5) for drinking, the Priest shall be the first to stretch out his hand (6) to bless the first-fruits of the bread and new wine.* (My italics).[17]

According to this text, the Qumranites eat in common,[18] and before the meal can begin, a "priest" is supposed to pronounce a blessing. This description of the common Qumran-Essenes meal corresponds closely to the traditions of the ordinary Jewish meal.[19] The only difference is the role of the "priest" in 1QS 6. In the Jewish family it is usually the head of the family, the father, who pronounces the initial blessing over the bread, but in 1QS 6 this prerogative is reserved for the "priest".[20]

Later, in 1QS 6.13 ff., regulations are given concerning the fellow Jew "who freely pledges himself to join the Council of the Community". In that case, "the Guardian at the head of the Congregation" shall examine the candidate "concerning his understanding and his deeds". If accepted, the candidate shall be admitted "into the Covenant" where he will be instructed "in all the rules of the Community". Later follows a questioning "before of the Congregation", who decides whether the candidate "shall ... enter or depart". If accepted, it is stipulated that

Fig. 5. Qumran. The main aqueduct. (Photo: Palestine Archaeological Museum.)

(16) he shall not touch the (17) pure Meal[21] of the Congregation until one full year is completed, and until he has been examined concerning his spirit and deeds; nor shall he have any share of the property of the Congregation (1QS 6.16-17).

The text continues by formulating further directions for the procedure of admission. After the first year a new test follows, and if the candidate is accepted by "the Priests and the multitude of the men of their Covenant", his "property and earnings shall be handed over to the Bursar of the Congregation..." (1QS 6.17-20). However: "He shall not touch the Drink of the Congregation until he has completed a second year among the men of the Community" (1QS 6.20-21).

The expression "the Congregation" is synonymous with the terms "the Community" and "the Covenant". They all refer to the complete community of the Qumran-Essenes.[22]

It seems obvious that "the pure meal of the Congregation" belongs to the same level as "the property of the Congregation", and both seem to symbolize the *partly* belonging to and membership of the community which is realized after one year plus a test. Full membership is symbolized by the "Drink of the Congregation", by the complete transfer of the candidate's belongings to the community and by his full participation in "the pure meal", and this is first realized after two years of preparation.[23]

In 1QS 6.24-25 the case of such a new member who has been found guilty of lying is discussed, and 1QS stipulates:

(24) If one of them has lied deliberately (25) in matters of property, he shall be excluded from the pure Meal of the Congregation for one year and shall do penance with respect to one quarter of his food.

In this text it seems obvious that participation in the common meal is the primary expression of full membership of the community.[24]

The Messianic Rule (1QSa/1Q28a) specifies the regulations for

(1) ... all the congregation of Israel in the last days, when they shall join <the Community to wa>lk (2) according to the law of *the sons of Zadok the Priests* and of the men of their Covenant who have turned aside <from the> way (3) of the people. (1.1-3). (My italics).

This rule gives directions for the various periods in the development of the young male member of the community (1.6-22), and further for the attitude of the congregation to defiled persons (2.3-10). The rest (2.11-22) describes the eschatological assembly, its ranks, hierarchy and meal: first comes the "(Priest-) Messiah ... <at> the head of the whole congregation of Israel", then follows "<his brethren, the sons> of Aaron the Priests <those called> to the assembly ..." Then, "<the Mess>iah of Israel shall <come>, and the chiefs of the <clans of Israel> shall sit before him ..." Finally follows the description of the eschatological meal:

(17) And <when> they shall gather for the common <tab>le, to eat and <to drink> new wine, when the common table shall be set for eating (18) and the new wine <poured> for drinking, let no man extend his hand over the first-fruits of bread (19) and wine before the Priest; for <it is he> who shall bless the first-fruits of bread and (20) wine, and shall be the first <to extend> his hand over the bread. Thereafter, the Messiah of Israel shall extend his hand (21) over the bread, <and> all the congregation of the Community <shall utter a> blessing, <each man in the order> of his dignity. It is according to this statute that they shall proceed (22) at every me<al at which> at least ten (cf. n. 16) men are gathered together (2.17-22).

This eschatological meal is described in the same terms as the community's ordinary daily meal. In both cases it is decisive that the "priest(s)" take(s) precedence of the non-priestly members of the community (cf. 1.1-3).

In these two writings we thus find a picture of a highly organized, hierarchic community, led by "priests" and characterized by common property and common meals, which are presided over by "priests".

Philo

In his stoicising treatise, *Qvod omnis probus liber sit* ("Every Good Man is Free"), presumably written at the beginning of the first century CE, the young Philo (c. 20 BCE-45 CE) presents the Essenes (§§ 75-91) in "Palestinian Syria" as a Jewish group "of high moral excellence".[25] In § 86 Philo characterizes the Essenes as a community with a high degree of social fellowship: they have a common economy and

> their clothes are held in common and also their food through their institution of public meals. In no other community can we find the custom of sharing roof, life and board more firmly established in actual practice.

In the concluding paragraph (§ 91) Philo sums up his account by mentioning that even cruel rulers show respect for the

> congregation of Essenes or holy ones here described. Unable to resist the high excellence of these people, they all treated them as selfgoverning and freemen by nature and extolled their communal meals and that ineffable sense of fellowship, which is the clearest evidence of a perfect and supremely happy life.

In his work, *Preparatio Evangelica* (8.6.1-8.7.20 and 8.11.1-18), Eusebius from Caesarea (c. 260 - c. 340 CE) brings two extracts from a (lost) work by Philo, both on the Essenes. In *Praep. Evang.* 8.5.11 Eusebius informs us that the first one comes from the second book of a work which he names *Hypothetica*. And in his introduction to the second extract (8.5.10) Eusebius remarks that this derives from another work by Philo entitled "Apology for the Jews".[26]

In the second extract (*Hyp.* 11.1-18) Philo gives a short account of the "Essenes" (§ 11.1). In § 11.5 he briefly describes their meal as follows: "They live together formed into clubs, bands of comradeship with common meals..."

Accordingly, in these two accounts of Philo — *Qvod omnis liber probus sit* and *Hypothetica* 11.1-18 — we have a vague picture of the "Essenes", similar to that of the Dead Sea Scrolls. Philo, however, does not mention the role of the "priests", nor the blessing at the beginning of the meal or its "purity".[27]

In his treatise, *De Vita Contemplativa*, Philo describes the so-called *Therapeutae*, a strange Jewish community — of men as well as women ("most of them aged virgins", § 68) — living near Alexandria, a group which Philo himself connects with the "Essenes" (§ 1a). As not only Philo but also (other) scholars of name regard the Therapeutes as related to the Essenes,[28] we have to include this description in our examination of the sources on meals in the Qumran-Essene communities.

In contrast to Philo's two other accounts, his description of the Therapeutes is more elaborate on our subject. In §§ 34-35 Philo describes the

Fig. 6. Qumran. Oven for production of bread. (Photo: Palestine Archaeological Museum.)

moderation and continence of the Therapeutes as the "foundation" for "their soul" and "the other virtues" (§ 34). They do not eat or drink before evening, and some of them fast for three or even for six days (§ 35). But on the "seventh day" — the Sabbath — "after providing for the soul" (§ 36) they allow themselves a modest meal:

Still they eat nothing costly, only common bread with salt for a relish flavoured further by the daintier with hyssop, and their drink is spring water. For as nature has set hunger and thirst as mistresses over mortal kind they propitiate them without using anything to curry favour but only such things as are actually needed and without which life cannot be maintained. Therefore they eat enough to keep from hunger and drink enough to keep from thirst but abhor surfeiting as a malignant enemy both to soul and body (§ 37).

As in the two other accounts, Philo does not refer to "priests", nor to the phenomena of "purity" and blessing. Instead, he reports that the Therapeutes are ascetics as regards food and drink, and he informs us about the actual contents of their Sabbath meal.

In § 40 Philo states that he "wish<es> also to speak of their common assemblages and the cheerfulness of their convivial meals as contrasted with those of other people". Then follows a long excursus (§§ 40-63) on the meals and banquets of the gentiles characterized by gluttony, drinking and noise.

Fig. 7. Qumran. Grinding mill made of basalt. (Photo: Palestine Archaeological Museum.)

In contradistinction to "such follies", Philo continues by describing the Therapeutes' celebration of the feast of seven weeks (§§ 64-65).[29] They meet "white robed" and begin the festival by a common prayer (§ 66). Then they lie down on the simple couches, men to the right and women to the left (§ 69). The service is provided, not by slaves, but by young free men (§§ 70-72). Next follows the description of the meal itself:

In this banquet — I know that some will laugh at this, but only those whose actions call for tears and lamentation — no wine is brought during those days but only water of the brightest and clearest, cold for the most of the guests but warm for such of the

Fig. 8. Qumran. Store room for tableware, attached to the dining hall. (Photo: Palestine Archaeological Museum.)

older men as live delicately. The table too is kept pure from the flesh of animals; the food laid on it is loaves of bread with salt as a seasoning, sometimes also flavoured with hyssop as a relish for the daintier appetites (§ 73).

However, before the beginning of the meal their "president" (*proedros*) "discusses some question arising in the Holy Scriptures or solves one that has been propounded by someone else" (§ 75). His explanation of the Holy Scriptures "treats the inner meaning conveyed in allegory" (§ 78). After his discourse, the president sings a hymn, followed by the audience (§ 80). Not until this moment comes the meal already described (§§ 81-82). After the meal there is a new service: all stand up, divide themselves into two choirs — of men and women — singing hymns to God (§§ 83-84). Later, the two choirs unite and sing together imitating the choir of the Israelites after they had been rescued by Yahweh through the Red Sea (§§ 85-87): "Thus they continue till dawn, drunk with this drunkenness in which there is no shame …" (§ 89a). In the early morning they stand up again "with their faces and whole body turned to the east, and when they see the sun rising they stretch their hands up to heaven and pray for bright days and knowledge of the truth …" (§ 89b).[30]

Accordingly, the festival meal of the Therapeutes is integrated in the festival of Pentecost as a whole. It is surrounded by prayers, hymns and alle-

Fig. 9. Qumran. Tableware and lamps. (Photo: Palestine Archaeological Museum.)

gorical interpretation of the Jewish Holy Scriptures. The meal itself is frugal consisting of the same ingredients as the Sabbath meal: bread, salt, hyssop and water. In the description of the festival meal, however, Philo strongly emphasizes that the Therapeutes neither drink wine nor eat animal flesh.[31]

Josephus

Josephus (37-c. 100 CE) brings a remarkable amount of material on the Essenes.[32] In these texts Josephus refers to their meals only once, in *BJ* 2.128-33, a piece which is part of the famous extensive account on the Essenes in *BJ* 2.119-61. This piece includes a description of the Essenes' morning prayer: "Before the sun is up they utter no word on mundane matters but offer to him certain prayers which have been handed down from their forefathers as though entreating him to rise."[33] Then they turn to their work which continues "until the fifth hour". At that time

> they again assemble in one place and, after girding their loins with linen cloths, bathe their bodies in cold water. After this purification, they assemble in a private apartment which none of the uninitiated is permitted to enter; pure now themselves, they repair to the refectory, as to some sacred shrine. When they have taken their seats in silence, the baker serves out the loaves to them in order, and the cook sets before each one

plate with a single course. Before meat[34] the priest says a grace, and none may partake until after the prayer. When breakfast is ended, he pronounces a further grace; thus at the beginning and at the close they do homage to God as the bountiful giver of life. Then laying aside the raiment, as holy vestments, they again betake themselves to their labours until the evening. On their return they sup in like manner, and any guests who may have arrived sit down with them. No clamour or disturbance ever pollutes their dwelling; they speak in turn, each making way for his neighbour. To persons outside the silence of those within appears like some awful mystery; it is in fact due to their invariable sobriety and to the limitation of their allotted portions of meat (cf. n. 34) and drink to the demands of nature (§§ 129-33).

This description is the most extensive of all our sources on the meals of the Qumran-Essenes (and Therapeutes). Josephus reports how, at noon, the full members of the community interrupt their work, purify themselves, change their clothes and move to their eating hall. Here they sit down quietly; the baker serves bread and the cook a single moderate dish; before they start eating, a "priest" pronounces a prayer and a blessing; after the meal the "priest" says another prayer[35] after which they leave the eating room, change their clothes and return to their work. In the evening, dinner is eaten in the same manner. In conclusion, Josephus underlines the impressive silence during the meals of the Essenes, and the modesty of their consumption of food.

Analysis

There is only a slight overlap among the six accounts we have looked at. In fact, their only common feature is that they all describe a common meal.

The descriptions in our two texts from the Dead Sea Scrolls are meagre. They only report that the full members of the community had a common "pure" meal, presided over by the "priests" who pronounced the initial blessing.

Philo's writings are not much informative either. In his two minor accounts, Philo only tells us that, among their various practices, the Essenes had a common meal. He has nothing to say about the role of the "priests" or of the "purity" of the meal.

In his long description of the meals of the Therapeutes, Philo reports in detail about the festival context of the meal, and he informs us about its modest, vegetarian and non-alcoholic character, a feature corresponding with Philo's general emphasis on the asceticism of the Therapeutes. These features could be connected to the "purity" we met in the Dead Sea Scrolls and Josephus,[36] but Philo does not say so explicitly, and, as already stated, he does not mention any "priest". Thus, Philo's description differs substantially from the other two.

In contrast to the accounts of Philo, Josephus does refer to the two features we met in the Dead Sea Scrolls: the role of the "priest" and the idea of "purity". This correspondence confirms the general impression that, to a large extent, Josephus agrees with the Dead Sea Scrolls.[37] This fact gives reasons to assume that Josephus had access to detailed information about the Essenes,[38] and this is one of the reasons why we believe that his description could be used as a supplementary source on the meals in the Qumran-Essene communities.[39]

Turning to the two important features, the "purity" and the "priest", we have to ask: what is the meaning of the presence and the position of the "priests" during the common meal, and what is meant by the "purity" of the meal? To answer these two questions I will have to give a (brief) account of the origin and early history of the community.

The basis of this account is the widespread consensus on these matters (cf. the references given in n. 7, 8 and 42). This common view explains the origins of the Qumran-Essenes in connection with the establishment of the Hasmonean high priesthood around 150-140 BCE. From 168 BCE, under the leadership, first of Judas the Maccabee and, after his death in 161 BCE, of his brother Jonathan, the Hasmonean family succeeded in the first phases of their revolt against the Seleucids: the recapture of Jerusalem and the Temple (164 BCE), the right to practice traditional Judaism (162 BCE), and exemption from taxation (152 BCE). During the war with the Seleucids Jonathan somehow managed to be installed as Jewish High Priest in Jerusalem. This event, however, was not received with unanimous satisfaction among the Jews. For the Hasmoneans did not belong to the high priestly family, the so-called "Sons of Zadok", the "Zadokites", who according to the "Law of Moses"[40] had monopoly on the high priesthood. Therefore, a group of "Zadokites", presumably supported by some of the so-called *Hasideans* (the "pious ones"),[41] turned against what they saw as the Hasmonean usurpation of the high priesthood, rejected the legitimacy of the Temple cult under Jonathan's auspicies, and possibly went into exile, either to Damascus, to Babylon or to Qumran.[42]

The main issue at stake was the legitimacy of high priesthood. Closely related to that issue, however, were the questions of the legitimacy of the general priesthood and, especially, the legitimacy of the actual cult and ritual worship going on in the Temple in Jerusalem. This implied that the whole status of the Jewish people was at stake because its "covenantal" relationship to their deity Yahweh was linked to its ritual "purity" which again was related to the whole cultic apparatus in Jerusalem[43] depending ultimately on the legitimacy of the officiating High Priest. Therefore, the disagreement on the legitimacy of the High Priest quickly developed into a fundamental disagreement on worship, cult, purity, calender and the general interpretation of the Mosaic Law, the *Torah*. Thus, the rejection of the legitimacy of the High Priest meant a rupture with the Temple cult and those who accepted it. In other words, the dissident "Zadokites" became a *sect* in the literal meaning of that word, a sect regarding the adherents of main stream Judaism as *heterodox*,[44] and being regarded by the others as similarly heterodox.

With this widespread consensus explanation we have pointed out the main reason why the dissident priestly group behind the Dead Sea Scrolls called themselves the *Sons of Zadok*, as we have seen above (e.g., 1QS 5.2; 1QSa 1.2). By this observation we have at the same time indicated the main reason for the unique position of the "priests" generally in the literature from the Qumran caves.

By this generally accepted hypothesis we have also found an explanation of the role of the "priests" being emphasized in connection with the common meal, both in the Scrolls and in Josephus. For the "priest" who pronounced the blessing at the beginning of the common meal was supposed to be a legitimate, "Zadokite" priest.

Finally, we also find an explanation here of the importance of "purity" among the Qumran-Essenes.[45] For the officiating priest was also the legal guarantor for the "purity" of the food served at the common meal.[46] This is one important reason why the Dead Sea Scrolls generally talk about the "the pure meal" (1QS 6.16-25).

We have seen that Josephus described the common meal of the Essenes almost as a holy or cultic act (*BJ* 2.129-33). M. Delcor and other scholars have related this text to *AJ* 18.19 (cf. n. 44), though preferring the Epitome's reading of *ouk*, corresponding to the old Latin version's *non*.[47] The meaning of this reading can be paraphrased as follows: They send their votive offerings to the Temple, but they do *not* sacrifice there because of their different concept of "purifications". Therefore "they are barred"[48] from the common sanctuary and practice their own sacrifices. According to these scholars, the idea is that the Qumran-Essenes understood and interpreted their common meal as a sort of substitute for the daily sacrificial service in the Temple in Jerusalem. In other words, they are supposed to have interpreted their common meal as a spiritualised version of the Temple cult.[49]

Even if this hypothesis is not accepted, it appears obvious that the common meal of the Qumran-Essenes had a ritual and priestly character.

Conclusion

All our sources agree that a common meal was practiced in the Qumran-Essene communities.

The Dead Sea Scrolls do not manifest any strong interest in the meals of the community. The few times they touch on them they stress the importance of the "priestly" presence at the common meals, of the "priestly" blessing, and of the "purity" of the meal.

Philo mentions neither the "purity" of the meal nor the presence of "priests". He is interested in the communal life of the Essenes and he extols the simplicity of their meal, their frugality and asceticism. As for the Therapeutes, he emphasizes their vegetarianism and their rejection of wine. Generally, Philo describes the Essenes/Therapeutes as the Jewish vanguard of an international movement towards frugality, asceticism and spirituality.

To some extent Josephus shares the interpretations of Philo, but at the same time he is interested in reproducing all available information. Josephus thus describes the communal meal of the Essenes as a holy act accompanied by "purifications", change of clothes and an impressive silence. Like the Dead Sea Scrolls, Josephus underlines the role of the "priests".

While Philo's (and Pliny's) accounts differ substantially from the Dead Sea Scrolls and, as far as Philo is concerned, might reflect the diaspora situation in Alexandria, Josephus' description fits the Qumran texts as well as the general priestly character of the Qumran community.

As to the discussion of the possibly "sacred" character of the meals, an answer obviously depends on the definition of the idea of "sacred". On the other hand, as the context of these meals is clearly "religious", this discussion seems to me to rest on false premises. As for me, I have no doubts that the Qumran texts as well as Josephus operate with a decisive distinction between the "sacred" — "pure" — room of the common meal and the profane world outside.

As regards the issue of the common Qumran-Essene meal as a substitution for the Temple cult, I have personally been convinced by the arguments of those scholars who interpret the common meal (and the other forms of worship) of the Qumran-Essene communities as the result of a spiritualised reinterpretation and transformation of the sacrificial cult at the Temple in Jerusalem.

At all events, the common meal in the Qumran-Essene communities seems to have had a crucial position as possibly the most tangible expression, not only of the communal character of the group but also of its "purity" and its genuine "priestly" stamp, in other words, of its collective identity. Access to the common "pure" meal of the Qumran-Essenes was only given to full members of the congregation who completely accepted its specific "Zadokite" interpretation of the Law of Moses.

In conclusion I wish to return to the general reflexions on the social function and symbolic meaning of the common meal in the first section of this paper and to apply them to our Qumran-Essene material. As it appears, I tend to emphasize the following features:

a) As to the *material culture* of the common meal, the general Jewish and the specific Qumran-Essene, "Zadokite" purity rules stipulated precisely what was allowed to be eaten and what not. The Qumran-Essenes were even more strict in their interpretation of the Jewish eating rules than the Pharisees.

b) As to the *tradition and history* of the common meal, the break of the Qumran-Essenes with the Temple cult in Jerusalem was decisive for their interpretation of the common meal: only the "Zadokite" priests and their *halakha* were accepted as valid.

c) As to the *social character* of the common meal, only full members of the "Zadokite" congregation were allowed to participate, whereas all others were categorically excluded.

d) As to the common meal as a *symbolic manifestation*, we may state that the common meal appears to have been a strong expression of the Qumran-Essene communities's common history, experiences, identity and solidarity. It manifested the congregation as the only legitimate expression as the "true", "pure", "holy" chosen people.

This interpretation implies that we can confirm the considerable applicability and the strong symbolic power of the common meal. It is no coincidence that a common meal almost always plays a central role in all sorts of social activity, from family life over clan and city life to politics and religion. It is difficult to imagine a more forceful and usable expression of social fellowship, and, at the same time, a stronger expression of social identity — and exclusivity.

Notes

1. For general analysis of the meal, its social function and symbolic significance, see, e.g., Douglas 1975, Feeley-Harnik 1981, 6-18, Corley 1993, 17-21, Holmberg 1995, 768-69. On meals in religious contexts, see also Bammel 1950, *JAAR* 1995. On meals in the ancient mystery cults, see Burkert 1987, 109-12.
2. This is best known from the eating rules in Judaism, cf. Douglas 1975, 262-73 (cf. Douglas 1966), Feeley-Harnik 1981, 85-106. Mary Douglas, however, also correctly refers to the Hinduistic eating rules (1975, 254).
3. Similarly Holmberg 1995, 769.
4. Thus, e.g., Bousset-Gressmann 1966, 459-62, Gnilka 1961, Delcor 1967-69. Against: van der Ploeg 1957, Schiffman 1979-81, Beall 1988, 62-63.
5. Thus, e.g., Gnilka 1961, Bousset-Gressmann 1966, 459-62, Delcor 1967-69. Against: Schiffman 1979-81.
6. Cf. Stegemann 1993, 98-193, Martínez 1994, xxxii-xliv, VanderKam 1994, 1-12. Complete lists of all the manuscripts can be found in Martínez 1994, 467-513, Vermes (1977) 1994, 202-25.
7. Cf. de Vaux 1973, especially 53-57, Stegemann 1993, 53-115, VanderKam 1994, 12-27; Vermes (1977) 1994, 26-40.
8. Cf. van der Ploeg 1957, 166, Dupont-Sommer 1959, 31-81, Gnilka 1961, 40, de

Vaux 1973, 91-138, especially 126-38, Stegemann 1993, 194-291, VanderKam 1994, 71-98, Vermes (1977) 1994, 100-18.
9. *HN* 5.17.4. Text and translation are borrowed from the Loeb Classical Library: Rackham 1969, 277. Notice, that common meals are not mentioned by Pliny.
10. Cf. the references given in n. 8 and the detailed examinations in Beall 1988 (only on Josephus), Vermes-Goodman 1989, Bergmeier 1993, Rajak 1994: 156-58 (only on *BJ*), Bilde 1998.
11. This terminology is also used by, e.g., Gnilka 1961, 54, VanderKam 1994, 99ff.
12. For a detailed exposition, see Bilde 1998.
13. Other remarkable differences between Philo and Josephus are treated below, in sections 4-6. For details, see the references given in n. 10.
14. Cf., e.g., 1QSa, quoted below in section 3.
15. For a detailed discussion of the character of Philo's and Josephus's accounts of the Essenes, see Bilde 1998, section 5.a.
16. The number "ten" refers to the phenomenon of the so-called *minyan*, the number of ten grown-up men as the minimal precondition for the performance of a Jewish religious service.
17. I follow the text in Lohse 1964, and the translations of the Dead Sea Scrolls are borrowed from Vermes (1962) 1995, this one from (1962) 1995, 77.
18. The literary evidence for this interpretation has been supplemented by de Vaux's excavation of an eating hall, a "refectory" at Khirbet Qumran, cf. de Vaux 1973, 11-14, 26-27, 110-11, Schiffman 1979-81, 47, see Fig. 8.
19. Cf. Gnilka 1961, 41, Feeley-Harnik 1981, 85-91, Berger 1993, 98-99.
20. This is the first sign in our material of the well-known outspoken "priestly" character of the Qumran-Essene community. Shortly, we will see more of that kind of signs (especially 1 QSa 1.1-3, 2.11-22), and in section 6 we shall return to this important issue.
21. The Hebrew text reads *bethaharat ha-rabbim* ("the purity of the many", and this expression may refer generally to membership of the community. The same expression appears in 1QS 3.13, 6.22. 25 and elsewhere, and Gnilka argues that this expression primarily refers to the common "pure" meal (1961, 44-47), as in Vermes (1962) 1995. More on the phenomenon of "purity" in section 6.
22. The most common Hebrew term in the Qumran manuscripts is *jachad* ("unity", "union", "community").
23. The text is not quite clear on the exact contents of the admission procedure. Compare Josephus' description of the admission procedure in *BJ* 2.137-42.
24. This is also the case in main stream Judaism and in Pauline Christianity, e.g., 1 Cor. 5.11, cf. Holmberg 1995, 771-4.
25. § 75. Text and translation are borrowed from the Loeb Classical Library: Colson (1941) 1967, 52-63.
26. These two titles together with a third one, "On the Jews", mentioned in Eusebius: *Historia Ecclesiastica* 2.18, are often believed to refer to one and the same work, thus Colson 1967, 407, Borgen 1984, 247. In the present paper we follow Colson in terming the two first mentioned *Hypothetica* (*Hyp.*).
27. Against Schiffman 1979-81, 50 n. 26.

28. Thus Vermes 1960, Schürer(-Vermes), vol. 2, 1979, 554-97, especially 595-97, Vermes-Goodman 1989, 15-17.
29. This festival — "after seven sets of seven days have passed" — seems to be identical with Pentecost, which takes place seven weeks after Passover, cf. Colson 1967, 152 n. a, Vermes-Goodman 1989, 90-91, n. 18.
30. The interesting question whether sun-worship was prevalent among the Qumran-Essenes cannot be treated here, apart from a necessary reference to Josephus: *BJ* 2.128 (cf. 2.148) where the same phenomenon is mentioned (cf. below in section 5).
31. As we saw above in section 3, the Qumran texts mention "wine" (and bread), but not animal flesh.
32. Cf. *BJ* 1.78-80, 2.113. 119-161. 567, 3.11, 5.145, *AJ* 13.171-73. 298. 311-13, 15.371-79, 17.346-48, 18.11. 18-22, *Vit.* 10-11. Beall 1988 presents a detailed examination of all texts in Josephus concerning the Essenes' relation to the Dead Sea Scrolls. Bergmeier 1993 analyses the same texts regarding the possibility of the existence of one or more source(s) behind Josephus (and Philo). This problem is also dealt with in Bilde 1998. See also n. 38.
33. 2.128. Text and translation are borrowed from the Loeb Classical Library edition of Josephus: Thackeray et al. (1927) 1967, here (1927) 1967, 373.
34. "Meat" translates *trophe* which is not "meat", but "food" or "meal".
35. This feature does not appear in the Dead Sea Scrolls examined above. This is not tantamount to its non-existence in the community because our two texts do not pretend to give complete descriptions of the common meal. In this connection it is interesting to note that Weinfeld (1992) has discovered a small fragment from cave 4 containing what he thinks is a grace after meal in Qumran.
36. Presumably, this "purity" should be understood in relation both to the community's radicalized interpretation of the Jewish eating rules and to the particular "priestly" character of the congregation (cf. below). For a general analysis of "purity", see Douglas 1966, 7-28.
37. Cf. especially Beall 1988, 52-64, Rajak 1994, 156-9.
38. On the issue of Josephus' possible use of sources, see Bergmeier 1993, Bilde 1998. Rajak emphasizes that Josephus had his information from his personal experience with the Essenes (*Vit.* 10-11) (1994, 144-45, 155, 159).
39. Cf. Rajak 1994, 156, Bilde 1998.
40. Cf. Lev. 6.15, 1 Sam. 2.35, 1 Kings 2.35, 4.4, 1 Chron. 29.22.
41. See 1 Macc. 2.42, 7.13, 2 Macc. 14.6.
42. Cf. Schürer(-Vermes), vol. 2, 1979, 585-87, VanderKam 1994, 99-108, Vermes (1977) 1994, 119-40.
43. Because transgressions of the Mosaic eating rules and other rules on "purity" had to be atoned for in the sacrificial cult in the Temple in Jerusalem.
44. Cf. Josephus: *AJ* 18,19: "They send votive offerings to the temple but <do not> perform their sacrifices employing a different ritual of purification. For this reason they are barred from those precincts of the temple that are frequented by all the people and perform the rites by themselves". On the debated "not", see below.

45. The same is true for the Qumran-Essene interpretation of the Mosaic Law on the Sabbath, on the Calender and many other "halakhic" issues.
46. See *AJ* 18.22: "They <The Essenes> elect by show of hands good men to receive their revenues and the produce of the earth *and priests to prepare the bread and other food ...*" (My italics).
47. Similarly Bousset-Gressmann 1966, 461, Gnilka 1961, 42-43, Delcor 1967-9, 403-6. See n. 44 above.
48. Bousset-Gressmann 1966 take *eirgomenoi* in the medium sense and, consequently, reads "barred themselves": "und deswegen schliessen sie sich vom gemeinsamen Heiligtum aus" (1966, 461).
49. Cf. van der Ploeg 1957, 170, Gnilka 1961, 50. 54, Delcor 1967-9, 425. On such spiritualized reinterpretation of traditional Jewish institutions in the Dead Sea Scrolls, see Philo: *Qvod omnis probus liber sit* § 75, cf. Gärtner 1965, Klinzing 1971, Bilde 1984.

Sacred Meal and Social Meeting: Paul's Argument in 1 Cor. 11.17-34

Geert Hallbäck

1 Cor. 11.17-34 is a famous text, because it contains the oldest known Eucharist formula. The synoptic gospels also have Eucharist formulas, but though these bear a traditional stamp, they are generally held to be younger than the Pauline formula. The Pauline text is also a much disputed text, because it is not immediately evident how the irregularities criticized by Paul are to be understood concretely, or how the relationship between the meal as such and the Lord's Supper as a religious ritual should be perceived.

In my analysis I shall start with a brief outline of the general argumentative structure of the text. Thereafter I shall discuss three specific problems, namely the question of what precisely it is Paul criticizes; how the Eucharist formula interferes with Paul's pragmatic criticism and admonition; and how Paul understands the Eucharist. The third and final part of my essay is devoted to considering the real focus of the text; is it a regulation of the meal practice in the Corinthian community, or is it the promotion of the significance of the Eucharist as a religious ritual? At first sight the argumentative structure of the text supports the first impression; but a closer examination seems to indicate a shift in Paul's admonition after the introduction of the Eucharist formula, which favors the latter interpretation.

In 1 Corinthians Paul goes over a number of problems in the Corinthian community. Some of these have been put to him in a letter from the congregation; others he tackles on his own accord, because he has heard rumors of abuses in Corinth. The present text relating to the communal meal belongs to the latter category. The previous chapters have been devoted to questions concerning the eating of sacrificial meat and the head-dresses worn by women during worship, and in the subsequent chapters Paul discusses the value of charismatic gifts such as prophesying, speaking in tongues etc. in connection with worship. In other words, this part of the letter is chiefly concerned with issues of a ritual character.

The argumentative structure

In my analysis of the text I shall distinguish between four different argumentative levels, each determined by their measure of either specificity or generality. As will be apparent, one of the key problems of the interpretation is the relationship between the more general and the more specific levels of the text.

Relative to specific level	1 Corinthians 11.17-34[1] 17 When I give this instruction, I do not praise you because you asemble not for the better but for the worse. 18 First of all, I keep hearing that when you assemble in church, there are divisions among you; and in part I believe it. 19 For indeed it is necessary that there be factions among you in order that those who are approved may become known among you.
The specific level	20 So when you assemble together, it is not to eat the Lord's Supper; 21 for each one takes his own supper ahead of time and eats, so that one person is hungry and another is drunk. 22 Do you not have houses for eating and drinking? Or do you despise the church of God and humiliate those who do not have anything? What am I to say to you? Shall I praise you? In this I do not praise you.
The general level	23 For I received from the Lord what I also delivered to you, that the Lord Jesus, on the night in which he was being betrayed, took bread, 24 gave thanks, broke it, and said: "This is my body for you; you are doing this for my remembrance." 25 Also in the same way he took the cup after eating supper and said: "This cup is the new covenant by my blood; you are doing this, as often as you drink it, for my remembrance." 26 For as often as you eat this bread and drink the cup, you are announcing the death of the Lord until he comes. 27 So whoever eats the bread or drinks the cup in an unworthy manner will be guilty of the body and the blood of the Lord.
Relative to the general level	28 Let a person examine himself, and thus let him eat from the bread drink from the cup. 29 For the one who eats and drinks is eating and drinking judgment upon himself if he does not discriminate the body. 30 On account of this many among you are weak and sickly, and a considerable number are dying. 31 Now if we discriminated ourselves, we would not be judged; 32 but when we are being judged, we are being disciplined by the Lord in order that we may not be condemned along with the world.
The specific level	33 So, my brothers, when you assemble to eat, wait for one another. 34 If anyone is hungry, let him eat at home in order that you may not be assembling to be judged. I will put in order the rest of the matters when I come.

In vv. 17-19 Paul engages the problem in a roundabout way. He will "not praise" them — an indirect way of saying that he is blaming them. The problem relates to their assembling as a congregation, for here Paul has heard rumors of divisions, *schismata*. Already in the first chapter of the letter we have heard about *schismata* in the Corinthian congregation (also known as "parties"), insofar as various factions followed various apostles. Thus, symptoms of divisions in the congregation is one of Paul's deep concerns. However, the kind of division mentioned here turns out to be of another character than in chap. 1.

These first verses reflect an articulation between the general worry conspicuous in the letter, and the specific problem, which Paul makes more explicit in the subsequent verses. I label this level as being "relative to the specific level" of argumentation.

In vv. 20-22 Paul introduces his concrete criticism of the irregularities at the communal meal of the Corinthians. Instead of eating the Lord's Supper, each one takes his own supper, the result being that one is hungry, another drunk. Instead, Paul recommends that they take their own supper with its eating and drinking in their own houses; this recommendation is repeated in vv. 33-34, thus establishing a close correlation to v. 22.

Consequently I consider vv. 20-22 together with vv. 33-34 to represent "the specific level" of argumentation of the text. Here Paul expresses his concrete criticism of and admonition regarding the way of practicing the communal meal in Corinth.

In vv. 23-25 Paul quotes the tradition which he has himself received from the Lord and delivered to the Corinthians, i.e. the Eucharist formula. In close connection with this, Paul, in vv. 26 and 27, comments on what this means for the celebration of the Eucharist, namely that it is a proclamation of the Lord's death, and that an unworthy participation makes the communicants guilty. It should be noted that, contrary to normal practice, I also interpret v. 27 as a direct comment on the Eucharist formula. Whereas the following v. 28 is an admonition to the reader, v. 27 is a general comment and should thus be read in connection with v. 26. I therefore define vv. 23-27 as being "the general level" of argumentation of the text.

Finally, v. 28 is an admonition for self-examination so as to be worthy to participate in the Eucharist, while vv. 29-32 are comments stating the reason for this admonition. On the one hand Paul quite shockingly connects the number of sickly and dying persons in the Corinthian congregation with its lack of "self-discrimination"; on the other hand he assures them that this is to be taken as disciplination, not as condemnation (one wonders what the deceased Corinthians would make of this!).

This piece of admonition is more relevant to the general significance of the Eucharist than to concrete problems in connection with the communal meal. I therefore label these verses "relative to the general level" of argumentation.

Three specific problems

I shall now take up three of the problems traditionally posed by the interpretation of this text.

First, how are we precisely to understand the irregularities criticized by Paul in connection with the communal meal in Corinth? Apparently the problem is that some have more to eat and drink than others: some go hungry while others get drunk. But is this because some start eating beforehand, or is it due to the fact that when they assemble to eat some have enough while others have next to nothing?[2] In connection with this issue I shall have to go into some details in the Greek text.

In v. 21 Paul says that each one *prolambanei* his own supper. In most cases the verb *pro-lambanein* has a temporal meaning like "taking or doing something in advance or beforehand". In that case the sentence will mean that some begin to eat before they are all assembled. This seems to fit in with the admonition of v. 33 where Paul tells them to wait for one another when assembling to eat. This translation refers to one possible signification of the verb *ekdekhestai* which also indicates a temporal relation: "wait for".

The presupposed scenario would be like this: The Corinthian congregation comprises people of varying social status and occupation, ranging from patrons to slaves, from rich people to day labourers.[3] At their communal meetings the rich patrons arrive early and eat a meal — which they have either brought with them, or which has been provided by their hosts.[4] Only later, when let off from work, do slaves and other workers arrive. Together they now celebrate the Eucharist, but the late-comers have neither had the time nor the means to eat beforehand, so some are hungry, others "drunk".[5]

However, in the Eucharist formula it is said, in connection with the cup (v. 25), that Jesus took the cup after eating supper: *meta to deipnesai* which seems to presuppose a proper meal between the breaking of the bread and the offering of the cup. Insofar as we must presume that the Eucharist was celebrated in the presence of the whole congregation the idea of a meal before the Eucharist, which only a few partook of, will therefore have to be abandoned, if we put forward this argument. The verbs *prolambanein* and *ekdekhestai* cannot then be understood temporarily, but will have to be read otherwise, which is also possible; *prolambanein* then means "to care for oneself", and *ekdekhestai* simply "to receive" or "to entertain".

We should then have to imagine the following picture: the Eucharist is administered as a communal meal, to which all contribute. Some, however, are rich and bring much food, while others are poor and bring little or nothing at all. But instead of sharing equally, every one eats his own supper, the result being that some go hungry, while others have plenty.[6]

In my opinion, the first possibility is the most convincing. I find it difficult to ignore the temporal aspect of the two verbs; especially when they correspond as in this case. Paul does not recommend an equal distribution of the food as would have been natural if that was the problem. On the contrary, he recommends that every one takes his supper at home, i.e. in advance and unequally. The expression of the Eucharist formula, *meta to deipnesai*, is to be seen as a stage direction corresponding to the remark respecting the bread: that it happened "on the night in which he was being betrayed"; these stage directions refer to the narrative setting of the Last Supper, not necessarily to the commemorative celebration of the Eucharist.

However this may be, it is imperative that we understand that what really worries Paul is not the unequal distribution of the food in itself. The problem is that it is done in public. What worries Paul is not hunger, but shame. He focusses on the social aspect of the meal, not the material.[7] It is certainly wrong that some have more to eat than others; but the reason why it is wrong is that it openly exhibits the divisions among the members of the congregation. The unequal distribution is a humiliation of those who have nothing, because their inferior status is thus publicly exposed. But it is not only the poor that are humiliated, it is the entire congregation; the Corinthians' way of practicing the communal meal reveals a contempt for the church of God. Apparently, Paul sees the communal meal primarily as a social meeting the purpose of which is to expose the unity of the church. He has not the abolition of material inequality in mind, but refers it to the houses, i.e. to the private, non-public sphere of life of the Corinthian community members.[8]

The second problem to be discussed refers to the relationship between Paul's criticism of the Corinthian meal practice and the Eucharist formula. What makes Paul suddenly introduce this formula, and what has it to do with the practical administration of the communal meal? Often interpreters have imagined a specific meal ethics to be implicit in the Eucharist; this, they say, is what Paul appeals to when trying to regulate the Corinthian practice.[9]

Advocates of this theory have pointed out two aspects of the Eucharist as examples of what this ethics implies. First they refer to the self-devotion of Christ as expressed in his inauguration of the Eucharist where Christ transforms himself into the bread and wine of the meal as a ritual prelude to his impending sacrificial death. The communicants thus bind themselves to a corresponding self-devotion which should be borne out in their sharing the food and drink of the meal. Secondly, they refer to an understanding of the Eucharist as symbolic of the unity of the congregation. In the Eucharist one loaf is distributed to all the communicants, who thus, by eating it, become one with the other communicants. Thus they commit themselves in the same way to sharing what else they eat.

The most striking aspect of this implicit Eucharist ethics is, however, that it remains implicit. It is not this meaning of the Eucharist which Paul emphasizes in his comments in vv. 26-27, but the proclamation of the Lord's death. If Paul quotes the Eucharist formula to assert an implicit ethics relevant to the Corinthians' meal practice, one would expect him to make the obligations of this ethics explicit in the text. Since this is not the case it may be assumed that this is not how he understands the Eucharist and not the reason why he quotes the formula.

On the other hand there is no doubt that the description he gives of the communal meal in Corinth in v. 21 is meant as a criticism, a description of abuses. But why is the practice in question wrong and where is the criterion for the criticism, if not in the Eucharist? I would suggest that the criterion might be found in the meal itself, or in the fact that it is a community meal. My impression is that there was, in antiquity, a meal ideology, prescribing an equal distribution of the available food. Presumably, this ideology presupposes that the participants in the meal are equal in respect of social status, which was certainly not the case in Corinth. But already Socrates criticized — according to Xenophon[10] — the unequal distribution of the food at a meal, where the participants were of varying social status; I find it quite possible that the ethics of this meal ideology is the criterion that Paul takes for granted in his criticism of the Corinthian practice.

Anyway, Paul is very insistent that the criticized meals take place when the Corinthians assemble. In the first four verses he uses the same Greek verb, *synerkhestai*, "come together" or "assemble", three times (the same verb is used again i v. 33). So it is their assembling that concerns Paul. It is by assembling they demonstrate their being a community. This is what makes the practice in question so fatal. It creates divisions instead of unity, factions instead of community, and this, I suppose, is the dominant criterion of Paul's criticism.

But then, if he does not want to plead an implicit ethics, why does Paul quote the Eucharist formula. I think he does so to underline the seriousness of the Eucharist and thus of the communal meal.[11] According to v. 30, the Eucharist is so grave that if you do not receive it worthily you may bring about your own death. The Eucharist is a proclamation of the death of the Lord; therefore it is no trivial matter how it is administered. The implication of the Eucharist is not communal ethics, but individual judgment: "Let a person examine himself" or he will be "eating and drinking judgment upon himself". Paul's criticism of the Corinthian meal practice should be seen in this perspective. The communal meal is the context of the Eucharist and should thus be taken as seriously as the Eucharist itself.

My third question is whether it is possible to say anything about Paul's view of the Eucharist, based on the preceding argumentation. Is his view a decent Protestant one or does he contend a massive sacramentalism, as coined by some interpreters.[12] What may be said with certainty is that he attributes to the Eucharist a certain content, and expects a certain effect on those who receive it.

As Paul sees it, the Eucharist is a proclamation of the Lord's death. He does not comment on how to comprehend the relationship between bread and wine, body and blood; what he emphasizes is the reference to body and blood as figurations of the Lord's death. The emphasis is not on the elements themselves, but on the eating and drinking of them as a commemoration of Christ's death. But why only His death and not His death and resurrection? First, I suppose, because death is the most powerful argument in any connection, the definitive argument; secondly, because death, according to Paul, was the ultimate act of Christ, his ultimate act of salvation. And thirdly, the proclamation of the death of Christ should correspond to the threat of death to all those who do not receive the Eucharist in a deserving manner.

After his proclamation of the extraordinary significance of the Eucharist, Paul reverts to its effect on the participants. This is awe-inspiring, causing sickness and even death for those who do not eat and drink it worthily. For they are "guilty of the body and the blood of the Lord". I agree with those interpreters who take this as an expression of Paul's seeing numinous forces at stake in the Eucharist.[13] It is not only a human "remembrance" of Christ, but it is a sacred meal eliciting divine judgment on the participants. That is why it takes special preparation and conscientiousness to participate. What Paul invokes is the threat of judgment as a warning to those Corinthians who celebrate the Eucharist unworthily.[14] However, if the Eucharist has such negative effect on the undeserving, it must have a corresponding positive effect on the "approved". If the Eucharist judges the undeserving, we must suppose that, as Paul sees it, it brings salvation to those who have "examined themselves" properly. So it seems that Paul is on the sacramentalist side regarding the Eucharist.

Communal meal and/or religious ritual

After this examination of the main problems of the text as I see them, I shall revert to a more all-round interpretation of the pericope and consider the question of the relationship between the specific and the general levels of the text.

With a view to a semiotic analysis of the New Testament letters, the French-American New Testament scholar Daniel Patte has suggested a distinction between a "dialogical" and a "warranting" level of the text.[15] The "dialogical" level comprises all direct appeals to the readers of the letter and the attempt to intervene in their present circumstances by means of comments or admonitions, exchange of questions and answers etc. The "warranting" level, on the other hand, includes all references to what is already common experience or shared convictions for the author of the letter and its recipients; such sections are introduced for the purpose of "warranting" the reliability and acceptability of what is being communicated on the "dialogical" level.

It is not difficult, in this text, to relate my "specific levels" to Patte's "dialogical" level. Here Paul seeks to intervene directly to regulate a behaviour peculiar to the Corinthian community. Nor is it difficult to identify "the general level", i.e. the Eucharist formula plus Paul's direct commentary as the "warranting" level, since this is introduced as common background, tradition, without any direct consequence for the Corinthian situation (Paul does not attempt to introduce a new Eucharist ritual or anything like that).

When we come to vv. 28-32, however, it is more muddled. On the one hand it is a clear admonition; there is even a reference to very concrete experiences of sickness and death in Corinth. On the other hand the admonition with its ensuing comments are more relevant for the understanding of the Eucharist than for the concrete regulation of the Corinthian meal abuses. I have therefore classified these verses as "relative to the general level". According to Patte's categories, then, these verses seem to be "dialogical" when seen in relation to the Eucharist, but "warranting" when seen in relation to the meal practice.

This confusion has made me wonder whether there is a shift in the focus of the text after the introduction of the Eucharist formula. Apparently the case is clear. Even if the information of the greatest theological relevance is often to be found on the "warranting" level, it will always be determined by the "dialogical" level; the "warranting" level does not exist for its own sake, but to support the "dialogical" level, which is textually the primary level. There can be no doubt that Paul has written these eighteen verses intentionally to regulate a critizisable meal practice in Corinth. The Eucharist formula is introduced to give weight to the seriousness of the admonition.

However, due to its great significance, by way of being a tradition that goes back to the Lord himself and proclaming His death, the Eucharist somehow assumes the argumentation and becomes the matter itself. Instead of using the formula in an admonition to administer the communal meal in a way that makes it truly communal, it is used in a general appeal to everybody to discriminate themselves before participating in the Eucharist.[16]

It is of course still possible to interpret this as emphasizing the sacredness of the Eucharist as a means to support the admonition regarding the meal practice. But it can also be interpreted as if the criticism of the communal meal is being reduced to an opportunity to emphasize the sacredness of the Eucharist itself. Thus the meal problems become not just symptoms of a non-communal attitude, but they become symptoms of a lack of appreciation that this communal meal is the setting for the holy Eucharist. The focus of the text is being shifted from the meal as a communal meeting to the meal as a religious ritual: the Lord's Supper.[17]

My intention is not to argue for these two readings as alternative interpretations of the text. Rather I would say that the argument of the text goes both ways at the same time. It is both an admonition to regulate a meal practice peculiar to the Corinthian congregation — in which respect the Eucharist formula represents the "warranting" level — and it is a promotion, occasioned only by the meal problems, of the Eucharist as a powerful religious ritual. Thus considered, the pericope exemplifies how a Pauline text generally operates. It revolves in a continuous movement from very concrete interventions in specific situations to theological reasoning in a highly principal perspective. The Pauline text intervenes theologically and theologizes specifically. In this way it resists both exhaustive historical and exhaustive theological readings. We cannot know from the text how the communal meal was really taken in Corinth, nor can we know how Paul "actually" understood the Eucharist. But we can continue to wrestle with the enigmas of the text — thus producing history and theology ourselves.

Notes

1. The translation has been taken from Orr & Walther 1976; the arrangement, however, is mine.
2. For a thorough discussion of these problems, see Theissen 1979b, 290-317.
3. On the question concerning the social structure of the Corinthian congregation, see Theissen 1979a. See also Judge 1960, Meeks 1983.
4. That a real meal was eaten before the celebration of the Eucharist is maintained by Neuenzeit 1960, Klauck 1982, Stuhlmacher 1988.
5. For this interpretation, see Lietzmann 1949, Bornkamm 1963, Conzelmann 1969, Lampe 1991.
6. For this interpretation, see von Dobschütz 1902, Weiss 1910, Theissen 1979b, Engberg-Pedersen 1991.
7. Cf. Theissen 1979b.
8. The difference between the assembly of the congregation and the private house is underlined by S.C. Barton (1986). The idea proposed by H.W. Bartsch (1962), that v. 33 refers to private meals alone and not to problems concerning the congregational meal, has not gained support.
9. For this interpretation, see Lampe 1991.
10. Xen. *Mem.* 3.14.1 (cf. Peter Lampe 1991).
11. Cf. Engberg-Pedersen 1991.
12. So Bornkamm 1963, von Soden 1963, Theissen 1979b.
13. So Kuss 1971.
14. For an interpretation emphasizing the judgemental aspect of Paul's understanding of the Eucharist, see Käsemann 1960.
15. See Patte 1983.

16. That the text has a double focus, both social and sacramental, has been pointed out by Weiss 1917; see also Theissen 1979b.
17. So von Dobschütz 1902, Weiss 1910.

Regulating Fellowship in the Communal Meal: Early Jewish and Christian Evidence

L. Michael White

At the opening of Book VII of his *Quaestiones convivales* or "Table Talk", Plutarch offers the following observation on a cultural idiom of dining practice in his day:

(My friend) Sossius Senecio, the Romans are fond of quoting a refined and sociable (*philanthropou*) man, who once said, after dining alone, "I have taken food (*bebrokenai*), but have not dined (*me dedeipnekenai*) today", since the dinner (*tou deipnou*) always requires fellowship and friendly affections (*koinonian kai philophrosynen*) for seasoning ... But the most truly godlike seasoning at the dining-table is the presence of a friend, an intimate and well-known companion — not merely because he eats and drinks with us, but because he participates in the give and take of conversation, at least if there is something profitable and reasonable in what is said ... Wherefore, it is right that discourse, no less than friends, should be welcomed to the dinner only if of proven quality (*Quaest. conv.* 697C-E).

Plutarch's comment shows that admission to the hospitality of the dinner-table was no idle consideration. It required both recognition and regulation of the fellowship there engaged, owing to the particular circumstances and, most of all, to the guests.

Whenever one is entertaining one's peers or equals, "young men, fellow citizens, and intimate friends" (*neous men ... kai politas kai synetheis*), says Plutarch (earlier in book I of the *Quaestiones convivales*), it is acceptable to disregard certain customs and conventions of formal dinner etiquette as in seating arrangements according to rank or status (617A). After all, the meal should ideally be a setting of equality and friendship, for, as he reminds us throughout the work, true friendship is the central character of the banquet table (612D, cf. 660B). On the other hand, Plutarch notes that in some contexts it is necessary to retain those formalities dictated by decorum and defined by "by custom and usage" (*synetheia ti kai nomo*), especially when at the symposium and "engaged in philosophical discourse" with "foreigners, magistrates, or one's elders" (*xenois e archousin e presbyterois* — 617A).[1]

Plutarch here touches on a basic principle regarding communal meals in the Graeco-Roman world, namely that there was an implicit grammar of etiquette which regulated the patterns of fellowship and social interaction that such meals fostered. This is hardly a novel observation today, given the extensive work done by Mary Douglas and others on the symbolic language of dining across all human cultures[2] (see Bradley in this volume). Still, we must remember that the grammar of symbols used in one culture may not be intelligible or meaningful to people from another culture. The scholar who seeks to interpret the significance of ancient dining practices, whether drawn from literary descriptions or archaeological remains, is no less at risk than the foreigner invited to dine in the tent of a bedouin sheik or to attend a Japanese tea ceremony. One must be sensitive to the particular grammar of etiquette, social convention, and cultural symbolism at work in each instance. What is *de rigueur* or "expected" in one might well be *faux pas* or "offensive" in the other. Each cultural context has its own grammar of symbols and etiquette, oftentimes lurking as an implicit template of values and behavior, that govern communal dining. Despite our sense of cultural heritage we are no less foreigners or outsiders when approaching the meal practices of Jews and Christians in the Roman world. For we also discover that there were some significant changes that occurred over time. Indeed, Jews and Christians of the first centuries might well have felt more at home dining with Plutarch than in attending a modern Passover seder or Eucharistic celebration.

My goal in this study is to trace some of the lines of dining practice among early Jews and Christians especially out in the cities of the Diaspora where the social etiquette of a Plutarch would have been closer to the norm. We will be focusing on the ways in which the communal meal regulated fellowship among these groups and how that regulation evolved over time. As reflected in the words of Plutarch, all dining assumes some such regulating of social interaction either by including or excluding individuals and by governing the status levels, modes, and symbols of interaction among them.

From supper to eucharist

In order to set Jewish and Christian practice into this broader context, therefore, we should note briefly four windows or observations on communal dining found in the earliest strata of the Christian movement (hence mid-first century CE) among the letters of a Diaspora Jew, Paul. The first comes from Gal 2.11-14 where Paul recounts his heated confrontation with Peter at Antioch after the latter had retreated from dining with gentile Christians.[3] At issue, however, was not the practice of circumcision *per se*, but one of fellowship within the still Jewish social matrix of the Antiochene Jesus movement. To dine with non-Jews in the context of a meal that had

Jewish religious significance was viewed by some, if not most, of the earliest Jewish Christians as a threat to their own sacred identity. While Paul's view was clearly at odds with this understanding, it nonetheless shows the sense of communal boundaries that were symbolized by the dining context and experience. But it is more than mere symbolism, for ritually enacted symbols serve as important boundary defining mechanisms for the identity of the group. By arguing over who may be admitted to their dinners, the members of the group are in reality arguing over who they are.[4]

The second comes from 1 Cor. 5.1-13 where Paul castigates the predominantly Greek Christians of Corinth for continuing to associate (*synanamignysthai* — 5.9, 11) with a man considered to be engaging in immoral practices (*porneia*). Paul ultimately tells them "not even to eat with such a person" (*to toiouto mede synesthiein* — 5.11). The implication is clear; to admit him to meal fellowship is to participate in his actions and thus pollute the group (cf. 1 Cor. 10.16, noting the word-play on the *koinonia* of the supper).[5] Third, in 1 Cor. 8-10 we may observe similar concerns over those with whom the Christian may or should dine, but now tilted on the opposite side of the communal boundaries, namely on issues of going to dinners with non-Christians. Here the concern on the part of some of Corinthian Christians with the food eaten — the so-called "meat offered to idols" (*eidolothyton*) — is not only a dietary matter, but also a symbol of social interaction and community ethos. But in this case Paul allows for Christians whose conscience is strong to go to dinners in the homes of their pagan neighbors (1 Cor. 10.27-28).[6]

Finally, we must note the influential passage regarding the Lord's Supper in 1 Cor. 11.23-35 (see also Hallbäck in this volume). It shows that the house church meetings of the Pauline tradition were regularly organized around the communal meal located in the dining room of the house. The Eucharist was part of the dinner. As is now well known, the concern over "abuses" at the dinner were primarily social in nature, but in Paul's view they threatened the religious character of the dining fellowship.[7] Consequently, he used the sacralizing elements of the Lord's Supper tradition to bracket, both literally/temporally and symbolically, the communal fellowship of the assembly. In each of these cases, the meal setting in the earliest stages of the Christian movement called forth key concerns about the communal nature of the group, its fellowship, and social dynamics. In the Pauline context, however, we see that communal dining was not yet the fully developed liturgical and sacramental ritual of an institutional church. It was first and foremost what Wayne Meeks has termed a ritual of group solidarity, a central moment of group integration, focused on the word *koinonia* ("fellowship" or "communion").[8]

Let us now jump ahead by approximately a century and a half, from the time of Paul to the time of Hippolytus of Rome. Now we discover that the basic pattern of communal dining among Christians has changed significantly. According to the church order of the so-called *Apostolic Tradition*, Hippolytus of Rome radically distinguishes the Eucharist as a ritualized meal from ordinary communal dining, usually referred to as the *agape* meal, but which he also calls the "Lord's Supper". Only baptized Christians were admitted to the Eucharist. All later Christian tradition has tended to preserve this basic distinction, and many attempts have been made to trace the lines of development back to the days of Jesus or Paul. So we may note in passing the widely repeated views of Joachim Jeremias and Hans Lietzmann, both of whom assume, albeit on quite different grounds, that the eucharistic memorial was from the beginning essentially separate from the communal meal.[9] But this view assumes that the practice found in Hippolytus had been the accepted norm rather than being a new set of regulations. The archaeological and historical evidence suggests the opposite.

In previous work on the development of Christian church building from the original house church setting I have argued that the separation of the eucharist from the *agape* meal coincided with a fundamental shift in the physical locus and social pattern of Christian assembly when renovation of church edifices began to develop into halls of assembly.[10] At this point, the gathering for worship no longer reflects the meal setting, even though the Lord's Supper tradition still stands at the center of the worship. Now, the Eucharistic celebration begins to take on a stylized and ritualized meal symbolism but no actual communal dining. Both the archaeological and literary evidence suggests that this shift began around the turn of the third century, although we must allow for local variations in this development. So, at the end of the second century (*c.* 197/8) Tertullian's description of the *agape* meal (*Apol.* 39) still assumes a fairly typical pattern of collegial dining. Here we may note its setting in the evening where a president presides over the fellowship and the festivities. By contrast the philosophical instructions of Clement of Alexandria (*c.* 203) are the first to reflect a clear separation of Eucharist from *agape* (*Paed.* 2.1). Even so Clement also gives clear indication and instruction in social etiquette for Christians who were expected to dine in polite society (see Bradley in this volume). By the middle of the third century the letters of Cyprian and the Syriac *Didascalia*, despite their regional differences, both offer carefully articulated spatial relationships in the church edifice, including patterns of seating in the worship assembly.[11]

Such changes may be partly a result of practical considerations, as increased group size may make table dining impossible. In such cases, stylizing or ritualizing the dining and meal elements might be a natural response. But at the same time, the meal ceased to be the setting for social interaction as found throughout Graeco-Roman society. We shall return to the implications of ritualizing the meal elements, but first we must focus on the regulations in Hippolytus regarding the *agape* or communal meal that coincided with the physical and spatial changes.

Regulation through ritual

The text of the *Apostolic Tradition*, which presumably goes back to the time of Hippolytus' days in Rome (*c.* 217-35), is notoriously difficult since a Greek original is no longer extant. There is a Latin version (known as the Verona ms.), but it appears to incorporate materials from later liturgical traditions at a number of points. Established critical editions of the Hippolytan text must rely on Syriac, Coptic, and Ethiopic versions which are themselves imbedded in later church order and liturgical texts. Still, there are clues to the original Greek text of Hippolytus, not the least of which are the numerous Greek loanwords and transliterations.[12]

The *Apostolic Tradition* marks off the Eucharist from ordinary dinners, even of a religious character among Christians. But the distinction is not, as is often assumed in modern liturgical contexts, one of a ritual meal versus an ordinary meal. As we have already seen, the dinners of the Graeco-Roman world, including those of earlier Christians, carried ritualized and symbolic import, even when no sacrifice was involved. Something else is at work in the Hippolytan regulations. The key passage, as reflected in the Latin (chap. 26) gives instructions to Christians in hosting or attending such private communal meals. It assumes that normally a bishop or other clergy will be in attendance at such meals to offer a proper blessing of the bread to be served. In other words, they still use features of the Lord's Supper tradition to sacralize the social interaction of the communal meal even though outside the framework of formal worship assembly. The text then continues:

> But at each act of offering <of bread> the offerer must remember the host, for he was invited to the latter's home for that purpose. But when you eat and drink, do so in an orderly manner and not so that anyone may mock, or so that your host be saddened by your unruliness. But behave so that he may pray to be made worthy that the saints may enter his dwelling: *"for ye"*, it says, *"are the salt of the earth"* (Matt. 5.13).
> If the offering should be made in common to all (the guests), what in Greek is called an *apoforetum*, accept it from him (the host). If all are to eat sufficiently (then and there), eat such that some remains ...[13]

Now what is most noteworthy about these instructions on private Christian dining is the use of *apoforetum*, a Latinized form of the Greek loanword (*apophoreton*), which may well be preserved from the original state of the text. Until recently most commentators looking at the liturgical development have disregarded the technical significance of this term.[14] Its basic meaning can be seen in two uses related to ancient dining practice. First, the root noun and verb forms (*apophoros* and *apophorein*) were used in ancient Greek cultic contexts to refer to the right sometimes granted to honored individuals to "carry away" portions of a sacrifice (see *SIG* 1025.46, 1026.4). This was a special privilege in most cultic or sacrificial contexts, especially since there were often regulations about completing the meal within the sacred *temenos*. Hence the term connotes some special features of cultic dining which may also link the food portions taken away to the sacral time and actions performed in service to the gods.

Second, by derivation the term *apophoreton* came to be used in Hellenistic and Roman times to refer to "gifts" that were given by hosts and patrons at dinner parties for the guests or clients "to take away". This is precisely the usage seen in two Latin texts also from Rome, one from Suetonius and the other from Petronius. In describing the generosity and largesse of Vespasian, traits perhaps not widely reputed to this emperor, Suetonius says:

He gave constant dinner parties, too, usually formally and sumptuously (*saepe recte et dapsile*), to support the *macellarios*. On the Saturnalia he used to give *apophoreta* to the men, and on the first of March [the Matronalia], also to the women (*Vesp.* 19).

Continuing on this same theme a bit later, Suetonius says further:

After his siesta (*secretum*) [usually with a favorite "concubine" (*pallaca*)], he would go to the baths and then to the dining room. It was said that at no time was he more good-natured or indulgent, so that members of his household (*domestici*) seized on such moments eagerly in order to request favors (*Vesp.* 21).

The point is that these *apophoreta* were demonstrations of patronage from the host to the guests, and often they symbolized the social relationship of hierarchy and depency that pervaded Roman society. The dinner setting described by Plutarch reflects these same relationships.

The first century novelist Petronius gives us something of the social flavor of these "gifts" offered to guests at dinners in his satirical sketch of the lavish parties of Trimalchio.[15] The pretentious former slave garners particular ridicule for the outlandish and tasteless fare and entertainment he provided. Similarly the guests, for daring to accept it without decorum and due indignation at the excesses.

He [Trimalchio] was just throwing the philosophers out of work, when tickets were carried around in a cup. And a boy (slave), having been assigned this duty, recited the *apophoreta* [for each, as the ticket was drawn] (*Sat.* 56).

In this case, each "gift" was personalized — a vulgar, even pornographic joke or a gag gift with a generous garnish of social insult, at least for some of the recipients. Most of the guests laughed and accepted these "gifts" graciously in the light of the sumptuous dinner. It suggests a good-natured acceptance of the social conventions by the use of satirical play. But not all were so amused. So Petronius notes that this ribaldry "annoyed one of Trimalchio's fellow freedmen (*conliberti*), the man sitting next above me" named Hermeros (*Sat.* 57, cf. 59 for the name). From Hermeros' reply, it is clearly the social abuse that most angered him; it involved biting ridicule directed at the social class and economic status of those from lower stations at the party, much to the amusement of others who felt they were better. Ultimately, however, the gag gifts were replaced with real *apophoreta* (*Sat.* 60) that made the party worthwhile.

Harking back to the Hippolytan exhortation for Christian diners to accept their "gifts" and properly "remember the host", it becomes clearer that the practice of distributing *apophoreta* was a formalized act of patronage in the customs of Roman dinners. Petronius lampoons some of its social edge; however, it was widely practiced as a means of clientellage and social dependency especially among familial networks. The host serves as patron and benefactor through the distribution of the gifts; the family and clients in turn must show loyalty and respect, and must know their place.

Martial notes that the dinner was liberally seasoned with social status implications especially for those to whom it was most significant as a source of economic distribution.

Since I am asked to dinner, no longer, as before, a purchased guest [i.e., a client], why is not the same dinner served to me as to you? You take oysters fattened in the Lucrine lake, I suck a mussel through a hole in the shell; you get mushrooms, I take hog-fungus; you tackle turbot, but I brill. Golden with fat, a turtledove gorges you with its bloated rump; there is set before me a magpie that has died in its cage. Why do I dine without you, even though, Ponticus, I am dining with you. The dole has gone; let us have the benefit of it — let us eat the same fare (*Epigr.* 3.60).

So also, we may compare Pliny, *Ep.* 2.6 who comments on the different fare offered to guests at a dinner, determined by rank and status — first the host and his "favorites", next other guests (including Pliny himself), and finally the freedmen of the host and his guests.[16] It is significant, too, that this kind of social dependency is reflected in the apocryphal *Acts of Peter* (c. 180-190), in a scene set in the *triclinium* or dining room of the senator Marcellus, who eventually becomes the leading member of the Christian community and patron of orphans, widows, and the poor (chap. 19-29).[17] Thus, the practice of giving *apophoreta* at dinners was an extended and encoded social ritual acted out both in the hierarchy of dining and in the social dependency of clientellage. On the surface, it would appear that by the time of Hippolytus

Site	No. of Phases	Building Type	Dates	1st cent. Synagogue Phase/Date
SYRIA				
Dura Europos	3	1. house 2. renovated 3. renovated 3a. paintings	Late first cent. c. 150-200 244/5	2/c. 150-200
LYDIA				
Sardis	4	1. apodyterion 2. hall 3. synagogue hall 4. synagogue/ 4a. reburbished	c. 166 late second cent. beginning of fourth cent.	3/third cent.
Priene	3	1-2. house 3. synagogue renovated	first cent. BCE	3/second cent.
AEGEAN ISLANDS				
Delos	2	1. house 2. synagogue 2a. reburbished?	second cent. BCE first cent. BCE first cent.	2/first cent. BCE
MACEDONIA				
Stobi	5	1-2. house 3. synagogue i 4. synagogue ii 5. Xenodochion basilica	first-second cent. third cent. third-fourth cent. fourth-fifth cent.	3/third cent.
ITALY				
Ostia	4	1. insula? 2. synagogue i 3. synagogue ii 3b. aedicula 4. synagogue iib	first cent. second-third cent. third-fourth cent. fourth cent. fourth-fifth cent.	2/third cent.

Table 1. *The Diaspora Synagogue. An Archaeological Survey of Building History.*

the communal meal tradition of the earliest Christian house churches has been reduced and regulated. The Eucharist has become a stylized and highly symbolic "meal" with many sacrificial overtones, but almost no real dining. Moreover it has been restricted to a morning practice in the worship assembly. The *agape* or supper, by contrast, has been restricted to privately hosted, exclusively Christian, gatherings at evening, and the tone of the Hippolytan church order implies that these gatherings require some

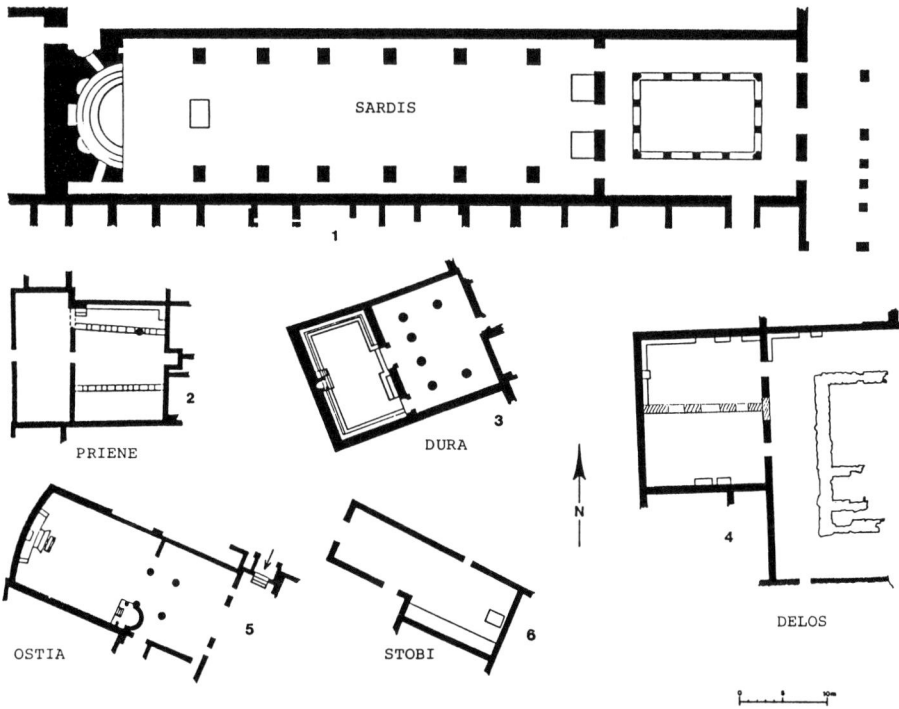

Fig. 1. Plans of the synagogues found in the Diaspora. (Drawing by S. Rand adapted by the author.)

monitoring by the bishop. For now the giving of gifts, and the social ties of exchange there implied, have been regulated. In the process, the bishop emerges as the ultimate mediator of the patronal benefits of the church, even when other networks of social hierarchy and dependency may still be operative within the local community. Networks of clintellage might fracture and split the congregations. In short, the Hippolytan church order tradition has stripped the communal dining of its typical collegial symbolism and social dependency, aspects that had been central in earlier Christian practice.

Archaeological evidence of Jewish and Christian dining

What may be reflected in the Hippolytan church order literature is not only a liturgical development but also a social shift in the ritualized interaction governed by the Eucharistic tradition. At stake is the notion of group boundaries and familial or collegial social structure, since by their very nature ancient meals served to regulate participation (by segregation or integration of individuals) and to order the interaction of those who participate. The non-literary evidence suggests that dining within Judaism and Christianity in the first three centuries started with some of the same

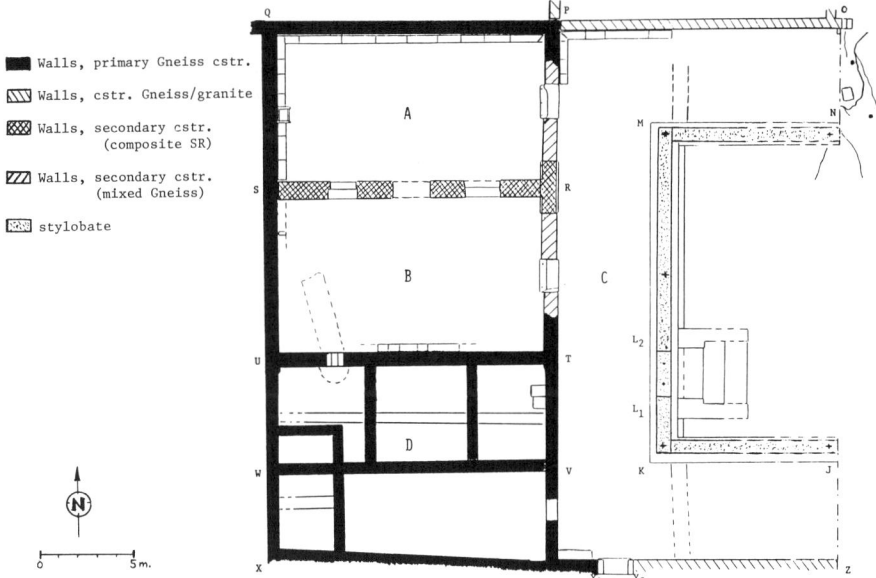

Fig. 2. Delos. The synagogue. Restored plan with the phases of construction indicated. (Drawing by the author.)

principles and practices, but that over time the traditions diverged, largely through the liturgical evolution of the Eucharist.

The archaeological evidence for Jewish synagogues of the Diaspora shows considerable social diversity among Jewish communities in the Graeco-Roman world. Indeed, throughout the earlier centuries, there was little or no sense of normative synagogue architecture.[18] Instead, Jewish congregations were often heavily influenced by local architectural and social traditions and by their own social and economic circumstances. Of the six known excavated synagogues from the Diaspora, five were renovated from private homes or apartments, and all were adapted from their existing form to serve Jewish congregational assembly[19] (Fig. 1 and Table 1).

The earliest Diaspora synagogue known from archaeological remains is that from the Greek island of Delos, dating from the late second to first centuries BCE. Analysis of the architectural development shows that an existing structure, probably a house, was adapted in at least two distinct stages.[20] Significantly, these renovations did little to transform the edifice from its basic domestic form. Still there is provision made for an assembly area (in room A, Fig. 2) with benches lining the walls. This type of bench configuration, moreover, shows notable similarities to that found in other collegial and religious halls on the island. In particular we may note the dining hall of the earliest Sarapis temple (Sarapeion A) (Fig. 3).[21] In addition to the synagogue edifice, two recently discovered inscriptions point to the

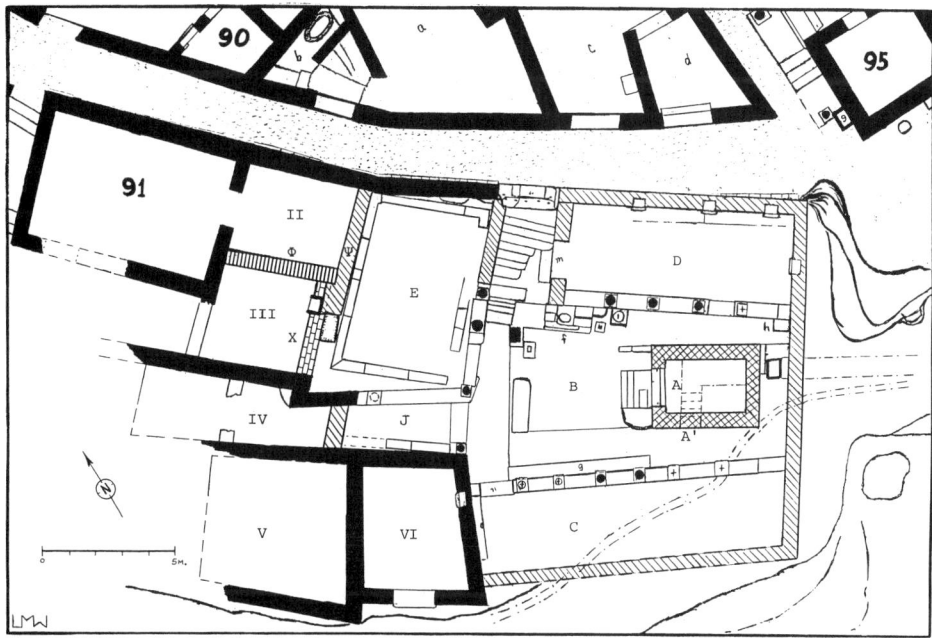

Fig. 3. Delos. Serapeion A. Restored plan with the phases of construction indicated. (Drawing by the author.)

existence of a second "synagogue" community nearby, but this one is for a Samaritan congregation. Moreover, the form of the existing building and the character of the Samaritan inscriptions both suggest affinities to other local collegial associations located on the island. The most notable example is the collegial hall known as the House of the Poseidoniasts from Berytus, an enclave of shippers and merchants whose house served both as sanctuary and social center.[22] While we do not have direct archaeological evidence that dinners were actually held in the synagogue itself, the surmise is not unreasonable based on similar social functions in other collegial halls and other Jewish evidence.

Other Jewish evidence is clearer on dining practices associated with synagogue edifices. The most explicit comes from the synagogue at Stobi, Macedonia (Fig. 4). The archaeological evidence points to a house that was renovated for synagogue use in two distinct phases from the second through the fourth centuries CE.[23] The form of the earlier of the two synagogues is not well known, but a hall for assembly associated with the house is made explicit in a building inscription of the donor, Claudius Tiberius Polycharmus, who calls himself "Father of the Synagogue" (Appendix, no. 1). The provisions of Polycharmus' bequest indicate that the edifice to be renovated was his own house, and special mention is made of the *triclinium* or dining room. It is also clear that portions of the house remained in private

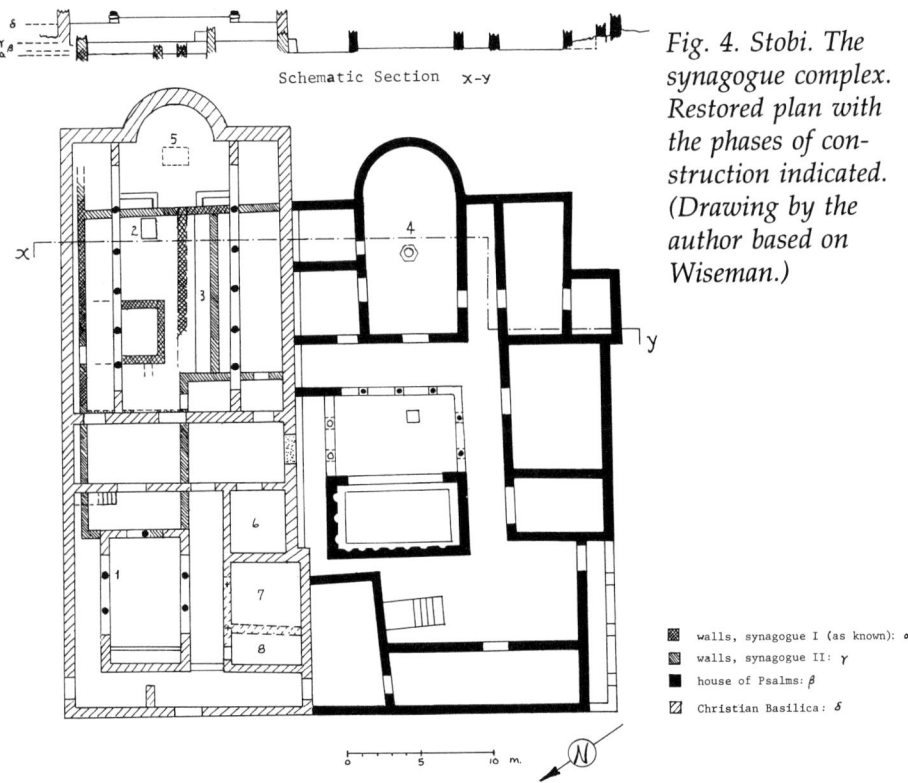

Fig. 4. Stobi. The synagogue complex. Restored plan with the phases of construction indicated. (Drawing by the author based on Wiseman.)

domestic usage throughout much of the life of the synagogue edifice. Furthermore, in the excavations of this earliest stratum of synagogue usage, a plastered floor was found to contain six iterations of the donor's honorific title, "Polycharmus, the Father".[24]

Another inscription from Caesarea Maritima, the Roman provincial capital of Judea, likewise points to the physical layout and decoration of a *triclinium* in conjunction with the local synagogue (Appendix, no. 2). The donor of the mosaic decoration for the dining room was, like Polycharmus, a leader of the synagogue; he is identified as Beryllos, an archisynagogus and curator. The nature of dinners held in these dining rooms may be guessed to include a range of social occasions for members of the local synagogue congregation and perhaps for a range of others. The meal, however, was not part of the worship proper, but remained, as it had been traditionally, a social function for the congregation. The question to be raised is to what extent Jews and non-Jews might have socialized in these dining contexts.

Two papyrus texts from Egypt dating to the later first century BCE yield different possibilities. One (Appendix, no. 3) seems to record the minutes of a burial club using collegial terminology (*synodos, koinos*) typical of other clubs from the wider environment. Such burial clubs held regular dinners along with business meetings for the members of the association. It would appear, however, that the club meets in the prayerhall of the Jewish congregation itself. While it is likely to be construed as a Jewish burial association affiliated with the synagogue, the precise relationship and the social makeup of the club is not specified. But it would have been typical for such burial clubs to conduct regular dinners as part of their social activity. Another papyrus (Appendix, no. 4) records specific provisions and contributions toward regular feasts by members of a Jewish congregation from Apollinopolis Magna. In this case the named individuals seem to be synagogue officials, and it is likely that the feasts under preparation are for the holy days.[25] This text is particularly significant because it does seem to reflect Jewish ritual meals in a diaspora synagogue context while the Temple at Jerusalem was still standing. Even so, the fragmentary nature of the text leaves many lacunae in our understanding of what happened at the feasts and who would have participated.

Some of the broader lines of Jewish and Christian dining practice may be seen from the evidence of Dura-Europos, where we have, virtually side-by-side, both a synagogue and a Christian *domus ecclesiae* in close proximity with a number of other religious edifices. At Dura, moreover, there seems to be a fairly common pattern of local adaptations in various temples to accommodate small collegial groups or sacred clubs attached to the larger temple. Many of the existing local temples that date from the Hellenistic and Parthian periods of the city's history (i.e., through the first and early second centuries CE), show continued architectural adaptation through the Roman period. For example, the Temple of Bel (also known as the Temple of the Palmyrene Gods) was renovated in the early Roman period (second century CE) to provide several dining rooms within the sacred precincts.[26] The fact that small dining confraternities were attached to these temple complexes, both ritually and socially, is further attested by three other examples: the Temple of Adonis, the Temple of Zeus Theos, and the Temple of Gadde.[27]

The site of the Temple of Adonis had earlier been a residential block, but the houses had for the most part been leveled to erect the temple precinct. On either end of the elongated complex, however, some houses were left intact and incorporated architecturally into the construction.[28] Also, along the west side of the complex some existing rooms were renovated to serve as "dining chapels" attached to the temple complex. These nine "chapels" each follow a regular *diwan* plan of low benches around the wall, typical of dining rooms in Durene domestic architecture. The dining rooms were dedicated privately by groups or individuals attached to the public cult of the temple, and were individually appointed and decorated as acts of private devotion. In at least one case, inscriptional evidence attests to the makeup of the cell group as a kind of small cultic confraternity.[29]

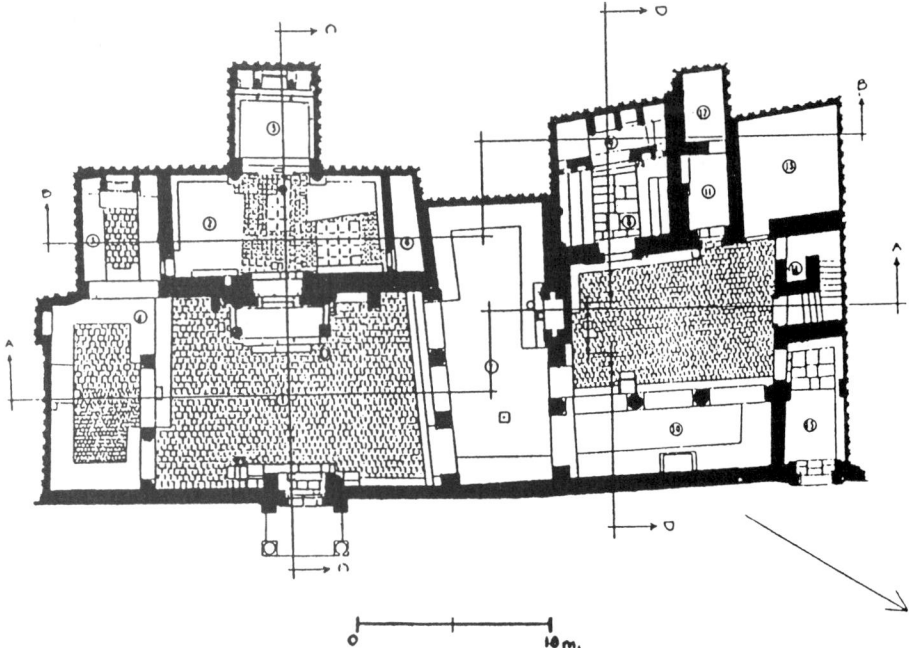

Fig. 5. Dura-Europos. Restored plan of the temple of the Gadde during the final period (IV). (Drawing by H. Pearson.)

In a similar fashion, the Temple of Zeus Theos was built over an *insula* block of private houses on the eve of the first Roman takeover (early second century CE). In much of the area the earlier houses were destroyed to make way for the open-air temenos; however, along the perimeter the houses were preserved and systematically refurbished to serve as dining chapels.[30] The private or individualized appropriation of these rooms may be signified by the idiosyncratic ways in which they were renovated; some were cut through two rooms, while others have thrones or other appointments in the dining form. The largest and most prominent double chapel (Rooms 24 & 31) was dedicated by a leading member of the temple who had also contributed to the construction of the temple complex.[31]

Finally, the case of the Temple of Gadde, a local Palmyrene deity, shows gradual adaptation from a cultic sanctuary in a single private house to a public temple complex in four phases.[32] The architectural form of the final public temple complex (Fig. 5) can be understood archaeologically by its renovation of three neighboring houses to retain some sense of location around the original private sanctuary. Also, specific provision was made for the incorporation of private and semi-private dining rooms in the temple complex. Analysis of the epigraphic remains associated with the building suggest that this architectural progression also had direct social implications,

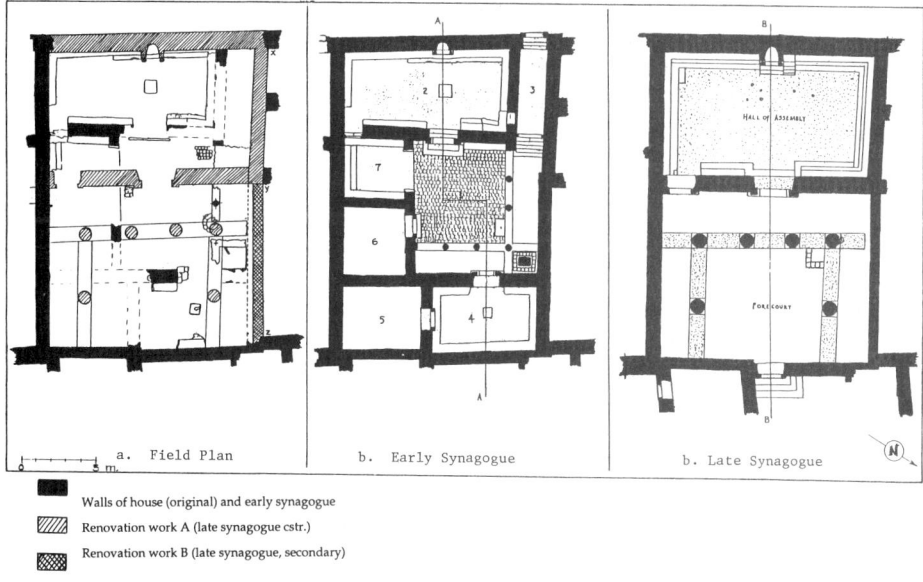

Fig. 6. Dura-Europos. The Synagogue. Field plan (a), and restored plans of the early (b) and the late (c) synagogue. (Drawing by the author based on Pearson.)

since a single family seems to be associated with the cult through all four phases. The sanctuary complex served both as ancestral religious center and collegial or guild hall for an enclave of Palmyrene merchants residing in Dura.[33] Thus, the provisions for dining served both religious and collegial functions within this enclave, and without much doubt the two sets of functions were delicately intertwined in the social life of the temple.

If we turn now to the Jewish and Christian buildings at Dura, we will find it far from surprising to notice that each one was renovated from an existing private house of a typical local character. In the case of the synagogue edifice, it went through two stages of renovation to reach its final form (Fig. 6).[34] In the first stage (Fig. 6b) the house retained much of its domestic character and plan, while two rooms (2 and 7) on the west side of the complex were modified on the interior to serve for assembly and other group functions. In another room of the house (4) a typical Durene domestic dining room (*diwan* type) was still functional apart from the assembly areas. Given the generally domestic character of these areas of the house it has been suggested that these rooms might have served as quarters for guests or a resident caretaker or for other, less formal group functions, including dining. In the final form of the building (Fig. 6c) these domestic quarters were subsumed in the enlargement and formalization of the assembly areas of the synagogue. But some of the domestic and guest-quarter functions likely continued with the annexation of a contiguous house to the east.

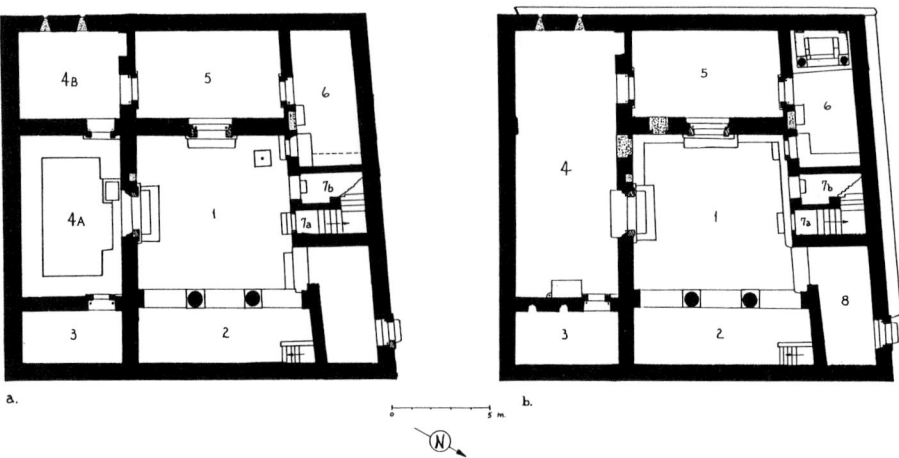

Fig. 7. Dura Europos. The Christian building. Reconstructed plans of the structure before (a) and after (b) the renovation as the domus ecclesiae. *(Drawing by the author.)*

What is perhaps worth noting here is that the form of the assembly seating in both the earlier and later synagogue phases seems to call for people sitting on narrow benches around the walls, while the focal point of the room was toward the center of the long west wall where the Torah niche was installed. This visual and spatial focus was further enhanced by the composition of the artwork on the walls of the hall of assembly. Thus, while there is resemblance between the seating of the assembly areas (both earlier and later) and that typical of dining, they would appear to be segregated activities in the actual usage of the building. It may well be the case that the introduction of the Torah niche as a focal point in the assembly and worship, dating most likely in the later second century, was a significant factor in this segregation of the two types of communal function.

By contrast, the renovations that produced the Christian building down the street treated the dining areas in a different way. The Christian building (Fig. 7) went through only one stage of renovation from its existing domestic form and dates to the middle portion of the third century (c. 241).[35] At this date it was contemporaneous with the renovations of the later synagogue (c. 244) even though it resembles more the stage of architectural development seen in the earlier synagogue (c. 175 CE). In other words, there is a slightly later process of development seen in the architectural renovation of the Christian building. In the renovation, it must be noted that the hall of assembly (Fig. 7b, room 4) was created by knocking out a partition wall and combining two rooms (4a and 4b) in the earlier house. It is significant, therefore, that room 4a was the original dining room of the house.

It is possible, but by no means demonstrable on any archaeological grounds, that the Christian group was used to meeting in the house prior to the renovations. Had they done so, then the courtyard and dining room would have been the most likely areas. On the other hand, after the renovation to serve as a *domus ecclesiae* it is clear that all the regular domestic functions of the house ceased, and the renovation of the dining room created a formal hall of assembly that no longer anticipates actual dining or meal preparation. Thus, if communal meals were practiced by this Christian community, it does not appear that they were held in the church edifice after its renovation, although it is possible (albeit doubtful in my opinion) that the courtyard could still be used in this way. The church house had become liturgically formalized for assembly and Eucharist, while other forms of communal dining, if they occurred at all, were relegated to different social locations.

By the end of the third century, we find that much of the architectural development of Christian buildings was moving in the direction of formal elongated halls to accommodate assembly, even before the introduction of monumental basilical architecture by the emperor Constantine. While these halls generally presuppose the liturgical formality of Eucharistic development, there does not seem to be regular provision for other types of communal dining in most of the known archaeological evidence. The original meal symbolism has been retained in the central place of the Eucharistic ritual; however, actual social dining has disappeared.

Both the similarities and the differences in the Jewish and Christian architectural development derive from their social location and their liturgical development. If we compare the synagogue building from Ostia, the port city of Rome, we see some features similar to that in synagogue from Dura-Europos. The Ostia synagogue also was renovated in two main phases from an existing private building (Fig. 8).[36] Significantly, in its earlier phase of Jewish usage, the hall of assembly (room D) had wide benches around the walls very much like those used in dining halls. Later, when the assembly hall was renovated and monumentalized, including the introduction of a fixed architectural Torah shrine, these benches were removed. Simultaneous with this renovation, a new dining hall (E) was annexed to the complex, while kitchen and storage areas (G and F) continued in use. In this case, it would appear that the introduction of the Torah Shrine and the liturgical development and formalization that it necessitated were correlated with the shifting of the dining functions of the group, even though an explicit provision was made to retain those communal dining functions within the architectural domain of the synagogue complex.

With this provision in mind, we may turn to a final piece of evidence from the Jewish tradition. One of the most outstanding recent archaeological discoveries from the Diaspora is an inscription found at Aphrodisias in Asia

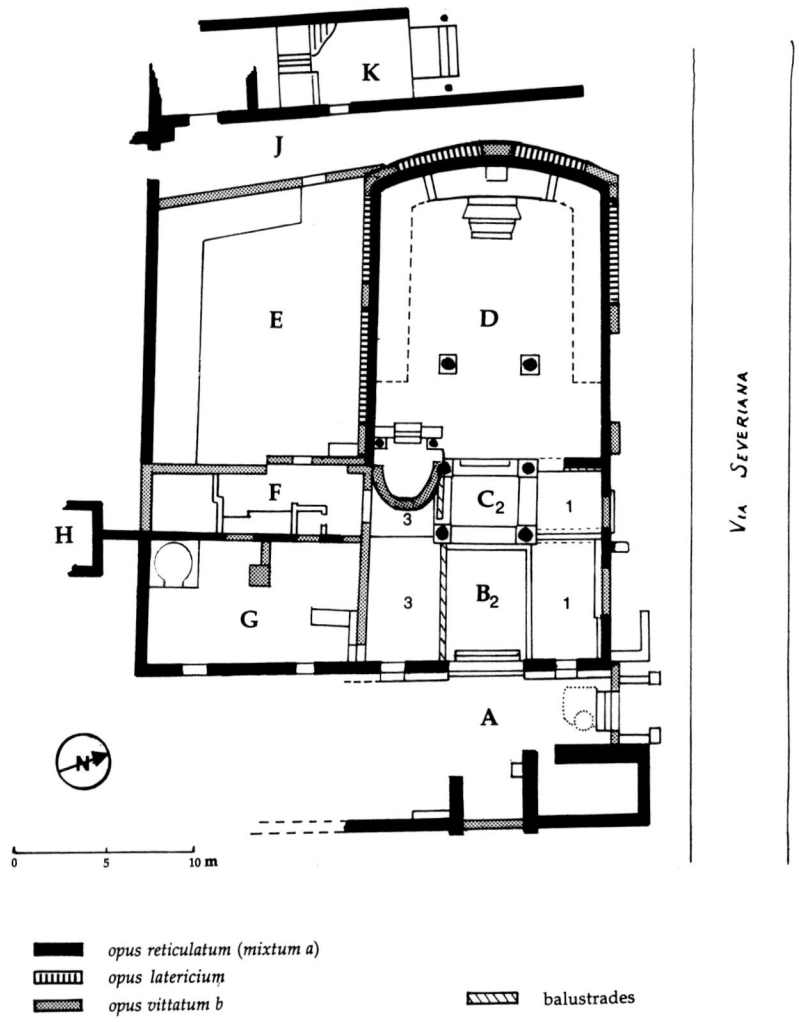

Fig. 8. Ostia. The synagogue. Restored plan showing the various types of construction. (Drawing by the author.)

Minor in 1976.[37] The text comprises three long columns and includes the names of over 80 individuals who appear to have been linked within the Jewish social matrix. The first column (Appendix, no. 5) describes the decision of the *dekania* (meaning governing council) of the group to establish what appears to be a building or foundation in connection with dining activities or food distribution. The other two columns list the names of the members of the group; these in turn seem to be divided between those individuals with semitic or Jewish names (column 2) and those with more Greek names (in column 3). Column 3 also carries the heading "and the rest of the godfearers (*theosebon*)".

Much has been made of this term as a technical designation for non-Jews who were attracted to the synagogue but who did not become full converts or proselytes.[38] So, it has been generally assumed that the inscription reflects the organization and actions of the actual synagogue community. But there is another possibility in reading this inscription as the activities of a Jewish collegial association or burial club that was attached in some way to the local synagogue, but is not identical with the actual synagogue congregation.[39] It may well reflect a social interaction of Jews and non-Jews who were considered to be pious and accepted through communal dining but in some way set apart from the actual liturgical contexts of the worship proper. In this way, Jewish social interaction and dining with non-Jews could be continued even after greater liturgical formality would have made traditional modes of communal activity less comfortable within the worship/assembly context.[40]

It seems to me that the self-designation of the group, which calls itself the "Lovers or Friends of Learning" and the "All-Blessing" likewise reflects intentionally ambiguous terminology for collegial groups within the local environment. Jews and non-Jews can dine together and socialize under this collegial self-designation.[41] Here we may note the use of similarly lofty titles employed by small religious clubs from the nearby regions of Galatia (Appendix, no. 6) that blend devotion to "the most high god" and the holy angels.[42] In some cases, these denote clearly pagan cultic and collegial activity (Appendix, no. 6a and 6b), while in other cases they appear to be more typically Jewish (Appendix, no. 6c). For both groups collegial organization and dining, just as suggested in the case of the Aphrodisias *dekania* inscription, appear to preserve networks of social integration and interaction with the larger environment. A final inscription from Mysia (Appendix, no. 7) shows the typicality of the language of collegial self-designations where the "cup", symbolic of the communal dining, has been personified and sacralized alongside the dedication to the most high god. Group identity and communal dining activity were the norm across the cultural and social expanse of the Roman world.

Conclusions

The evidence here assembled suggests that the liturgical and architectural specialization that developed in the Jewish and Christian traditions respectively from the second century onward resulted in different treatments of the communal significance of dining as a cultural idiom of the Graeco-Roman world. The social significance of dining began in the Christian tradition as a communal solidarity ritual, and was exploited for this symbolism especially within the Pauline tradition, with its emphasis on integrating Jews and Gentiles in fellowship. In this way, it is proper to think of Paul's instructions regarding the fellowship meal practice in 1 Cor. 11.17-34 as using the Lord's Supper elements to sacralize the social order of the meal by linking it through ritual and symbol to the Jesus tradition. But the meal was still a real communal meal and remained within the cultural traditions of dining fellowship.

By contrast, the further development of the Eucharistic ritual and its architectural setting, so that the meal was reduced to schematic and symbolic elements, had the effect of retaining some elements of incorporation language, but at the same time removing most of the integrative functions of the actual dining. In other words, the Eucharistic ritual was becoming a symbol of in-group identity only; admission or exclusion from the Eucharist was a sign of membership. Other aspects of communal dining, therefore, as seen in the Hippolytan church order tradition, show that there are potential conflicts with this emerging liturgical function under ecclesiastical control. To the extent that communal dining in the extended household was symbolically and practically linked to the patronage networks of Roman social life it could be viewed as competing with the controlled sense of incorporation symbolism evolving within the ecclesiastical Eucharist. At stake was the symbolism of patronage and hierarchy implicit within at least some aspects of the meal tradition. Of course there are other forms of early Christian dining that have not been explored in this discussion, most notably the meals for the dead. Also, it must be remembered that the process of liturgical specialization likely proceeded at different rates in different localities in the early centuries. Nonetheless, the increasing liturgical centralization of the meal symbolism in the development of the Eucharist within orthodox Christian tradition tended to delimit the roles of dining in relation to worship and assembly.

From virtually the same beginning point, one may watch the Jewish tradition take a different line of development in its use of dining. Of course, here too there are ranges of dining practice that have not been explored in detail, as in the case of the developments of the Passover meal tradition as a ritual of home and family observance in the Rabbinic tradition after the destruction of the Temple in 70 CE. But in the final analysis, it appears that communal dining remained in the Jewish tradition a form of social interaction that was kept somewhat separate from the central features of the worship assembly, especially as time passed and liturgical formalization occurred around the Torah shrine. Thus, while there may have been less division in earlier days, dining practices were increasingly removed from the central acts of worship in the institutionalization of the synagogue. This development allowed, however, for the communal aspects of dining, both in the family and in contexts of social integration, to continue with direct religious symbolism. Thus, provisions for communal dining are seen within synagogue architecture throughout the Roman period and into late Antiquity. We also see continued provisions for dining as a mechanism for social integration within the broader lines of the community and even between Jews and non-Jews, depending on the local circumstances of the Jewish community.

In both sets of developments, the basic cultural template of the meal as ritually regulated fellowship was operative. It was a multiplex set of symbols that was derived from the Graeco-Roman religious and social environment, but that allowed for specialized adaptations over time. The adaptation of dining practice, symbolically, ritually, and architecturally, is an important indicator of the cultural roots as well as the historic development of the Jewish and Christian traditions.

Notes

1. For this reason, Plutarch recommends that the size of such dinners should remain small, since too large a crowd interferes "with sociability and conversation" (*Quaest. conv.* 679A). In general on Plutarch and his writings, see Jones 1971, especially 39-64. On the literary tradition of the symposium, see Martin 1931, passim; for its relation to Jewish tradition, see Stein 1957.
2. Douglas 1971 and 1974, especially 59-77, Detienne 1981, Smith, forthcoming. I am grateful to Dr. Smith for allowing me to see this work in ms. form.
3. See Meeks & Wilken 1981, 24-30.
4. Meeks 1983, 155-73. See also Essler 1994, 52-69.
5. Meeks, 1983, 94-96, 130. See also below n. 10.
6. Willis 1985, passim. See also Theissen 1982b. Here, too, it is recognized that some of the tensions over pagan dinners comes from traditional Jewish scruples about eating and social interaction; however, Theissen is correct, I think, in suggesting that the impulse of Diaspora Jews to participate in such dinners was already an operative force in the debate. See also Borgen 1995.
7. Theissen 1982a, 148-56, Meeks 1983, 77-80, 155-60. See also Malherbe 1983, 55-70. Barton 1986.
8. Meeks 1983, 78, 115, 157-62. See also Feely-Harnik 1981, 11, Theissen 1982a, 163-75, Lampe 1991, Smith & Taussig 1990, 21-69, White 1996 (1990), 118-9.
9. Jeremias 1966, 118-20, Lietzmann 1972, 123, 187-88. Contrast Bornkamm 1969, 129. It should be stated that the notion of Christian eucharistic practice deriving primarily from the Jewish Passover meal, a claim central to Jeremias' argument, is no longer viable. Paul's dining practice in the house church assumes no such connection whatsoever; the Last Supper tradition found in the synoptic gospels reflects later literary and theological efforts to link Passover symbolism with the death of Jesus, rather than its point of origin. Consequently, for the remainder of this study, I will be concentrating on developments in communal dining in both Jewish and Christian practice but apart from the Passover meal proper.
10. White, 1996 (1990), 119-20. Some degree of development from the Pauline meal as the center of social inclusion may be seen in 2 Jn 9-10, where an injunction is given to use a creedal test before admitting traveling Christians "into the house (of the church)". Now the boundaries of the patron"s home — rather than the

fellowship of the table proper — have become the boundaries of the sacralized community. While hospitality and fellowship language would have been operative in both realms, there seems to be some degree of formalization to the sense of place of assembly among the Christian communities reflected in Johannine epistles. So see White 1996 (1990), 145. See now also Osiek & Balch 1997, especially 200, 207, 212.

11. White 1996 (1990), 123-6. For the relevant texts and archaeological evidence, see White 1997a, nos. 16 and 18.
12. For the history of the reconstruction of the "lost" text of Hippolytus, see the work of Connolly 1916, Dix 1968, and Botte 1963 and 1968.
13. *The Apostolic Tradition*, 27-28. The complete Latin text (from Botte), is as follows: 27 ... *Per omnem vero oblationem memor sit qui offert eius qui illum vocavit; propterea enim depraecatus est ut ingrediator sub tecto eius. 28 Edentes vero et bibentes cum id agite et non ad ebrietatum, et non ut aliquis inrideat, aut tristetur, qui vocat vos, in vestra inquietudine, sed oret ut dignus efficiatur ut ingrediantur sancti ad eum. Vos enim, inquit, estis sal terrae. Si communiter vero omnibus oblatum fuerit quot dicitur graece apoforetum, accipite ab eo. Si autem ut omnes gustent sufficienter, gustate ut et superet ...*
14. The first to propose this reading of the social context is Bobertz 1993, and the discussion that follows here is indebted to his article.
15. On Trimalchio's dinners relative to common social practice see the discussion of Dennis Smith, forthcoming. On the "typicality" of Trimalchio as a social description see D'Arms 1981, 97-120.
16. On the implications of the social stratification inscribed through dining conventions, see also Meeks 1983, 68 following Theissen 1982a, 156-60.
17. See the discussion by Stoops 1986 and 1991.
18. Kraabel 1981a.
19. Kraabel 1979, White 1996 (1990), 60-85.
20. White 1987, also summarized in White 1997a, nos. 70-71.
21. White 1987, 153, White 1996 (1990), 33-37, figs. 1-2 (with further bibliography for the site).
22. White 1987, 152-5, White 1996 (1990), 82, Picard 1921.
23. White 1997a, no. 72.
24. White 1997a, no. 73 and n. 123.
25. This is the conclusion of the editors of the *Corpus Papyrorum Iudaicarum*, III.254-55, since the days of the feasts would correspond to the observance of Passover, even though the precise month is not given. Even so, the feasts need not be thought of strictly as Passover meals according to later custom. The editors also note, however, that the constitution of the group is much like that of other clubs in first century Egypt. In general on Jewish associations in Egypt, see also Richardson & Heuchan 1996. That synagogal organization, especially in the Diaspora, originated after the model of clubs or *collegia* is supported by Richardson 1996, especially 97-98.
26. In general on local developments in Durene temple architecture, see Perkins 1973, 15-32. The typical Durene temple described by Perkins shows evidence of considerable adaptation over time. The courtyard of the Temple of Bel, originally built during the Parthian period, was renovated in at least two subsequent phases

in order to make more rooms for dining. For the archaeological report see *Excavations at Dura-Europos: Preliminary Reports IV*, 1933, 16-18.
27. See the discussion of patterns of renovation for cultic usage in these temples at Dura in White, 1996 (1990), 40-44.
28. *Excavations at Dura-Europos: Preliminary Reports VII-VIII*, 1939, 135-50. The temple dates to the late Parthian period (late first - early second centuries CE), but was renovated substantially in the second century CE. The epigraphic remains for this period of activity indicate a date range from 150-175 CE, or just about the same time that the first *mithraeum* and early synagogue buildings were also being established by renovation.
29. The dining chapels conform to a rather standard plan (usually called the *diwan* type by the excavators) found commonly among the different temples and houses at Dura. They are squarish rooms with a low, plastered bench built along the walls. See *Dura-Europos: Preliminary Reports VII-VIII*, 1939, 168-70 and inscription no. 871 (dated 153 CE) for chapel 38 and its "confraternity".
30. *Dura-Europos: Preliminary Reports VII-VIII*, 1939, 181-195. The construction of the Temple dates to the early second century CE. The renovations continued into the Roman period.
31. *Dura Europos, Preliminary Reports VII-VIIII*, 1939, 190-91, 213-15, White 1996 (1990), 41.
32. *Dura-Europos: Preliminary Reports VII-VIII*, 1939, 222-80.
33. *Dura-Europos: Preliminary Reports VII-VIII*, 1939, 278-79, White, 1996 (1990), 41-43.
34. White 1997a, nos. 60-61, White 1996 (1990), 74-75, 93-97. The archaeological analysis is based on the final report of Kraeling 1956, passim, but also uses the extensive discussion of the building by Goodenough 1964.
35. White 1997a, nos. 36-37, White 1996 (1990), 120-22. The archaeological analysis is based on the final report of Kraeling 1964.
36. White 1997a, nos. 83-85, White 1996 (1990), 69-70. The archaeological analysis is based on fieldwork published as an article: White 1997b.
37. The critical edition of the inscription was first published by Reynolds and Tannenbaum 1987. The text is reproduced with critical discussion in White 1997a, no. 64.
38. For the debate over the term "godfearers" (*theoseboi*) see the articles by Kraabel 1981a, reprinted with responses in Kraabel 1992. In the final analysis, the issue is whether the term "godfearer" in this period reflects a technical designation for a class of gentiles who were sympathetic toward Judaism but who did not fully convert. As such, the godfearer would have had a secondary status in relation to the Jewish community, even though the person might have been included in some communal functions. Most scholars have read the Aphrodisias inscription to affirm this view, despite Kraabel's arguments that the term actually refers to Jews instead. My own view differs from both positions, since I would argue that the term was intentionally ambiguous and can be found applied to Jews by non-Jews and to non-Jews by Jews, depending on the context in which it is found. It is a term that reflects life on the social boundary of Jews living in Greek and Roman cities. It was designed to preserve an arena of interaction between Jews and non-Jews by allowing each to call the other in effect "pious". Thus, it does show considerable respect and sympathy for Jews in those particular

Diaspora contexts. Given the tensions that one sees in certain Jewish contexts over dining with non-Jews (as noted earlier in the case of Paul in Antioch), it would not be surprising to think of these social interactions between Diaspora Jews and their pagan neighbors, at least in some localities, as including communal dining, whether or not the pagans were considering possible conversion to Judaism.

39. This is the view reached in my *Building God's House* 1996 (1990), 88-89. Similarly, Williams (1992) concluded that the inscription describes the activities of a burial association attached, loosely perhaps, to a local Jewish synagogue. The social composition of the group thus included both Jews and non-Jews, as well as some who had become Jewish converts or proselytes. She also concludes that the terminology of the dedication formula specifically refers to the celebration of a typical funerary meal by the members of the association.

40. In this sense, my own guess is that the situation reflected in the Aphrodisias inscription is a kind of local social compromise, whereby some members of the Aphrodisian Jewish community could have an ongoing social relationship with non-Jews through a collegial association only loosely affiliated with the synagogue congregation itself. By separating this dining and social activity from worship, it would thereby preserve the sacral integrity of the Jewish community in assembly and worship and at the same time it would allow for another locus of social interaction. To be sure this kind of compromise must have been a local development owing to the particular circumstances of the Jewish congregation; Jewish groups in other cities will have reached different solutions for dealing with issues of religious identity and acculturation. I would argue, however, that the kind of architectural evolution seen in the Ostia synagogue would compare favorably with this reading of the Aphrodisias inscription. Whereas earlier the provision for communal dining was in the same space as the main assembly, later — as the assembly hall came to have a more formal liturgical articulation around the Torah shrine — social dining was segregated into a separate area of the building. The two aspects of Jewish practice could thereby be kept in creative harmony.

41. So see the article by Rutgers 1992.

42. For the texts and discussions see Sheppard 1980-81.

Appendix

1. *Donation of Polycharmos for a Synagogue*
   (CIJ I.694: Stobi, Macedonia, IIIrd CE)

   [Κλ.] Τιβέριοσ Πολύ-
   χαρμος ὁ καὶ 'Αχύρι-
   ος ὁ πατὴρ τῆς ἐν
   4 Στόβοις συναγωγῆς
   ὃς πολειτευσάμε-
   νος πᾶσαν πολειτεί-
   αν κατὰ τὸν 'Ιουδαϊ-
   8 σμὸν εὐχῆς ἕνεκεν
   τοὺς μὲν οἴκους τῷ
   ἁγίῳ τόπῳ καὶ τὸ
   τρίκλεινον σὺν τῷ
   12 τετραστόῳ ἐκ τῶν
   οἰκείων χρημάτων
   μηδὲν ὅλως παραψά-
   μενος τῶν ἁγίων, τὴν
   16 δὲ ἐξουσίαν τῶν ὑπερώων πάντων πᾶσαν
   καὶ τὴν (δ)εσποτείαν
   ἔχειν ἐμὲ τὸν Κλ. Τιβέρι-
   20 ον Πολύχαρμον καὶ τοὺς
   <καὶ τοὺς> κληρονόμους
   τοὺς ἐμοὺς διὰ παντὸς
   βίου, ὃς ἂν δὲ βουληθῆ
   24 τι καινοτομῆσαι παρὰ τὰ ὑπ'
   ἐμοῦ δοχθέντα, δώσει τῷ
   πατριάρχῃ δηναρίων (μ)υριά-
   δας εἴκοσι πέντε· ουτω γάρ
   28 μοι συνέδοξεν, τὴν δὲ ἐπι-
   σκευὴν τῆς κεράμου τῶν
   ὑπερώων ποιεῖσθ(α)ι ἐμὲ
   καὶ κληρονόμους
   32 ἐμούς.

Translation: [...] Claudius Tiberius Polycharmus, also called Achyrius, father of the synagogue at Stobi, having lived my entire life according to Judaism, in accordance with a vow (gave) my houses to the holy place along with the *triclinum* and its *tetrastoa* out of my household accounts without touching the sacred (treasury). However, (I retain) the ownership and disposition of all the upper chambers for myself, Cl. Tiberius Polycharmus, and for my heirs, for life. If anyone seeks to make changes beyond what has been set down by me, he shall give the patriarch 250,000 denarii; for this have I agreed. As for the upkeep of the rooftiles of the upper chambers, it will be done by me and my heirs.

2. *Donation of Beryllos of a Dining Room for the Synagogue*
   (Lifshitz, Donateurs, No. 66: Caesarea Maritima, Palaestina prima, IIIrd-Vth CE).

   Βη[ρ]ύλλοσ ἀρχις(υνάγωγος)
   καὶ φροντιστὴς
   ὑ(ι)ὸς ᾽Ιούτου, ἐποί-
4 ησε τὴν ψηφο-
   θεσίαν τοῦ τρι-
   κλίνου τῷ ἰδίῳ.

Translation: Beryllos, son of Judah (or Justus), archisynagogos and curator, made the mosaic of the *triclinium* from his own funds.

3. *Papyrus Resolution of a Burial Association meeting in the Synagogue*
   (CPJ 138 (= P.Ryl. 590): Egypt, provenance unknown, c. 49-31 BCE)

   ]. —ἐπὶ τῆς γ[ε]νηθείσης συναγωγῆς ἐν τῆι προσευχῆι
   Δημητ]ρίωι τῶν [(πρώτων)] φίλων καὶ θ[υ(ρωρῶν)] (?) καὶ εἰσαγγελέων
                                                    καὶ ἀρχυπηρε(τῶν)
   ]-Κάμακος […]..[……]ξ[……..].[..γραμ]ματεὺς
   ..]…..[   ]κυον εἰς τὴν σ[ύνοδον
5 .]ου σὺν τοῖ[ς.] …. [……].ρασιος καὶ συλλελόχισται
   ]ρκως το ε.[.].αλλ εμ [….]υ ἐν τοῖς ἐρχο.[.]…..ντας
   .]με δικαι .[..]……[……] ειν ἐφ᾽ ᾧιτε ἐτεάς [.]ς
   σ]υνόδου[   ].φ[.]..[…]καιροις
   .]ωι κατ᾽ ἔτο[ς.]ει επτ.[……..]ιου γ.ιλι…ωι με[.]ε
10 .]ινων ε.[.]σου κ[οινου(?) … ταφιαστῶν ἐκ τῆς
   ..]τε ατε[.].πον[……….]φαλλισμων κα [2-5 lett.]
   ]. ὁ τοῦ ἐσομένου και[νοῦ…..οὐ]δ᾽ [ι] ἐν αὐλῷ [ι 2-6 lett.]
   ..]μαι Ευδ[..].ι[12 lett.   ]του συνταφι α[στου]
   ..]σεται [ο]ἷς προσ[ήκει   7 lett.   γ]ραμματεῖ ἀκολ[ούθως]
15 .]εἰς ἱερο.[…].απ[12 lett.   ]ια τοῦ δελ.[
   τοῖς λει[του]ρ[γ   12 lett.   ]συνόδου τοῦ[
   …]……[15 lett.   ].θησεται ξ[

Translation: ... at the session held in the prayerhall
... To (...) Demetrius of the First Friends and the door-keepers (?) and
      the ushers and chief overseers.
... of Kamax ... secretary ...
                      to the association
with ...   and has been incorporated
                      on the condition that
association   the times
... every year
...   the corporation of *(syn)taphiastai*
future new
                      the *syntaphiastai*
... whom it concerns   to the secretary
                      according to the association ...

4. *Papyrus list of contributors to a Jewish Dining Club*
   [CPJ 139 (=O.E. 368): Apollinopolis Magna, Egypt Ist BCE].

ιε τρίτη πόσις | Θευξου[...] | Λυσίμαχος σο[φός? | Σεφθαῖς ἐνα(γωγὸς)
ε[| 5 | ᾽Ιώσηπος ἱερεὺ(ς) ἐν[(γίνονται) ᾽Α | ις τετάρτη πόσις | Θημᾶς ισο-
τοντ.[| ᾽Ιώσηπος ἱερε(ὺς) [| 10 | Τεύφιλος τ[| τὰ ἐπιδόμ[α | τα].ας φ | φ.

Translation: (on the) 15th. Third feast: Theux[?] ... Lysimachos, the
philosopher(?), Sephthais, ... Josep(h)os, the priest; (total) 1,000 (drachmae?).
(On the) 16th. Fourth feast: Themas, Josep(h)os, the priest ... Teuphilos ...,
the contributions ...

5. *The Jewish* Dekania *of Aphrodisias*
   (Reynolds-Tannenbaum, Jews and Godfearers at Aphrodisias *(Cambridge,*
   1987): Aphrodisias, Caria, c. late IIIrd CE)

Col. (i)	θεὸς βοηθός, πατέλλα? δο[.1 or 2.]
	Οἱ ὑποτεταγμέ-
	νοι τῆς δεκαν(ίας)
	τῶν φιλομαθῶ[ν]
5	τῶν κὲ παντευλογ(--ων)
	εἰς ἀπενθησίαν
	τῷ πλήθι ἔκτισα[ν]
	ἐξ ἰδίων μνῆμα
Σα-	᾽Ιαηλ προστάτης.
μου 10	υ σὺν υἱῷ ᾽Ιωσούα ἀρχ(οντι?)
ηλ	Θεόδοτος Παλατῖν(ος?) σὺν

πρες-	υ υἱῷ Ἱλαριανῷ vac.
βευ-	Σαμουηλ ἀρχιδ(έκανος?) προσήλ(υτος)
τῆς	Ἰωσῆς Ἰεσσέου vacat
Περ-	15 Βενιαμιν ψαλμο(λόγος?)
γε-	Ἰούδας εὔκολος vacat
οὺς	Ιωσῆς προσήλυ(τος)
	Σαββάτιος Ἀμαχίου
	Ἐμμόνιος θεοσεβ(ής) v.v.
	20 Ἀντωνῖνος θεοσεβ(ής)
	Σαμουηλ Πολιτιανοῦ
	Εἰωσηφ Εὐσεβίου προσή(λυτος)
	κα[ὶ] Εἰούδας Θεοδώρ(ου)
	καὶ Ἀντιπέος Ἑρμή(ου?)
	25 καὶ Σαβάθιος νεκτάρις
	[?κα]ὶ Σαμο[υ]ηλ πρεσ-
	βευτῆς ἱερεύς

Translation: God help the (builders, donors?) of the Patella. The undersigned, (members) of the *dekania* of the "Friends of Learning," also called the "All-Blessing," for the relief of grief (or suffering) in the community, built this memorial from their own ressources.
Jael, the president; Samuel of Perge, presbyter, with his son Joshua, archon; Theodotos Palatinos with his son Hilarion; Samuel the archidekanos, proselyte; Joses, son of Jesse; Benjamin, Psamologist(?); Judas Eukolos; Joses; proselyte; Sabbatios, son of Amachios; Emmonios, godfearer; Samuel son of Politianos;
(2nd hand) Joseph, son of Eusebius, proselyte; Judas, son of Theodoros; and Antipios, son of Hermeos; and Sabathios Nektaris
[erased: and Samuel, the elder, priest].

6. Hypsistians and cults or Collegia of Angels
 (from A.R.R. Sheppard, "Pagan Cults of Angels in Roman Asia Minor,"
 Talanta 12/13 (1980-81) 77-101: Phrygia, IInd-IIIrd CE)

6a. Stratonicea (No. 1, p. 78)

Δὺ ὑψίστω καὶ ἀγαθῷ
ἀγγέλῳ Κλαύδιος Ἀχιλλεὺς
καὶ Γαλάτ[ι]α ὑπὲρ σωτηρίας
4 μετὰ τῶν ἰδίων πάντων
χαριστήριον.

Translation: To Zeus Most High and
the Good Angel, Claudius Achilles and
Galatia, with all their household,
made a thank offering for salvation.

6b. Yala Baba Köy (No. 8, p. 88)

Αὐρ(ήλιος)
[----]
Φιλανγέλων συνβι
ώσις Ὁσίῳ Δικέῳ εὐ-
χήν.

Translation: Aurelius ... (and) The "Association of the Friends of Angels" made (this) for a vow to Holiness and Justice.

6c. Kalecik (No. 11, p. 94)

τῷ μεγάλῳ
Θεῷ Ὑψίστῳ καὶ
Ἐπουρανίῳ καὶ
τοῖς ἁγίοις αὐτοῦ
ἀνγέλοις καὶ τῇ
προσκυνητῇ αὐ-
τοῦ προσευχῇ τὰ
ὧδε ἔργα γείνεται

Translation: The works here set forth are dedicated to The Great and Most High God of Heaven and his Holy Angels, and to his venerable house of prayer ...

7. Athenische Mitteilungen 30.145: *Mysia (date uncertain)*

Διὶ Ὑψίστῳ καὶ τῷ Χῷ

Translation: To Zeus Most High and to The Decanter (*chous*).

Bibliography

Ahern, E.M. 1973. *The Cult of the Dead in a Chinese Village*, Stanford.
Alarcao, J. de 1988. *Roman Portugal*, Warminster.
Alexiou, M. 1974. *The Ritual Lament in Greek Tradition*, Cambridge.
Amedick, R. 1993. "*Stibadia* in Herculaneum und Pompeji", in: *Ercolano 1738-1988. 250 anni di ricerca archeologica. Atti del Convegno Internazionale Ravello-Ercolano-Napoli-Pompei 30 ottobre - 4 novembre 1988*, ed. L. Franchi dell'Orto, Rome, 179-92.
Amedick, R. 1994. "Herakles im Speisesaale", *Mitteilungen des Deutschen Archäologischen Instituts, Römische Abteilung* 101, 103-19.
André, J. 1961. *L'Alimentation et la cuisine à Rome*, Paris.
Andronicos, M. 1984. *Vergina. The Royal Tombs and the Ancient City*, Athens.
Astin, A.E. 1967. *Scipio Aemilianus*, Oxford.
Bagnall, R.S. & Frier, B.W. 1995. *The Demography of Roman Egypt*, Cambridge.
Baldassarre, I. 1976. "Mosaici ellenistici a Cirene e a Delo: rapporti e differenze", *Quaderni di archeologia della Libia* 8, 193-221.
Balty, J.Ch. 1984. "Notes sur l'habitat romain, byzantin et arabe d'Apamée. Rapport de synthèse", in: *Actes du Colloque Apamée de Syrie. Aspects de l'Architecture domestique d'Apamée, Brussels 1980*, ed. J. Balty, Brussels, 473-78.
Bammel, F. 1950. *Das heilige Mahl im Glauben der Völker*, Gütersloh.
Banks, R.M. 1979. *Paul's Idea of Community*, Sydney.
Barton, S.C. 1986. "Paul's Sense of Place: An Anthropological Approach to Community Formation in Corinth", *New Testament Studies* 32, 225-46.
Bartsch, H.W. 1962. "Der korintische Missbrauch des Abendmahls. Zur Situation und Struktur von I Korinther 8-11", in: *Entmythologisierende Auslegung*, Hamburg, 169-83.
Beall, T.S. 1988. *Josephus' Description of the Essenes Illustrated by the Dead Sea Scrolls*, Cambridge.
Beek, B.L. van 1983. "*Salinatores* and *Sigillata*: The Coastal Areas of North Holland and Flanders and Their Economic Differences in the 1st Century AD", *Helinium* 23, 3-13.
Bek, L. 1983. "*Questiones Convivales*. The Idea of the *Triclinium* and the Staging of Convivial Ceremony from Rome to Byzantium", *Analecta romana Instituti danici* 12, 81-107.
Benedict, R. 1934. *Patterns of Culture*, Boston.
Benoît, F. 1959. "L'économie du littoral de la Narbonnaise à l'époque antique: Le commerce du sel et les pêcheries", *Rivista di studi liguri* 25.

Berger, K. 1993. *Manna, Mehl und Sauerteig. Korn und Brot im Alltag der frühen Christen*, Stuttgart.
Bergmeier, R. 1993. *Die Essener-Berichte des Flavius Josephus: Quellen-studien zu den Essenertexten im Werk des jüdischen Historiographen*, Kampen.
Bergquist, B. 1990. "Sympotic space: A functional aspect of Greek dining-rooms", in: *Sympotica: A Symposium on the Symposion*, ed. O. Murray, Oxford, 37-65.
Bilde, P. 1984. "Templets betydning i jødedommen på Jesu tid", *Religionsvidenskabeligt Tidsskrift* 4, 41-68.
Bilde, P. 1998. "The Essenes in Philo and Josephus", in press.
Blümmer 1920. Art. "Salz", *RE* I, A2, cols. 2075-99.
Bobertz, C. 1993. "The Role of the Patron in the *Cena Dominica* of Hippolytus' *Apostolic Tradition*", *Journal of Theological Studies* 44, 170-84.
Bohlen, D. 1937. *Die Bedeutung der Fischerei für die antike Wirtschaft*, Hamburg.
Bokser, B.M. 1984. *The Origins of the Seder. The Passover Rite and Early Rabbinic Judaism*, Berkeley.
Bokser, B.M. 1990. "Todos and Rabbinic Authority in Rome", in: *New Perspectives on Ancient Judaism*, vol. 1: *Religion, Literature and Society in Ancient Israel, Formative Christianity and Judaism*, eds. J. Neusner et al. (Brown Judaic Studies, vol. 206), Atlanta, 117-30.
Booth, A. 1991. "The Age for Reclining and its Attendant Perils", in: *Dining in a Classical Context*, ed. W.J. Slater, Ann Arbor, 105-20.
Borgen, P. 1984. "Philo of Alexandria", in: *Jewish Writings of the Second Temple Period. Apocrypha, Pseudepigrapha, Qumran Sectarian Writings, Philo, Josephus*, ed. M.E. Stone (CRINT, vol. 2.2), Assen-Philadelphia, 233-82.
Borgen, P. 1995. "'Yes,' 'No,' 'How Far?': The Participation of Jews and Christians in Pagan Cults", in: *Paul in His Hellenistic Context*, ed. T. Engberg-Pedersen, Minneapolis, 30-59.
Bornkamm, G. 1963. "Herrenmahl und Kirche bei Paulus", in: *Studien zur Antike und Urchristentum*, Munich, 138-76.
Bornkamm, G. 1969. *Early Christian Experience*, London.
Borza, E.N. 1983. "The Symposium at Alexander's court", in: *Ancient Macedonia* 3, Thesssaloniki, 45-55.
Botte, B. 1963. *La Tradition Apostolique de Saint Hippolyte: Essai de Réconstitution*, Münster.
Botte B. 1968. *Hippolyte de Rome, La Tradition Apostolique d'apres les anciennes versions* (2nd ed.), (Sources chrétiennes), Paris.
Bousset-Gressmann, W. 1966. *Die Religion des Judentums im späthellenistischen Zeitalter* (3rd ed. 1927 by H. Gressmann, rp.), Tübingen.
Bradley, K.R. 1986. "Wet-nursing at Rome: A Study in Social Relations", in: *The Family in Ancient Rome: New Perspectives*, ed. B. Rawson, Sydney and London, 201-29.

Bradley, K.R. 1991a. *Discovering the Roman Family: Studies in Roman Social History*, New York and Oxford.

Bradley, K.R. 1991b, Review of Wiedemann (1989), *Classical Philology* 86, 258-63.

Bradley, K.R. 1992. "'The Regular, Daily Traffic in Slaves': Roman History and Contemporary History", *The Classical Journal* 87, 125-38.

Bradley, K.R. 1994. "The Nurse and the Child at Rome: Duty, Affect and Socialisation", *Thamyris* 1, 137-56.

Bragantini, I. 1990: "Il lato ovest: L'occupazione dello spazio: lo spazio rituale", in: *Sepolture e riti nella necropoli dell'Isola Sacra*, eds. I. Baldassarre et al., (Bolletino di archeologia) 5-6, 61-70.

Brewster, E.H. 1918. "The Synthesis of the Romans", *Transactions and Proceedings of the American Philological Association* 49, 131-43.

Brisay, K.W. de & Evans K.A. 1975. *Salt. The Study of an Ancient Industry*, Colchester.

Brown, P. 1988. *The Body and Society*, New York.

Bruneau, P. & Siebert, G. 1969. "Une nouvelle mosaïque délienne à sujet mythologique", *Bulletin de correspondance hellénique* 93, 261-307.

Bruneau, P. & Vatin, C. 1970. *Délos*, vol. 27, *L'Ilot de la Maison des Comédiens*, Paris.

Bruneau, P. 1972. *Délos*, vol. 39, *Les Mosaïques*, Paris.

Burkert, W. 1987. *Ancient Mystery Cults*, Cambridge, Mass. and London.

Cabal, M. 1973. "Le site archéologique d'Ardes Pas-de-Calais", *Revue du Nord* 55, 126, 17-28.

Cabourdin, G. (ed.) 1981. *Le sel et son histoire*. Actes du colloque de l'association interuniversitaire de l'est (1979), Nancy.

Carlsen, J. 1995. *Vilici and Roman Estate Managers until AD 284*, Rome.

Casparri, F. 1916. "Das Nilschiff Ptolemaios IV", *Jahrbuch des Deutschen Archäologischen Instituts* 31, 1-74.

Casson, L. 1986. *Ships and Seamanship in the Ancient World*, Princeton (1971).

Castillo, C. 1991. "Epigrafía Romana en Hispania (1983-87)", *Emerita: revista de lingüística y filologia clásica* 59, 225-73.

Chadwick, H. 1966. *Early Christian Thought and the Classical Tradition: Studies in Justin, Clement and Origen*, Oxford.

Chamonard, J. 1922. *Délos*, vol. 8, *Le Quartier du Théâtre*, Paris.

Charles N. & Kerr M. 1988. *Women, Food and Families*, Manchester and New York.

Charlesworth, M.P. 1926. *Trade Routes and Commerce of the Roman Empire*, London.

Chrysostomou, P. 1988. *Arkaiologikon Deltion* 35, 1980, B1, 307-11.

Cimma, M.R. 1981. *Ricerche sulle società di publicani*, Milan.

Cohen, Y.A. 1968. "Food: Consumption Patterns", *International Encyclopedia of the Social Sciences* 5, 508-13.
Colson, F.H. 1967. *Philo* (LCL), London and Cambridge, Mass.
Connolly, R.H. 1916. *The So-Called Egyptian Church Order and Derived Documents*, Cambridge.
Conzelmann, H. 1969. *Der erste Brief an die Korinther* (Kritisch-exegetischer Kommentar über das Neue Testament, vol. 5), Göttingen.
Corley, K.E. 1993. *Private Women, Public Meals. Social Conflict in the Synoptic Tradition*, Peabody, Mass.
Corpus juris civilis (Translated by S.P. Scott, *The Civil Law*, 1973, New York).
Courtney, E. 1980, *A Commentary on the Satires of Juvenal*, London.
Curtis, R.I. 1991. *Garum and Salsamenta*, Leiden.
D'Arms, J.H. 1981. *Commerce and Social Standing in Ancient Rome*, Cambridge.
D'Arms, J.H. 1984. "Control, Companionship, and *Clientela*: Some Social Functions of the Roman Communal Meal", *Échos du monde classique* 28, 327-48.
D'Arms, J.H. 1990. "The Roman *Convivium* and the Idea of Equality", in: *Sympotica: A Symposium on the Symposion*, ed. O. Murray, Oxford, 308-20.
D'Arms, J.H. 1991. "Slaves at Roman *Convivia*", in: *Dining in a Classical Context*, ed. W.J. Slater, Ann Arbor, 171-83.
D'Arms, J.H. 1995. "Heavy Drinking and Drunkenness in the Roman World: Four Questions for Historians", in: *In Vino Veritas*, eds. O. Murray & M. Tecuşan, London, 304-17.
Degrassi, A. 1965. *Inscriptiones latinae liberae rei publicae*, Berlin.
Delcor, M. 1967-69. "Repas cultuels esséniens et thérapeutes, thiases et haburoth", *Revue de Qumran* 6, 401-25.
Deonna, W. & Renard, M. 1961. *Croyances et superstitions de table dans la Rome antique*, Brussels.
Detienne, M. 1981. "Culinary Practices and the Spirit of Sacrifice", in: *The Cuisine of Sacrifice among the Greeks*, eds. M. Detienne & J.-P. Vernant, Berkeley, 1-20.
DeVault, M.L. 1991. *Feeding the Family. The Social Organization of Caring as Gendered Work*, Chicago.
Dionisotti, A.C. 1982. "From Ausonius' Schooldays? A Schoolbook and its Relatives", *Journal of Roman Studies* 72, 83-125.
Dix, G. 1968. *The Treatise on the Apostolic Tradition of St. Hippolytus of Rome* (revised ed.), London.
Dixon, S. 1992. *The Roman Family*, Baltimore and London.
Dobschütz, E. von 1902. *Die Urchristlichen Gemeinden. Sittengeschichtlichen Bilder*, Leipzig.
Domus Aurea 1995, AAVV, "Domus Aurea". In: *LTUR*, vol. 2, Rome, 49-64.

Douglas, M. 1966. *Purity and Danger. An analysis of concepts of pollution and taboo*, London.
Douglas, M. 1971. "Deciphering a Meal", in: *Myth, Symbol, and Culture*, ed. C. Geertz, New York.
Douglas, M. 1974. *Natural Symbols*, London.
Douglas, M. 1975. "Deciphering a Meal", in M. Douglas, *Implicit Meanings: Essays in Anthropology*, London and Boston, Henley, 249-75.
Douglas, M. 1982. "Food as a System of Communication", in M. Douglas, *In the Active Voice*, London, Boston, Henley, 82-124.
Douglas, M. 1984. "Standard Social Uses of Food", in: *Food in the Social Order*, ed. M. Douglas, New York, 1-39.
Dreliossi-Herakleidou, A. 1996. "Späthellenistische palastartige Gebäude in der Nähe der Akropolis von Rhodos", in: *Basileia. Die Paläste der hellenistischen Könige*", eds. W. Hoepfner & G. Brands, Mainz, 182-92.
Ducrey, P., Metzger, I. & Reber, K. 1993. *Eretria*, vol. 8, *Le Quartier de la Maison aux mosaïques*, Lausanne.
Dumont, J. 1976-77. "La pêche du thon à Byzance à l'époque Hellénistique", *Revue des études anciennes* 78-79, 96-120.
Dumont, J. 1977. "Liberté des mers et territoire de pêche en droit grec", *Revue historique de droit français et étranger* 1, 53-57.
Dunbabin, K.M.D. 1991. "*Triclinium* and *Stibadium*", in: *Dining in a Classical Context*, ed. W.J. Slater, Ann Arbor, 121-48.
Dunbabin, K.M.D. 1993. "Wine and Water at the Roman *Convivium*", *Journal of Roman Archaeology* 6, 116-42.
Dunbabin, K.M.D. 1995. "Scenes from the Roman *Convivium*: Frigida non derit, non derit calda petenti (Martial XIV.105)", in: *In Vino Veritas*, eds. O. Murray & M. Tecuşan, Rome and London, 252-65.
Dunbabin, K. 1996. "Convivial Spaces: Dining and Entertainment in the Roman Villa", *Journal of Roman Archaeology* 9, 66-80.
Duncan-Jones, R. 1990. *Structure and Scale in the Roman Economy*, Cambridge.
Duncan-Jones, R. 1994. *Money and Government in the Roman Empire*, Cambridge.
Dupont-Sommer, A. 1959. *Les écrits esséniens découverts près de la Mer Morte*, Paris.
Duval, N. 1984. "Les Maisons d'Apamée et l'architecture 'palatiale' de l'Antiquité tardive", in: *Actes du Colloque Apamée de Syrie. Aspects de l'Architecture domestique d'Apamée, Brussels 1980*, ed. J. Balty, Brussels, 457-64.
Edmondson, J.C. 1987. *Two Industries in Roman Lusitania* (BAR, Int. ser. vol. 362), Oxford.
Elias, N. 1978. *The History of Manners. The Civilizing Process*, vol. 1, New York.

Elsner, J. 1995. *Art and the Roman Viewer: The Transformation of Art from the Pagan World to Christianity*, Cambridge.

Engberg-Pedersen, T. 1991. "Proclaiming the Lord's Death: 1 Corinthians 11:17-34 and the Forms of Paul's Theological Argument", *Society of Biblical Literature Seminar Papers* series 30, Atlanta, 592-617.

Engelmann, H., Knibbe, D. & Hüber F. 1989. "Das Zollgesetz der Provinz Asia", *Epigraphica anatolica. Zeitschrift für Epigraphik und historische Geographie Anatoliens* 14, 1-206.

Essler, P. 1994. *The First Christians in their Social World: Social Scientific Approaches to New Testament Interpretation*, London.

Étienne, R. 1970. "A propos du 'garum sociorum'", *Latomus* 29.1, 297-313.

Étienne, R., Makaroun, Y. & Mayet, F. 1994. *Un grand complexe industrielle à Tróia*, Paris.

Faye, E. de 1906. *Clément d'Alexandrie: Etude sur les rapports du Christianisme et de la philosophie grecque au IIe siècle*, Paris.

Feeley-Harnik, G. 1981. *The Lord's Table. Eucharist and Passover in Early Christianity*, Philadelphia.

Ferdière, A. 1988. *Les Campagnes en Gaule Romaine*, vols. 1-2, Paris.

Fernández Gómez, F. 1991. "Nuevos fragmentos de leyes municipales y octros bronces epigarficos de la Betica", *Zeitschrift für Papyrologie und Epigraphik* 86, 121-36.

Finsen, H. 1969. *La residence de Domitian sur le Palatin* (Analecta romana Instituti danici, Suppl. vol. 5), Copenhagen.

Franceschini, M. De 1991. *Villa Adriana. Mosaici – pavimenti – Edifici*, Rome.

Frey, J.B. 1936. *Corpus inscriptionum judaicarum*, vol. 1, Vatican City.

Gabelmann, H. 1985. "Römische Kinder in Toga Praetexta", *Jahrbuch des Deutschen Archäologischen Instituts* 100, 497-541.

Gärtner, B. 1965. *The Temple and the Community in Qumran and the New Testament*, Cambridge.

Garland, R. 1985. *The Greek Way of Death*, London.

Gauthier, Ph. 1980. "Études sur des inscriptions d'Amorgos", *Bulletin de correspondance hellénique* 104, 197-20.

Gennep, A. van 1960, *The Rites of Passage* (translation M. Vizedom & G.L. Caffee), London.

Giannouli, V. & Guimier-Sorbets, A.-M. 1988. "Deux mosaïques hellénistiques à Samos", *Bulletin de correspondance hellénique* 112, 545-68.

Giangrotta, P.A. 1983. "Indagine archeologica e lo scavo – Baia", In: *Il ninfeo imperiale sommerso di Punta Epitaffio*, Napoli, 25-39.

Gibson, S, DeLaine, J. & Claridge, A. 1994. "The *Triclinium* of the Domus Flavia: A new reconstruction", *Papers of the British School at Rome* n.s. 99, 67-97.

Ginouvès, R. 1977. "La mosaïque de Délos", *Revue archéologique*, 99-107.

Gnilka, J. 1961. "Das Gemeinschaftsmahl der Essener", *Biblische Zeitschrift* 3, 39-55.

Goette, H.R. 1986. "Die Bulla", *Bonner Jahrbücher des Rheinischen Landesmuseums in Bonn und des Vereins von Altertumsfreunden im Rheinlande* 186, 133-64.

Goldman, N. 1994. "Reconstructing Roman Clothing", in: *The World of Roman Costume*, eds. J.L. Sebasta & L. Bonfante, Madison and London, 213-37.

Goodenough, E.R. 1964. *Jewish Symbols in the Graeco-Roman Period*, vols. 9-11, New York.

Goody, J. 1982. *Cooking, Cuisine and Class*, Cambridge.

Gowers, E. 1993. *The Loaded Table: Representations of Food in Roman Literature*, Oxford.

Haley, E.W. 1990. "The Fish Sauce Trader L. Junius Puteolanus", *Zeitschrift für Papyrologie und Epigraphik* 80, 72-78.

Hands, A.R. 1967. *Charities and Social Aid in Greece and Rome*, New York.

Harmon, D.P. 1978. "The Family Festivals of Rome", *Aufstieg und Niedergang der römischen Welt: Geschichte und Kultur Roms im Spiegel der neueren Forschung* 2.16.2., 1592-1603.

Harvey, R.A. 1981. *A Commentary on Persius*, Leiden.

Heermann, V. 1986. *Studien zur Makedonischen Palastarchitektur*, Berlin.

Hellström, P. 1989. "Formal Banqueting at Labraunda", in: *Architecture and Society in Hecatomnid Caria*, Boreas 17, 99-104.

Hellström, P. 1990. "Hellenistic Architecture in Light of Late Classical Labraunda", in *Akten des XIII. Internationalen Kongresses für klassische Archäologie, Berlin 1988*, Mainz, 243-52.

Hellström, P. 1996. "The Andrones at Labraunda. Dining Halls of Protohellenistic Kings", in: *Basileia. Die Paläste der hellenistischen Könige*, eds. W. Hoepfner & G. Brands, Mainz, 164-69.

Heskel, J. 1994. "Cicero as Evidence for Attitudes to Dress in The Late Republic", in: *The World of Roman Costume*, eds. J.L. Sebasta & L. Bonfante, Madison and London, 133-45.

Hirschfeld, O. 1905. *Die kaiserlichen Verwaltungsbeamten bis auf Diocletian* (2nd ed.), Berlin.

Hoepfner, W. 1996. "Zum Typus der Basileia und der königlichen Androines", in: *Basileia. Die Paläste der hellenistischen Könige*, eds. W. Hoepfner & G. Brands, Mainz, 1-43.

Hoepfner, W. & Schwandner, E.-L. 1994. *Haus und Stadt im klassischen Griechenland* (Wohnen in der klassischen Polis, vol. 1, new ed.), Munich.

Höppener, H. 1931. *Halieutica. Bijdrage tot de Kennis der oud-griekse Visscherij*, Amsterdam.

Holmberg, Bengt 1995. "Paul and Commensality", in: *Texts and Contexts*.

Biblical Texts in their Textual and Situational Contexts. Essays in Honor of Lars Hartman, eds. Tord Fornberg & David Hellholm, Oslo, 767-80.

Hopkins, K. 1983. *Death and Renewal: Sociological Studies in Roman History*, Cambridge.

Horbury, W. 1991. "Herod's Temple and 'Herod's days'", in: *Templum amicitiae*, ed. W. Horbury, Sheffield, 103-49.

Hudson, N.A. 1989. "Food in Roman Satire", in: *Satire and Society in Ancient Rome*, ed. S.H. Braund, Exeter, 69-87.

Humphrey, S.G. 1993. *The Family, Women and Death*, Michigan.

Husson, G. 1983. *OIKIA. Le vocabulaire de la maison privée en Égypte d'après les papyrus grecs*, Paris.

JAAR 1995. Thematic Issue on "Religion and Food", *JAAR* 43.

Jacobi, I. 1995, "Domus Augustus (Palatium)", in: *LTUR*, vol. 2, Rome, 46-48.

Jacobsen, G. 1995. *Primitiver Austausch oder freier Markt* (*Pharos*, vol. 5), St. Katharinen.

Jeremias, J. 1966. *The Eucharistic Words of Jesus*, London.

Jobst, W. 1977. *Römische Mosaiken aus Ephesos*, vol. 1, *Die Hanghäuser des Embolos* (FiE VIII/2), Vienna.

Johnson, J. 1935. *Excavations at Minturnae*, vol. 1, Philadelphia.

Jolowitz, J.H. & Nicholas, B. 1972. *Historical Introduction to the Study of Roman Law* (3rd ed.), Cambridge.

Jones, B. & Mattingly, D. 1990. *An Atlas of Roman Britain*, Cambridge.

Jones, C.P. 1971. *Plutarch and Rome*, Oxford.

Jones, C.P. 1991. "Dinner Theater", in: *Dining in a Classical Context*, ed. W.J. Slater, Ann Arbor, 185-98.

Judge, E.A. 1960. *The Social Pattern of Christian Groups in the First Century*, London.

Käsemann, E. 1960. "Anliegen und Eigenart der paulinischen Abendmahlslehre", in: *Exegetische Versuche und Besinnungen*, vol. 1, Göttingen, 11-34.

Kaser, M. 1972. *Das römische Privatrecht. Handbuch der Altertumswissenschaft*, Munich.

Kawerau, G & Wiegand, Th. 1930. *Die Paläste der Hochburg* (Altertümer von Pergamon, vol. 5.1), Berlin.

Klauck, H.J. 1982. *Herrenmahl und hellenistischer Kult. Eine religionsgeschichtliche Untersuchung zum ersten Korintherbrief*, Münster.

Klinzing, G. 1971. *Die Umdeutung des Kultes in der Qumrangemeinde und im Neuen Testament*, Göttingen.

Kniep, F. 1896. *Societas Publicanorum*, Jena.

Koch, G. 1988. *Roman Funerary Sculpture*, Malibu.

Kraabel, A.T. 1979. "The Diaspora Synagogue: Archaeological and Epigraphic Evidence since Sukenik", *Aufstieg und Niedergang der römischen Welt: Geschichte und Kultur Roms im Spiegel der neueren Forschung* 2.19.1, 488-510.

Kraabel, A.T. 1981a. "The Disappearance of the Godfearers", *Numen: international review for the history of religions* 28, 113-26
Kraabel, A.T. 1981b. "The Social Systems of Six Diaspora Synagogues", in *Ancient Synagogues: The State of Research*, ed. J. Gutmann, Atlanta, 71-81.
Kraabel, A.T. 1992. "The Disappearance of the Godfearers", in: *Diaspora Jews and Judaism: Essays in Honor of, and in Dialogue with, A. Thomas Kraabel*, eds. J. Andrew Overman & Robert S. MacLennan, Atlanta, 119-236.
Kraeling, C.H. 1956. *The Synagogue. The Excavations of Dura-Europos. Final Report*, vol. 8.1, New Haven.
Kraeling, C.H. 1964. *The Christian Building. The Excavations at Dura-Europos. Final Report*, vol. 8.2, New Haven.
Krause, C. 1995. "Wo residierten die Flavier? Überlegungen zur flavischen Bautätigkeit auf dem Platin", in: *Aculiana*. Recuil d'hommages offerts à H. Bögli, Avenches, 459-68.
Kuss, O. 1971. *Paulus. Die Rolle des Apostels in der theologischen Entwiklung der Urkirche*, Regensburg.
La Rocca, E. 1986. "Il lusso come espressione di potere", in: *Le tranquille dimore degli dei*, eds. M. Cima, & La Rocca, E., Venice, 3-35.
Laet, S.J. de 1949. *Portorium. Étude sur l'organisation douanière chez les Romains*, Bruges.
Lampe, P. 1991. "Das korinthische Herrenmahl im Schnittpunkt hellenistisch-römischer Mahlpraxis und paulinischer Theologia Crucis (1 Kor 11,17-34)", *Zeitschrift für die Neutestamentliche Wissenschaft und die Kunde der älteren Kirche* 82, 183-213.
Lassère, J-M. 1977, *Ubique Populus*, Paris.
Lauter, H. 1971. "Ptolemais in Libyen. Ein Beitrag zur Baukunst Alexandrias", *Jahrbuch des Deutschen Archäologischen Instituts* 86, 149-78.
Lauter-Bufe, H. 1987. *Die Geschichte des sikeliotisch-korinthischen Kapitells*, Mainz.
Lavin, I. 1962. "The house of the Lord. Aspects of the Role of Palace *Triclinia* in the Architecture of Late Antiquity and the Early Middle Ages", *The Art Bulletin* 44, 1-27.
Le Bonniec, H. 1958. *Le culte de Cérès à Rome, des origines à la fin de la république*, Paris.
Lehner, H. 1930. "Römischer Steindenkmäler von der Bonner Münsterkirsche", *Bonner Jahrbücher des Rheinischen Landesmuseums in Bonn und des Vereins von Altertumsfreunden im Rheinlande* 135 (= Nesselhauf, H. *Bericht der römisch-germanischen Kommission* 1937 (1939)).
Lembke, K. 1994. *Das Iseum Campense in Rom. Studie über dem Isiskult unter Domitian* (Archäologie und Geschichte, vol. 3), Heidelberg.
Leveau, P. 1984. *Caesarea de Maurétanie. Une ville Romaine et ses campagnes*, Rome.

Levi, D. 1947. *Antioch Mosaic Pavements*, Princeton.
Levine, L.I. 1979. "The Jewish Patriarch (Nasi) in Third Century Palestine", *Aufstieg und Niedergang der römischen Welt: Geschichte und Kultur Roms im Spiegel der neueren Forschung* 2.19.2, 649-88.
Lewis, D.M. 1987. "The King's Dinner (Polyaenus 4.3.32)", in: *Achaemenid History*, vol. 2, Leiden, 79-87.
Leyerle, B. 1995. "Clement of Alexandria on the Importance of Table Etiquette", *Journal of Early Christian Studies* 3, 123-41.
Lietzmann, H. 1949. *An die Korinther. Handbuch zum Neuen Testament* 9, Tübingen.
Lietzmann, H. 1972. *Mass and Lord's Supper*, Leiden.
Lindsay, H.M. 1993. *Suetonius, Caligula*, Bristol.
Lindsay, H.M. 1995. *Suetonius, Tiberius*, Bristol.
Lindsay, H.M. 1996. "The Romans and Ancestor Worship", in: *Religion in the Ancient World: New Themes and Approaches*, Amsterdam.
Ling, R. 1995. "The Decoration of Roman *Triclinia*", in: *In Vino Veritas*, eds. O. Murray & M. Tecuşan, London, 239-51.
Littlewood, A.R. 1987. "Ancient Literary Evidence for the Pleasure Gardens of Roman Country Villas", in: *Ancient Roman Villa Gardens*, ed. E. Blair Macdougall, Washington, D.C., 9-30.
Lohse, E. (ed.) 1964. *Die Texte aus Qumran. Hebräisch und deutsch, mit masoretischer Punktuation, Übersetzung, Einführung und Anmerkungen*, Darmstadt.
Lutz, C. 1947. "Musonius Rufus 'The Roman Socrates'", *Yale Classical Studies* 10, 3-147.
Maas, M. 1992. *John Lydus and the Roman Past*, London.
McCartney, E. 1934. "The Couch as a Unit of Measurement", *Classical Philology* 29, 30-5.
McDaniel, W.B. 1925. "Roman Dinner-Garments", *Classical Philology* 20, 268-70.
McKenzie, J. 1990. *The Architecture of Petra*, Oxford.
Malherbe, A.J. 1983. *Social Aspects of Early Christianity* (2nd ed.), Philadelphia.
Marquardt, J. 1876. *Römische Staatsverwaltung*, vols. 1-2, Leipzig.
Marquardt, J. 1886. *Das Privatleben der Römer* (4th ed. rev. A. Mau), Leipzig.
Marrou, H.-I. 1957, "Humanisme et Christianisme chez Clément d'Alexandrie d'après le 'Pédagogue'", in: *Recherches sur la tradition platonicienne. Entretiens sur l'antiquité classique*, vol. 3, Verona, 183-200.
Marrou, H.-I. & Hart, M. 1960, *Clément d'Alexandrie, Le Pédagogue*, vol. 1, Paris.
Martin J. 1931. *Symposion: Die Geschichte einer literarischen Form*, Paderborn.
Martin-Kilcher, S. 1990, "Fischsaucen und Fischkonserven aus dem

römischen Gallien", *Archäologie der Schweiz: Mitteilungsblatt der Schweizerischen Gesellschafft für Ur- und Frühgeschichte* 13.1, 37-44.

Martínez, F.G. 1994. *The Dead Sea Scrolls Translated. The Qumran Texts in English*, Leiden.

Mau, A. 1885. *BdI* 69-70.

Mau, A. 1901. "Convivium", *RE* IV, cols. 1201-8.

Meeks, Wayne A. 1981 & Wilken, R.L. 1981. *Jews and Christians in Antioch*, Chico.

Meeks, Wayne A. 1983, *The First Urban Christians: The Social World of Paul*, New Haven.

Meiggs, R. 1982. *Trees and Timber in the Ancient Mediterranean World*, Oxford.

Meyboom, P.G.P. 1995. *The Nile Mosaic of Palestrina* (Religions in the Graeco-Roman World, vol. 121), Leiden.

Millar, F. 1992. "The Jews of the Graeco-Roman Diaspora between Paganism and Christianity", in: *The Jews among Pagans and Christians*, eds. J. Lieu, J. North & T. Rajak, London, 97-123.

Miller, S.G. 1972. "A Mosaic Floor from a Roman Villa at Anaploga", *Hesperia: Journal of the American School of Classical Studies at Athens* 41, 332-54.

Miller, S. 1978. *The Prytaneion*, Berkeley.

Mitchell, T. 1986. Cicero, *Verrines* 2.1 (translation and commentary), Warminster.

Murphy-O'Connor, B.J. 1983. *St. Paul's Corinth*, Wilmington, Delaware.

Murray, O. (ed.) 1990. *Sympotica. A Symposium on the Symposion*, Oxford.

Musurillo, H. 1972. *The Acts of the Christian Martyrs*, Oxford.

Maas, M. 1992. *John Lydus and the Roman Past*, London.

Nenquin, J. 1961. *Salt. A Study in Economic Prehistory*, Brugge.

Nesselhauf, H. 1937. *Bericht der römisch-germanischen Kommission des Deutchen Archäologischen Institut*.

Netzer, E. 1990. "Architecture in Palaestina Prior to and During the Days of Herod the Great", in: *Akten des XIII Internationalen Kongresses für klassische Archäologie Berlin 1988*, Mainz, 37-50.

Netzer, E. 1991. *Masada III. The Buildings. Stratigraphy and Architecture. The Yigael Yadin Excavations 1963-65. Final Reports*, Jerusalem.

Netzer, E. 1996. "The Hasmonean Palaces in Palestine", in: *Basileia. Die Paläste der hellenistischen Könige*, eds. W. Hoepfner & G. Brands, Mainz, 203-8.

Netzer, E. & Weiss, Z. 1994. *Zippori*, Jerusalem.

Neuenzeit, P. 1960. *Das Herrenmahl. Studien zur Paulinischen Eucharistieauffassung*, Munich.

Nicolet, C. 1976. *L'ordre equestre à l'époque républicaine*, Paris.

Nielsen, I. 1994a. "The Hellenistic Palaces of the Jewish Kings", in: *In the Last*

Days. On Jewish and Christian Apocalyptic and its Period, eds. K. Jeppesen, K. Nielsen & B. Rosendal, Aarhus.

Nielsen, I. 1994b. *Hellenistic Palaces. Tradition and Renewal* (Studies in Hellenistic Civilisation, vol. 5), Aarhus.

Nowicka, M. 1969. *La Maison privée dans l'Égypte ptolémaique*, Wroclaw.

Noy, D. 1995. *Jewish Inscriptions of Western Europe*, vol. 2, Cambridge.

Ørsted, P. 1994. "From Henchir Mettich to the Albertini tablets", in: *Landuse in the Roman Empire*, Eds. J. Carlsen, J.E. Skydsgaard, & P. Ørsted (Analecta romana Instituti danici, Suppl. vol. 22), Rome, 115-27.

Ørsted, P. 1985. *Roman Imperial Economy and Romanization*, Copenhagen.

Orr, D.G. 1978. "Roman Domestic Religion: The Evidence of Household Shrines", *Aufstieg und Niedergang der römischen Welt: Geschichte und Kultur im Spiegel der neueren Forschung* 2.16.2., 1559-91

Orr, W.F. & Walther, J.A. 1976. *I Corinthians*. The Anchor Bible, vol. 32, New York.

Osiek, C. & Balch D.L. 1997. *Families in the New Testament World: Households and House Churches*, Louisville, Ky.

Overbeck, J. 1884. *Pompeji in seinen Gebäuden, Althertümern und Kunstwerken* Leipzig.

Parker, J.A. 1992. *Ancient Shipwrecks of the Mediterranean and the Roman Provinces* (BAR, int. ser. vol. 580), Oxford.

Parkin, T.G. 1992. *Demography and Roman Society*, Oxford.

Parkin, T.G. 1994. Review of Bradley (1991a), Dixon (1992) et al., *Journal of Roman Studies* 84, 178-85.

Patte, D. 1983. *Paul's Faith and the Power of the Gospel. A Structural Introduction to the Pauline Letters*, Philadelphia.

Perkins, A. 1973. *The Art of Dura-Europos*, Oxford.

Pesce, G. 1950. *Il "Palazzo delle Colonne" in Tolemaide di Cirenaica*, Rome.

Picard, C. 1921. *L'établissement des Poseidoniastes de Berytos*, (Exploration Archéologique de Délos, vol. 6), Paris.

Ploeg, J. van der 1957. "The Meals of the Essenes", *Journal of Semitic Studies* 2, 163-75.

Ponsich, M. & Tarradell, M. 1965. *Garum et industries antiques de salaison dans la Méditerranée Occidentale*, Paris.

Pozzi, E., Boriello, M.R. et al. 1986. *Le Collezioni del Museo Nazionale di Napoli. I mosaici, le pitture, gli oggetti di uso quotidiano, gli argenti, le terrecotte invetriate, i vetri, i cristalli, gli avori*, Rome

Prévost, M.-H. 1949. *Les Adoptions politiques à Rome sous la République et le Principat*, Paris.

Prieur, J. 1984. *La mort dans l'antiquité romaine*, Rennes.

Purcell, N. 1995. "The Roman *Villa* and the Landscape of Production", in: *Urban Society in Roman Italy*, eds. T.J. Cornell & K. Lomas, London 151-79.

Rackham, H. 1969. *Pliny: "Natural History" in Ten Volumes*, vol. 2, London-Cambridge, Mass. (1942).

Radt, W. 1988. *Pergamon. Geschichte und Bauten. Funde und Erforschung einer antiken Metropole*, Köln.

Raeder, J. 1988. "Vitruv, *de architectura* VI 7 (*aedificia Graecorum*) und die hellenistische Wohnhaus- und Palastarchitektur", *Gymnasium: Zeitschrift für Kultur der Antike und humanistische Bildung* 95, 316-68.

Rajak, T. 1994. "Ciò che Giuseppe vide: Josephus and the Essenes", in: *Josephus and the History of the Greco-Roman Period. Essays in Memory of Morton Smith*, eds. F. Parente & J. Sievers, Leiden, 141-60.

Rakob, F. 1987. "Ambivalente Apsiden — Zur Zeichensprache der römischen Architektur", *Mitteilung des Deutschen Archäologischen Instituts, Römische Abteilung* 94, 1-28.

Rathje, A. 1995. "Il banchetto in Italia centrale: quale stile di vita?", in: *In Vino Veritas*, eds. O. Murray & M. Tecuşan, Rome, 167-75.

Rauh, N. 1993. *The Sacred Bonds of Commerce. Religion, Economy, and Trade Society at Hellenistic Roman Delos, 166-87 BC*, Amsterdam.

Rawson, E. 1987. "*Discrimina Ordinum*: The *Lex Julia Theatralis*", *Papers of the British School at Rome* 55, 83-114 (= *Roman Culture and Society* (Oxford 1991), 508-45).

Reynolds, J. & Tannenbaum, R. 1987. *Jews and Godfearers at Aphrodisias: Greek Inscriptions with Commentary*, Cambridge.

Richardson, P. 1996. "Early Synagogues as Collegia in the Diaspora and Palestine", in: *Voluntary Associations in the Graeco-Roman World*, eds. J. Kloppenborg & S.G. Wilson, London, 90-109.

Richardson, P. & Heuchan, V. 1996. "Jewish Voluntary Associations in Egypt and the Roles of Women", in: *Voluntary Associations in the Graeco-Roman World*, eds. J. Kloppenborg & S.G. Wilson, London, 226-51.

Richter, G.M.A. 1966. *The Furniture of the Greeks, Etruscans and Romans*, London.

Rickman, G. 1980. *The Corn Supply of Ancient Rome*, Oxford.

Robert, L. 1960. "Recueil d'épigraphie de numismatique et d'antiquité grecques", *Hellenika* 11-12, especially 21-53. ("Pêcheurs de Corinthe", 42-53).

Rops, D. 1962. *Daily Life in Palestine at the Time of Christ* (translation P. O'Brien), London.

Rossiter, J. 1991. "*Convivium* and Villa in Late Antiquity", in: *Dining in a Classical Context*, ed. J.W. Slater, Ann Arbor, 199-214.

Rostovtzeff, M. 1902. *Geschichte der Staatspacht in der römischen Kaiserzeit* (Philologus: Zeitschrift für das klassische Philologie, Suppl. vol. 9), Leipzig.

Rutgers, L.V. 1992. "Archaeological Evidence for Interaction of Jews and Non-Jews in Late Antiquity", *American Journal of Archaeology* 96, 101-18.

Saddington, D.B. 1988. "*Praefecti classis, orae maritimae* and *ripae* of the second triumvirate and the Early Empire", *Jahrbuch des römisch-germanischen Zentralmuseums*, 35, 299-313.

Safrai, S. 1976. "Home and Family", in: *The Jewish People in the First Century*, vol. 2, eds. S. Safrai & M. Stern, Assen, 728-92; "Religion and Everyday Life", ibid., 793-833.

Saller, R.P. & Shaw, B.D. 1984. "Tombstones and Roman Family Relations in the Principate: Civilians, Soldiers and Slaves", *Journal of Roman Studies* 74, 124-56.

Saller, R.P. 1994. *Patriarchy, Property and Death in the Roman Family*, Cambridge.

Salza Prina Ricotti, E. 1983. *L'arte del convito nella Roma antica*, Rome.

Salza Prina Ricotti, E. 1987 "The Importance of Water in Roman Garden *Triclinia*", in: *Ancient Roman Villa Gardens*, ed. E.B. Macdougal, Washington, D.C., 137-84.

Salza Prina Ricotti, E. 1988-89. "Le tende conviviali e la tenda di Tolomeo Filadelfo", in: *Studia Pompeiana et Classica in honor of Wilhelmina F. Jashemski*, vol. 2, ed. R. Curtis, New Rochelle, 199-239.

Sanders, E.P. 1992. *Judaism: Practice and Belief*, London.

Sanquer, R., Galliou, P. 1972. "Garum, sel, et salaisons en Armorique Gallo-Romaine", *Gallia* 30.1, 200-23.

Sanquer, R. 1973. "L'inscription à Neptune", *Annales de Bretagne et des Pays de l'Ouest* 80, 215-36.

Schama, S. 1987. *The Embarrassment of Riches: An Interpretation of Dutch Culture in the Golden Age*, London.

Scherrer, P. 1985. "Zur Lage der Statio Esc(ensis) in Noricum", in: *Lebendige Altertumswissenschaft*. Festschrift Hermann Vetters, Wien.

Schiffman, L.H. 1979-81. "Communal Meals at Qumran", *Revue de Qumran* 25, 45-56.

Schürer, E. 1979. *The History of the Jewish People in the Age of Jesus Christ (175 BC-AD 135)* (New English Version Revised by Geza Vermes, Fergus Millar & Matthew Black), Edinburgh.

Schürmann, H. 1970. "Die Gestalt der urchristlichen Eucharistie-feier", in: *Ursprung und Gestalt. Erörterungen und Besinnungen zum Neuen Testament*, Düsseldorf, 87-90.

Sciallano, M. 1987. "Une collection de plombs Romains trouvés à Fos-sur-Mer", *Archaeonautica* 7, 193-203.

Sheppard, A.R.R. 1980-81. "Pagan Cults of Angels in Roman Asia Minor", *Talanta: Proceedings of the Dutch Archaeological and Historical Society* 12-13, 81-102.

Sigismund Nielsen, H. 1987. "*Alumnus*, a Term of Relation Denoting Quasi-Adoption", *Classica et Mediaevalia* 38, 141-88.

Sigismund Nielsen, H. 1996. "The Physical Context of Roman Epitaphs and the Structure of 'The Roman family'", *Analecta romana Instituti danici* 23, 35-60.

Sigismund Nielsen, H. forthcoming. *Roman family, the evidence of the epitaphs*.

Slater, W.J. (ed.) 1991. *Dining in a Classical Context*, Ann Arbor.

Smith, D.E. 1980. Social Obligation in the Context of Communal Meal. A Study of the Christian Meal in 1 Corinthians in Comparison with Greco-Roman Communal Meals, Diss., Harvard.

Smith, D.E. & Taussig, H.E. 1990. *Many Tables: The Eucharist in the New Testament and Liturgy Today*, Philadelphia.

Smith, Dennis E. forthcoming. *From Symposium to Eucharist*, Minneapolis.

Soden, H. von 1963. "Sakrament und Etik bei Paulus", in: *Urchristentum und Geschichte*, Munich 138-76.

Sodini, J-P. 1984. "L'habitat urbain en Grèce à le veille des invasions", in: *Villes et peuplement dans l'Illyricum protobyzantin. Actes du colloque organisé par l'École française de Rome, 1982* (CEFR, vol. 77), Rome, 375-83.

Sotgiu, G. 1961. *Iscrizioni latine della Sardegna*, Padova.

Spinazzola, V. 1953. *Pompei alla luce degli Scavi Nuovi della Via dell'Abbondanza*, vols. 1-2, Rome.

Stegemann, H. 1993. *Die Essener, Qumran, Johannes der Täufer und Jesus*, Freiburg.

Stein, S. 1957. "The Influence of Symposia Literature on the literary Form of the Pesach Haggadah", *Journal of Jewish Studies* 8, 13-44.

Steinby, M. 1987. "La necropoli della Via Triumphalis", in: *Römische Gräberstrassen, Selbstdarstellung – Status – Standard*, eds. H. von Hesberg & P. Zanker, 85-110.

Stern, M. 1976. *Greek and Latin Authors on Jews and Judaism*, vol. 1, Jerusalem.

Stevenson, J. 1978. *The Catacombs*, London.

Stillwell, R. 1961. "Houses of Antioch", *Dumbarton Oaks Papers* 15, 47-57.

Stöckle 1924. Art. "Fischereigewerbe", *RE*, Suppl. vol. 4, cols. 456-62.

Stone, L. 1981. *The Past and the Present Revisited*, London and New York.

Stoops, R. 1986. "Patronage in the *Acts of Peter*", in *The Apocryphal Acts of Apostles*, ed. D. McDonald (*Semeia* 38), Atlanta 91-100.

Stoops, R. 1991. "Christ as Patron in the *Acts of Peter*", in *Social Networks in the Early Christian Environment*, ed. L.M. White (*Semeia* 56), Atlanta, 143-57.

Stuart, P. & Bogears, J.E. 1971. "Catalogus van de monumenten", in: *Deae Nehalenniae, Rijksmuseum van Oudheiden*, Leiden.

Studniczka, F. 1914. Das Symposium Ptolemaios II (*Abhandlungen der Sächsischen Akademie der Wissenschaften zu Leipzig*, vol. 30.2), Leipzig.

Stuhlmacher, P. 1988. *Jesus von Nazareth – Christus des Glaubens*, Stuttgart.
Tamm, B. 1963. *Auditorium and Palatium*, Stockholm.
Tcherikover, V., Fuks, A. & Stern, M. 1957-64. *Corpus papyrorum judaicarum*, vols. 1-3, Cambridge, Mass.
Thackeray, H.St.J, Marcus R. & Feldman, L.H. *et al.* 1926-69. Josephus (LCL), London and Cambridge, Mass.
Theissen, G. 1979a. "Soziale Schichtung in der korinthischen Gemeinde. Ein Beitrag zur Sociologie des hellenistischen Urchristentums", in: *Studien zur Soziologie des Urchristentums*, Tübingen, 231-71.
Theissen, G. 1979b." Soziale Integration und sakramentales Handeln. Eine Analyse von 1 Cor 11:17-34", in: *Studien zur Soziologie des Urchristentums*, Tübingen, 290-317.
Theissen, G. 1982a. "Social Integration and Sacramental Activity: An Analysis of 1 Cor 11:17-34," in *Social Setting of Pauline Christianity: Essays on Corinth*, Philadelphia, 148-75.
Theissen, G. 1982b. "The Strong and the Weak in Corinth", in: *The Social Setting of Pauline Christianity: Essays on Corinth*, Philadelphia, 121-44.
Thoen, H. 1978. *De belgische Kustvlakte in de romeinse Tijd*, Brussel.
Thoen, H. 1981. "The Third Century Roman Occupation in Belgium: the Evidence of the Coastal Plain" (BAR, Int. ser. vol. 109), Oxford, 245-57.
Thompson, E. Stuart 1988. "Death, Food and Fertility", in: *Death Ritual in Late Imperial and Modern China*, eds. J.L. Watson & E.S Rawski, Berkeley and Los Angeles.
Thylander, H. 1952. *Inscriptions du port d'Ostie* (Opuscula Romana: Acta Instituti Romani Regni Sueciae, vols. 1-2), Lund.
Toynbee, J.M.C. 1964. *Art in Britain under the Romans*, Oxford.
Toynbee, J.M.C. 1971. *Death and Burial in the Roman World*, London.
Traina, G. 1992. "Sale e saline nel Mediterraneo antico", *La parola del passato* vol. 47.5, 363-79.
Trillmich, W., et al. 1933. *Hispania Antiqua. Denkmäler der Römerzeit*, Mainz.
Tufi, S.R. 1983. *Corpus Signorum Imperii Romani*, vol. 1.3, Oxford.
VanderKam, J.C. 1994. *The Dead Sea Scrolls Today*, Grand Rapids, Mich.
Vaux, R. de 1973. *Archeology and the Dead Sea Scrolls*, London.
Vermes, G. 1960. "Essenes – Therapeutai – Qumran", *Durham University Journal* 52, 97-115.
Vermes, G. 1994. *The Dead Sea Scrolls. Qumran in Perspective* (3rd ed.), London.
Vermes, G. 1995. *The Dead Sea Scrolls in English* (4th ed.), London.
Vermes, G. & Goodman, M.D. (eds.) 1989. *The Essenes According to the Classical Sources*, Sheffield.
Vernant, J.-P. 1982. "La belle mort et le cadavre outragé", in: *La mort, les morts dans les societés anciennes*, eds. G. Gnoli & J.-P. Vernant, Cambridge.

Visser, M. 1991. *The Rituals of Dinner: The Origins, Evolution, Eccentricities and Meaning of Table Manners*, Toronto.

Väänänen, V. 1973. *La necropoli dell'autoparco vaticano* (Acta Instituti romani Finlandiae, vol. 6), Rome.

Waell, F.J. de 1961. *Corinthe et St. Paul*, Paris.

Watson, J.L. 1988. "Funeral Specialists in Cantonese Society: Pollution, Performance, and Social Hierarchy", in: *Death Ritual in Late Imperial and Modern China*, eds. J.L. Watson & E.S Rawski, Berkeley and Los Angeles.

Weinfeld, M. 1992. "Grace After Meals in Qumran", *Journal of Biblical Studies* 111, 427-40.

Weiss, J. 1910. *Der erste Korintherbrief* (Kritisch-exegetischer Kommentar über das Neue Testament, vol. 5), Göttingen.

Weiss, J. 1917. *Das Urchristentum*, Göttingen.

White, L.M. 1987. "The Delos Synagogue Revisited: Recent Fieldwork in the Graeco-Roman Diaspora", *Harvard Theological Studies* 80, 133-66.

White, L.M. 1996. *The Social Origins of Christian Architecture*, vol. 1, *Building God's House in the Roman World: Architectural Adaptation among Pagans, Jews, and Christians* (originally published as separate volume, Baltimore, 1990), Valley Forge.

White L.M. 1997a. *Texts and Monuments of the Christian Domus Ecclesiae in its Environment* (Social Origins of Christian Architecture, vol. 2), Valley Forge.

White, L.M. 1997b. "Synagogue and Society in Imperial Ostia: Archaeological and Epigraphic Evidence", *Harvard Theological Review* 90, 23-58.

Vidman, L. 1971. "Inferiae und iustitium", *Klio: Beiträge zur alten Geschichte*, 53, 209-12.

Wiedemann, T. 1989. *Adults and Children in the Roman Empire*, New Haven and London.

Will, E. 1962. "Le sel des Morins et des Ménapiens", *Latomus* 58, 1649-57.

Williams, M.H. 1992. "The Jews and Godfearers Inscription from Aphrodisias — A case of Patriarchal Interference in Early 3rd Century Caria?", *Historia: revue d'histoire ancienne* 41, 297-310.

Willis, Wendel E. 1985. *Idol Meat at Corinth*, Atlanta.

Winter, F. & Christie, A. 1985. "The Symposium-Tent of Ptolemy II: a new proposal", *Échos du monde classique* 4.2, 289-308.

Wiseman, T.P. 1987. "*Conspicui postes tectaque digna deo*: The Public Image of Aristocratic and Imperial Houses in the Late Republic and Early Empire", in: *L'Urbs: Espace urbain et historique (I^e siècle av. J.-C. - IIIe siècle ap. J.-C.)*, Paris and Rome, 393-413.

Wood, S.P. 1954. *Clement of Alexandria, Christ the Educator*, Washington, DC.

Zangemeister, C. 1889. (on the Dea Hludana-inscription), *Westdeutche Zeitschrift für Geschichte und Kunst, (Trier) Korrespondenzblatt* no. 1.

Contributors

Per Bilde
Department of the Study of Religion
Aarhus University
DK-8000 Aarhus C
Denmark

Keith Bradley
Department of Greek and Roman Studies
University of Victoria
V8W 3P4 Victoria, BC, Canada

Katherine Dunbabin
Department of Classics
McMaster University
Hamilton, Ont. L8S 4M2
Canada

Geert Hallbäck
Institute of Biblical Exegesis
University of Copenhagen
Købmagergade 44-46
DK-1150 Copenhagen K
Denmark

Hugh Lindsay
Department of Classics
University of Newcastle
Callaghan NSW 2308
Australia

Inge Nielsen
The Danish Institute at Athens
Herefondos 14
GR-10558 Athens
Greece

David Noy
Department of Classics
University of Wales
Lampeter, Dyfed SA48 7ED
UK

Peter Ørsted
Institute of History
University of Copenhagen
Njalsgade 102
DK-2300 Copenhagen S
Denmark

Hanne Sigismund Nielsen
Department of Greek and Latin
University of Aarhus
DK-8000 Aarhus C
Denmark

L. Michael White
Department of Classics and Religious Studies Program
University of Texas
Waggener Hall 212
Austin, Texas 78 712
USA

Index of Names

Aaron, 153
Abaye, 136
Abraham, 63
Achilles, 45, 74
Achilles, Claudius
Acis, 54 n. 17
Adrastus, 45
Aelia Aeliana, 46, 47, 54 n. 18
Aelian, 130 n. 2, 3
Aelius Marus, Publius, 32 n. 59
Aemilius Paullus, L., 45, 54 n. 17, 130 n. 4
Aeneas, 76
Agathocles of Syracuse, 107, 131 n. 16, 133 n. 57
Agrippa, 137, 142 n. 17
Agrippina, 47, 55 n. 19
Ahern, E., 70, 78 n. 19
Alarcao, J. de, 30 n. 36, 34 n. 73
Alcibiades, 45
Alexander the Great, 45, 100 n. 22, 102-4, 118, 125, 131 n. 16
Alexandra, Queen, 101 n. 44
Alexiou, M., 77 n. 2-4
Amachios, 204
Amarantos, 140
Ambrose, 57, 63
Amedick, R., 100 n. 33, 104, 132 n. 45
Andronicos, M., 131 30
Antichos IV, 105, 130 n. 9
Antipios, 204
Antonia, 122
Apuleius, 41, 47, 53 n. 12, 54 n. 19
Aqiba, R., 140
Aristeas, 104, 125
Aristotle, 15, 28 n. 13-14, 30 n. 42
Artemidorus, 68, 77 n. 8
Assubanipal, 118

Astin, A.E., 54 n. 17
Athenaeus, 38, 53 n. 8, n. 12, 54 n. 15, 79 n. 52, 87, 98 n. 18, 100 n. 22, n.24, 130 n. 1-4, n. 6, n. 9, 131 n. 16, 22, 132 n. 35, 133 n. 52-53, n. 57
Athis, 54 n. 17
Atticus, 52, 57
Augustine, 41, 57, 62-63, 65 n. 29, 66 n. 19
Augustus, 46, 53 n. 7, 58, 69, 107, 126, 140
Aurelius, 205
Aurelius Victor, 32 n. 57
Ausonius, 79 n. 65
Bagnall, R.S., 54 n. 17
Balch, D.L., 198 n. 10
Baldassarre, I, 86, 99 n. 16
Balty, J.Ch., 101 n. 35
Bammel, F., 163 n. 1
Barton, S.C., 175 n. 8, 197 n. 7
Bartsch, H.W., 175 n. 8
Baucis, 55 n. 19
Beall, T.S., 164 n. 10, 165 n. 32, n. 37
Beek, B.L., 31 n. 51, 33 n. 61, n. 68-69, 34 n. 82, n. 87, 35 n. 90
Bek, L., 52 n. 4, 55 n. 26, 110-12, 131 n. 15, n. 28 ,132 n. 43, n. 45, 133 n. 59-60
Benedict, R., 52 n. 3
Benjamin, 204
Benoît, F., 23, 28 n. 23, 32 n. 60-61, 34 n. 74
Berger, K., 164 n. 19
Bergilianus, P. Luscius, 29 n. 24
Bergmeier, R., 164 n. 10, 165 n. 32, 38
Bergquist, Birgitta, 84, 98 n. 3, 99 n. 4, 6, 9, 15, 124, 133 n. 48-49
Beryllos, 188, 202

Betiliena Antiochis, 60, 65 n. 20-21
Betilienus Synegdemus, Publius, 60, 65 n. 20-21
Bilde, P., 11-12, 142 n. 16, 144 n. 76, 164 n. 10, n. 12, n. 15, 165 n. 32, n. 38-39, 166 n. 49
Blackman, P., 142 n. 6
Blümmer, 32 n. 5, 57, 60-61, 33 n. 61, 34 n. 82, 35 n. 97
Bobertz, C., 198 n. 14
Bogears, J.E., 34 n. 90
Bohlen, D., 27 n. 8, 12, 28 n. 19, 29 n. 27, 30 n. 41-42, 31 n. 47, 51, 34 n. 82, 35 n. 97
Bokser, B.M., 140, 142 n. 7, 143 n. 55, n. 57-59, 144 n. 77
Borgen, P., 197 n. 6
Bornkamm, G., 175 n. 5, 12, 197 n. 9
Borza, E.N., 130 n. 1
Botte, B., 198 n. 12-13
Bousset-Gressmann, W., 163 n. 4-5, 166 n. 47-48
Bradley, K., 10, 52 n. 2, 53 n. 12, 54 n. 17, 55 n. 28, 58, 89, 98 n. 2, 178, 180
Bragantini, I, 65 n. 28
Brewster, E.H., 53 n. 8
Britannicus, 58
Brown, P., 53 n. 13
Bruneau, P., 85, 99 n. 11-12, 100 n. 19
Brutus, 39
Burkert, W., 163 n. 1
Cabal, M., 34 n. 87
Caecilius, 39
Caesar, 38, 53 n. 9, 75, 104, 130 n. 4, 135
Caligula, 47, 58-59, 71, 74, 122, 133 n. 47
Callixenus, 109, 130 n. 6
Calpurnia, 38
Carlsen, J., 29 n. 29
Carna, 76
Casparri, F., 100 n. 22
Cassius, 30 n. 34, 39
Cato, 33 n. 61, 53 n. 9, 79 n. 38
Cato Censorius, 11
Catullus, 53 n. 8

Cephisus, 45
Cestius Pius, 91
Chadwick, H., 53 n. 13
Chamonard, J., 84, 99 n. 10-11
Chares, 130 n. 2
Charles, N., 63 n. 1
Charybdis, 50
Chione, 54 n. 17
Christie, A., 100 n. 22
Chrysostomou, P., 99 n. 8
Cicero, 13-14, 17, 27 n. 2-3, 28 n. 18, 20-21, 29 n. 27, 33 n. 61, 38, 40, 45, 47, 51-52, 53 n. 7, n. 11, 57-58, 69, 72-74, 79 n. 36, n. 55, n. 61, 81, 91, 98 n. 1
Cimma, M.R., 28 n. 21, 31 n. 51, 32 n. 60
Claudius, 38, 46, 58
Clement of Alexandria, 42-46, 180
Cleopatra, 104, 132 n. 37
Clodius Pulcher, P., 55 n. 26
Coarelli, P., 110
Cohen, Y.A., 52 n. 3, 55 n. 27
Colson, F.H., 164 n. 25-26, 165 n. 29
Columella, 34 n. 79, 39, 78 n. 33
Connolly, R.H., 198 n. 12
Conzelmann, H., 175 n. 5
Corley, K.E., 163 n. 1
Cornelius Nepos, 38
Cosconius Hyginus, Marcus, 60, 65 n. 21
Courtney, E., 55 n. 23
Critias, 98 n. 1
Croesus, 45
Cuq, E, 78 n. 13,23
Curtis, R.I., 25, 27 n. 8, n. 12, 28 n. 19, 30 n. 36, n. 38, 31 n. 51, 32 n. 53, 34 n. 73, n. 79, n. 86, 35 n. 90, n. 97
Cyrus the Great, 117
Cytheris, 47, 55 n. 19
Daedalus, 54 n. 17
Daremberg, 77 n. 6, 78 n. 12-13, n. 22-23, 79 n. 59, n. 63, n. 68
D'Arms, J.H., 54 n. 15-16, 55 n. 26-27, 89, 100 n. 28, 198 n. 15
David, 62

Index of names

Delcor, M., 161, 163 n. 4, n. 5, 166 n. 47, n. 49
Demetrius of the First Friends, 203
Demetrios of Phaleron Poliorketes, 103
Deonna, W., 53 n. 8
Detienne, M., 197 n. 2
DeVault, M.L., 63 n. 4
Dihle, A, 78 n. 15
Dio Chrysostom, 47, 55 n. 26
Diodorus Siculus, 100 n. 22, 131 n. 16
Dionisotti, A.C., 53 n. 12
Dionysius of Halicarnassus, 79 n. 66
Dionysius the Younger of Syracuse, 100 n. 22
Dionysius II, 133 n. 57
Dix, G., 198 n. 12
Dixon, S., 54 n. 17, 63 n. 3
Dobschütz, E. von, 175 n. 6, 176 n. 17
Domitian, 44, 122-24, 126, 129
Douglas, M., 52 n. 3, 53 n. 9-10, 78 n. 25-26, 163 n. 1-2, 165 n. 36, 178, 197 n. 2
Dreliossi-Herakleidou, A., 133 n. 58
Drusilla, 58, 71, 78 n. 24
Ducrey, P., 99 n. 5
Dumont, J., 30 n. 37, 42, 31 n. 44-45, 47
Dunbabin, K., 11, 53 n. 5, 55 n. 22, n. 24, 99 n. 3, 100 n. 26, n. 32, 101 n. 35, n. 38, 109, 112, 130 n. 8-9, 131 n. 19-20, n. 27-29, n. 31, 132 n. 38, 133 n. 49, n. 54
Duncan-Jones, R., 27 n. 5
Dupont-Sommer, A., 163 n. 8
Duris, 130 n. 3
Duval, N., 101 n. 35
Edmondson, J.C., 23, 25, 27 n. 8, n. 12, 30 n. 36, 31 n. 47, 33 n. 66, 34 n. 73, n. 89, 35 n. 90
Elagabal, 132 n. 42, 133 n. 47
Elias, N., 54 n. 15
Elsner, J., 55 n. 27
Emmonios, 204
Engberg-Pedersen, T., 175 n. 6, 11
Engelmann, H., 31 n. 43
Ephippus, 132 n. 25

Essler, P., 197 n. 4
Étienne, R., 30 n. 38, 33 n. 61-62, n. 64, 34 n. 80, n. 89, 35 n. 90, n. 94, n. 96-97
Euphemus, 61, 65 n. 25
Euphrates, the Stoic, 135
Eusebius from Caesarea, 154, 164 n. 26, 204
Faye, E. de, 53 n. 13
Favonius, M., 39, 53 n. 9
Feeley-Harnik, G., 163 n. 1-2, 164 n. 19, 197 n. 8
Felix, 66 n. 29
Finsen, H., 132 n. 43
Ferdiére, A., 34 n. 83
Fernandez Gómez, F., 34 n. 83
Festus, 29 n. 27, 69
Festus-Paulus, 72, 78 n. 14, n. 28-30, n. 34, n. 36, 79 n. 38, n. 42-44, 80 n. 71
Flavius Callimorphus, 54 n. 18
Fortunata, 47
Franceschini, M. De, 121, 131 n. 26, 132 n. 46
Freedman, H., 142 n. 15
Frier, B.W., 54 n. 17
Fuscus Salinator, 57
Gabelmann, H., 54 n. 18
Gaius the jurist, 14, 17, 21
Gaius Augustus' grandchild, 46
Galatia, 205
Galliou, P., 31 n. 53
Gamaliel, Rabban, 135, 141
Garland, R., 77 n. 7
Gärtner, B., 166 n. 49
Gaothier, Ph., 100 n. 24-25, n. 30
Gellius, 52 n. 4, 53 n. 5, 78 n. 32, 79 n. 38
Gennep, A. van, 77 n. 9
Giangrotta, P.A., 132 n. 44
Giannouli, V., 99 n. 12
Gibson, S., 120, 132 n. 43
Ginouvès, R., 99 n. 14, 100 n. 19
Ginsberg, M., 142 n. 6
Gnilka, J., 163 n. 4-5, n. 8, 164 n. 11, n. 19, n. 21, 166 n. 47, n. 49

Goette, H.R., 54 n. 18
Goldman, N., 53 n. 8
Goodenough, E.R., 199 n. 34
Goody, J., 52 n. 3
Gowers, E., 53 n. 5
Guimier-Sorbets, A.-M., 99 n. 12
Habinnas, 47
Hades, 68
Haley, E.W., 32 n. 53, 33 n. 71, 35 n. 90
Hallbäck, G., 12, 79
Hands, A.R., 13, 27 n. 1 ,
Harmon, D.P., 80 n. 75
Hart, M., 54 n. 13
Harvey, R.A., 134-135
Hector, 74
Heermann, V., 99 n. 4-5, n. 13, 100 n. 23, 131 n. 17
Hellström, Pontus, 87, 99 n. 17, 133 n. 51
Heracleides, 130 n. 1
Hermaphroditus, 54 n. 17
Hermeos, 204
Hermeros, 183
Herod the Great, 96, 104, 109, 126, 131 n. 16, 134-135, 142 n. 2
Heuchan, V., 198 n. 25
Hieron II, 109
Hilarion, 204
Hippolytus of Rome, 180-181, 183, 198 n. 12
Hirschfeld, O., 28 n. 23, 32 n. 60-61, 33 n. 61
Hoepfner, W., 82, 98 n. 3, 59, 10, 18, 131 n. 19
Holmberg, B., 163 n. 1, n. 3, 164 n. 24
Homer, 74
Hopkins, K., 55 n. 25, 78 n. 13
Höppener, H., 30 n. 37, 31 n. 47
Horace, 50, 53 n. 8, 55 n. 26, 57-58, 79 n. 49, 135, 142 n. 4
Horbury, W., 135, 143 n. 58
Hortensius, Q., 133 n. 47
Hudson, N. A., 55 n. 26
Hug, A., 99 n. 7
Humphrey, S.G., 78 n. 11

Husson, G., 100 n. 21
Hymnis, 47
Iphis, 54 n. 17
Jacobi, I., 132 n. 39
Jacobsen, G., 32 n. 53, 35 n. 90
Jael, 204
Jeremias, Joachim, 180, 197 n. 9
Jerome, 57
Jesse, 204
Jobst, W., 94, 101 n. 36
Johnson, J., 28 n. 21, 29 n. 29, 32 n. 60, 33 n. 61
Jolowitz, J.H., 27 n. 11, 28 n. 13, n. 18
Jonathan, 160
Jones, B., 28 n. 23, 33 n. 68, 53 n. 5, 133 n. 50, 197 n. 1
Joseph, 204
Josephus, 104, 119, 130 n. 5, 132 n. 36, 141-142 n. 8, n. 16, 144 n. 60, n. 72, 146, 148-50, 158-62, 164 n. 10, n. 13, n. 15, n. 23, 165 n. 30, n. 32-33, n. 38, n. 44, 203
Joses, 204
Joshua, 204
Joshua, R., 141
Judah, R., 136-37
Judas Eukolos, 204
Judas the Maccabee, 160
Judge, E.A., 175 n. 3
Julia Felix, 131 n. 20
Julian, 143 n. 58
Julia Velva, 54 n. 18
Julius Valentinus, Gajus, 32 n. 59
Juvenal, 27 n. 7, 29 n. 29, n. 38, 53 n. 7, 55 n. 23, 59, 64 n. 14, 79 n. 47, 143 n. 46
Justinian, 29 n. 25
Kaser, M., 27 n. 10-12, 28 n. 16, n. 19, 30 n. 35
Käsemann, E., 175 n. 14
Kawerau, G., 131 n. 30
Kerr, M., 63 n. 1
Klauck, H.J., 175 n. 4
Klinzing, G., 166 n. 49
Knibbe, D., 31 n. 43

Kniep, F., 32 n. 57, n. 60-61, 33 n. 61
Koch, G., 54 n. 19
Kraabel, A.T., 198 n. 18-19, 199 n. 38
Kraeling, C.H., 199 n. 34-35
Krause,C., 132 n. 41
Kritolaos, 92
Kuss, O., 175 n. 13
Laet, S.J. de, 30 n. 38
Lampe, P., 175 n. 5, n. 9-10, 197 n. 8
La Rocca, E., 132 n. 46
Lassère, J-M., 33 n. 65
Lauter, H., 96, 101 n. 41-42, 131 n. 21
Lauter-Bufe, H., 101 n. 42
Lavin, I., 131 n. 28, 133 n. 60
Le Bonniec, H., 78 n. 35, 79 n. 38
Lecrivain, C., 77 n. 6, 78 n. 12
Lehner, H., 31 n. 52
Lentulus, 57
Leonidas, 45
Lepidius Proculus, Lucius, 24
Leveau, P., 33 n. 65
Levi, D., 93, 101 n. 34
Levine, L.I., 144 n. 64
Lewis, D.M., 130 n. 1
Leyerle, B., 54 n. 13, n. 15
Licinia Helena, 61, 65 n. 24
Licinius Felix, Gaius, 61, 65 n. 23
Licinius Lucullus, L., 37, 52 n. 4, 58, 133 n. 47
Licinius Syneros, Gaius, 61, 65 n. 23-25
Lietzmann, H., 175 n. 5, 180, 197 n. 9
Lindsay, H., 10-11, 78 n. 17, n. 24, 79 n. 58, 80 n. 74
Lindsay, W.M., 78 n. 14
Ling, R., 55 n. 26
Liriope, 45
Littlewood, A.R., 133 n. 47
Livius Drusus, 50
Livy, 22, 32 n. 57, n. 60-61, 55 n. 19
Lohse, E., 164 n. 17
Lucan, 130 n. 4
Lucian, 39, 43, 53 n. 5, n. 8, 68, 79 n. 47
Lucius, Augustus' grandchild 46
Lutz, C., 54 n. 16
Lycurgus, 36
Lydus, 79 n. 62
Lysimachos, 203
Maas, M., 79 n. 62
Malherbe, A.J., 197 n. 7
Manilius, 23, 34 n. 76
Mantinia Maerica, 54 n. 18
Marcianus, 14, 15
Marcus Cicero's son, 91
Mark Antony, 104, 130 n. 4, 133 n. 53
Marquardt, J., 32 n. 61, 52 n. 4, 98 n. 1-2
Marrou, H.-I., 53 n. 13, 54 n. 16
Martial, 33 n. 61, 44, 53 n. 5, n. 8, 55 n. 19, 59, 109, 131 n. 25, 143 n. 45, 183
Martin, J., 197 n. 1
Martínez, F.G., 163 n. 6
Martin-Kilcher, S., 27 n. 8
Masurius Pothinus, Marcus, 61, 65 n. 26
Mattingly, D., 28 n. 23, 33 n. 68
Mau, 100 n. 27
Mausolus, 125-26
Mayboom, P.G.P, 131 n. 20
McCartney, E., 100 n. 23
McDaniel, W.B., 53 n. 8
McKenzie, J., 101 n. 41
Meeks, W.A., 175 n. 3, 179, 197 n. 3-5, n. 7-8, 198 n. 16
Meiggs, R., 55 n. 23
Menecrates of Syracuse, 87
Meniskos, 47
Mercury, 55 n. 19
Metellus Pius, 132 n. 37
Metzger, I., 99 n. 5
Millar, F., 143 n. 58
Miller, S., 99 n. 6, 101 n. 34
Milo, 47, 54 n. 19
Mitchell, T., 98 n. 1
Mithridates, 132 n. 37
Mommsen, 27 n. 11, 31 n. 51, 32 n. 60
Monnica, 63, 66 n. 29
Moschion, 130 n. 9, 131 n. 22
Moses, 13
Mummius, Cornelius L., 28 n. 21
Musonius Rufus, 44, 54 n. 16
Musorillo, H., 143 n. 58
Nahman, R. 137

Narcissus, 45
Nasidienus Rufus, 50
Nausithoon, 45
Nero, 46-47, 54 n. 18, 122, 132 n. 41
Nesselhauf, H., 29 n. 29, 31 n. 52
Netzer, E., 97, 101 n. 36, 101 n. 43-44, 131 n. 23
Neuenzeit, P., 175 n. 4
Nicholas, B., 27 n. 11, 28 n. 13, n. 18
Nicolet, C., 30 n. 39
Nielsen, I., 11, 101 n. 41, n. 43-45, 113-14, 117, 119, 130 n. 14, 131 n, 15, n. 17-19, n. 21, n. 23, n. 30, n. 32, n. 34, 132 n. 36, n. 39, 133 n. 51, n. 56
Nowicka, M., 199 n. 21
Noy, D., 11,
Numa, 75
Octavian, 92
Oculatia Daphne, 61, 65 n. 26
Ørsted, Peter, 10, 28 n. 15, n. 17, n. 22, 30 n. 32, n. 38, 31 n. 43, n. 52, 32 n. 58-60, 34 n. 84-85
Oppianus, 23, 34 n. 75
Orr, W.F., 80 n. 75, 175 n. 1
Osiek, C., 198 n. 10
Ovid, 39, 45, 55 n. 19, 74, 76, 79 n. 60, n. 69-70, 80 n. 73
Pamphile, 47, 54 n. 19
Papa, R., 136, 138
Parkin, T.G., 52 n. 3, 54 n. 17, 65 n. 15
Patte, Daniel, 173-75 n. 15
Paul, 12, 42, 69, 167-75, 178-80, 197 n. 9, 200 n. 38
Perkins, A., 198 n. 26
Perseus, king, 45, 132 n. 37
Persius, 79 n. 51, 134-35, 141 n. 2
Pesce, G., 95-96, 101 n. 41, 131 n. 21
Peter, 178, 183
Petronius, 47, 53 n. 8, 132 n. 42, 143 n. 45, 182-83
Philemon, 55 n. 19
Phileas, 143 n. 58
Philip II of Macedon, 87
Philip V of Macedon, 99 n. 18
Philippus, 13

Philo, 12, 142 n. 10, 144 n. 63, 146, 148-53, 158-59, 162, 164 n. 13, n. 15, 165 n. 32, 166 n. 49
Philodamus, 81, 91
Philostratus, 135, 142 n. 9
Phoenix, 45
Picard, C., 198 n. 22
Plato, 19, 28 n. 13, 30 n. 37, 36, 99 n. 7
Plautus, 73, 105
Pliny, 37-38, 44, 50-51, 53 n. 5, n. 7, 57-58, 75, 109, 129, 131 n. 25, 133 n. 55, 183
Pliny the Elder, 32 n. 56-57, 33 n. 70, 35 n. 94, 37, 53 n. 5, n. 8, 54 n. 15, 55 n. 23, 58, 133 n. 47, 147-50, 164 n. 9
Ploeg, J. van der, 163 n. 4, 8, 166 n. 49
Plutarch, 36-38, 41, 46, 50, 52 n. 1, n. 4, 53 n. 5-7, n. 9, n. 11-12, 54 n. 15, n. 17, 55 n. 23, n. 26, 77 n. 6, 79 n. 48, n. 50, 95, 101 n. 37, n. 39, 130 n. 9, 132 n. 37, 133 n. 47, 135, 139, 142 n. 10, 143 n. 46, 177-78, 181, 197 n. 1
Pollux, 100 n. 23
Polybius, 76, 105, 130 n. 9, 132 n. 37
Pompeius Potens, 29 n. 29
Pomponia, 38, 52, 57
Ponsich, M., 27 n. 8, 30 n. 36, 33 n. 63, 66, 69, 34 n. 78, 86, 89
Poppaea Sabina, 38
Porphyrius, 80 n. 72
Posidonius, 133 n. 53
Pozzi, E., 100 n. 27
Prévost, M.-H., 54 n. 17
Prieur, J., 78 n. 13, 79 n. 57
Ptolemy II Philadelphus, 100 n. 22, 104, 130 n. 6, 130 n. 16
Ptolemy IV Philopator, 100 n. 22, 104, 109, 110, 130 n. 9
Pupius Piso, 55 n. 26
Purcell, N., 53 n. 5
Pythagoras, 75
Quintus, 38, 52, 57
Quintilian, 44, 53 n. 8
Rackham, H., 164 n. 9
Radt, W., 131 n. 30

Raeder, J., 99 n. 10, n. 14, 133 n. 49
Rajak, T., 164 n. 10, 165 n. 37-39
Rakob, F., 99 n. 14
Rathje, A., 130 n. 10
Rauh, N., 100 n. 29
Rawson, E., 55 n. 20
Reber, K., 99 n. 5
Remus, 75
Renard, M., 53 n. 8
Reynolds, J., 199 n. 37
Richardson, P., 198 n. 25
Richter, G.M.A., 54 n. 19, 55 n. 22
Rickman, G., 27 n. 6
Rose, H.J., 52 n. 1
Rossiter, J., 131 n. 28
Rostovtzeff, M., 30 n. 41, 31 n. 47, 51, 32 n. 61
Rubrius, 81
Rudd, N., 141 n. 2
Rutgers, L.V., 200 n. 41
Sabbatios, 204
Sabathios Nektaris, 204
Saddington, D.B., 30 n. 33
Safrai, S., 142 n. 3, n. 21, n. 24, 143 n. 50-52, n. 54-55, 144 n. 65, n. 72-74
Saglio, 78 n. 12-13, n. 22-23, 79 n. 59, n. 63, n. 68
Saller, R.P., 54 n. 17, 55 n. 27, 63 n. 2
Salza Prina Ricotti, E., 100 n. 22, 109, 129-30 n. 11, 131 n. 16, n. 26, n. 34, 132 n. 44, n. 47, 133 n. 47
Samuel, 204
Sanders, E.P., 141-142 n. 21, 143 n. 50-51, n. 53-54, n. 58, 144 n. 77
Sanquer, R., 31 n. 53, 33 n. 67, n. 69, n. 71, 34 n. 73, n. 82
Sasso 'Elia, L., 132 n. 43
Schama, S., 55 n. 27
Scherrer, P., 32 n. 58
Schiffman, L.H., 163 n. 4-5, 164 n. 18, n. 27
Schürer, E., 165 n. 28, 42
Schwandner, E.-L., 82, 99 n. 3, n. 5, n. 10, 131 n. 19
Scintilla, 47

Scylla, 50
Seneca, 51, 53 n. 7-8, 12, 54 n. 15, 55 n. 19, 91, 107, 130 n. 13, 142 n. 3
Septhais, 203
Septimius Severus, 38
Serapion, 54 n. 18
Servius, 29 n. 27, 54 n. 15, 78 n. 34, 79 n. 45
Shackleton Bailey, 53 n. 7, 55 n. 19
Shaw, B.D., 55 n. 27, 63 n. 2
Sheppard, A.R.R., 200 n. 42
Sicinius Pudens, 41
Siebert, G., 99 n. 12
Sigismund Nielsen, H., 10, 65 n. 18, 66 n. 30, n. 32
Smith, D.E., 197 n. 2, n. 8, 198 n. 15
Socrates, 172
Socrates of Rhodes, 130 n. 4, 133 n. 53
Soden, H. von, 175 n. 12
Sodini, J.-P., 101 n. 35
Solon, 6, 78 n. 12
Soranos, 66 n. 30
Sosius Senecio, 37, 177
Sotgiu, G., 33 n. 61
Spinazzola, V., 90-91, 100 n. 26
Stegemann, H., 163 n. 6-8
Stein, S., 197 n. 1
Steinby, M., 65 n. 27
Stern, M., 134
Stevenson, J., 144 n. 71
Stillwell, R., 101 n. 34
Stone, L., 53 n. 12
Stoops, R., 198 n. 16
Strabo, 20, 29 n. 27, 30 n. 38, n. 41-42, 34 n. 87, 35 n. 96, 132 n. 44
Stöckle, 28 n. 13, 30 n. 37, 41, 34 n. 77
Stronach, 117
Stuart, P., 34 n. 90
Studniczka, F., 113, 124, 131 n. 16
Stuhlmacher, P., 175 n. 4
Suetonius, 46-47, 53 n. 7, n. 9, 54 n. 18, 58-59, 64 n. 6, 78 n. 15-16, n. 24, 79 n. 58, 100 n. 31, 107, 130 n. 13, 132 n. 40, n. 42, n. 44, 143 n. 45, 181
Tacita, 76

Tacitus, 33 n. 70, 46, 53 n. 7, 55 n. 19, 58, 79 n. 46-47, 132 n. 44, 135, 142 n. 9
Tamm, B., 130 n. 7, 132 n. 43
Tannenbaum, R., 199 n. 37
Tarpeia, 75
Tarradell, M., 27 n. 8, 30 n. 36, 33 n. 63, n. 66, n. 69, 34 n. 78, n. 86, n. 89
Taussig, H.E., 197 n. 8
Tellus, 72
Temkin, O., 66 n. 30
Terence, 39, 53 n. 9
Tertullian, 57, 75, 79 n. 64, 142 n. 3, 180
Tetrarchs, 102
Teuphilos, 203
Theissen, G., 175 n. 2-3, n. 6-7, n. 12, 176 n. 16, 197 n. 6-8, 198 n. 16
Themas, 203
Theodoros, 204
Theodosius, R., 135
Theodotos Palatinos, 204
Theophrastus, 54 n. 15
Thoen, H., 33 n. 68, 34 n. 82
Thompson, S., 70-71, 73, 78 n. 18, n. 20-21, 79 n. 40-41, n. 56
Thylander, H., 65 n. 16
Tiberius, 123, 133 n. 47
Tiberius Polycharmus, C., 187, 201-2
Tibullus, 59
Tiberius, 79 n. 73
Tosefta, 142 n. 7
Toynbee, J.M.C., 53 n. 7, 54 n. 18, 78 n. 13
Traina, G., 30 n. 36, 32 n. 57, 59
Trajan, 31 n. 51, 44, 129
Trebius, 38, 53 n. 7
Trillmich, W., 29 n. 29
Trimalchio, 182-83, 198 n. 15
Tufi, S.R., 54 n. 18
Tullius, Marcus, 29 n. 25
Turtura, 62
`Ulla, R., 138
Ulpianus, 17, 18, 21
Väänänen, V., 65 n. 22
Valerius Maximus, 54 n. 19, 132 n. 37

Valerius, Quintus Secundus, 20-21, 24, 31 n. 52
VanderKam, J.C., 163 n. 6-8, 164 n. 11 165 n. 42
Varia Ennuchis, 60, 65 n. 17
Varia Servanda, 60, 65 n. 17
Varius Ampelus, Publius, 60, 65 n. 17
Varro, 32 n. 56, n. 37, n. 48, n. 58, 34 n. 79, 52 n. 4, 53 n. 5, n. 8, 54 n. 19, 55 n. 23, 72, 79 n. 38, 105, 107, 109, 131 n. 24, 133 n. 47
Vatin, C., 85, 99 n. 11, 100 n. 19
Vatinius, P., 40
Vaux, Roland de, 146, 163 n. 7-8, 165 n. 18
Veranius Flaccus, 72, 79 n. 37
Vergil, 76
Vermes, G., 163 n. 6-8, 164, n. 10, n. 17, n. 21, 165 n. 28-29, n. 42
Vernant, J.-P., 77 n. 5
Verres, 81, 91, 133 n. 57
Verrius Eucharistus, Lucius, 60, 62, 65 n. 19
Verrius Flaccus, 69, 72, 78 n. 15
Vespasian, 30 n. 42, 31 n. 51, 61, 181
Vestals, 75
Vestricius Spurinna, 37, 53 n. 5
Vidmann, L., 78 n. 23
Ville de Mirmont, H. de la, 98 n. 1
Visser, M., 52 n. 2, 53 n. 10, 55 n. 21
Vitellius, 64 n. 6, 122
Vitruvius, 32 n. 56, n. 59, 51, 53 n. 8, 86, 96, 99 n. 14, 107, 117, 122, 124, 130 n. 12, 133 n. 49
Walther, J.A., 175 n. 1
Watson, J.L., 78 n. 27
Weinfeld, M., 165 n. 35
Weiss, Z., 101 n. 36, 175 n. 6, 176 n. 16-17
White, L.M., 12, 140, 197 n. 8, n. 10, 198 n. 11, n. 19-24, 199 n. 27, n. 31, n. 33-37
Wiedemann, T., 54 n. 18
Wiegand, Th., 131 n. 30

Wilken, R.L., 197 n. 3
Will, E., 28 n. 23, 32 n. 61, 33 n. 68, 34 n. 82
Williams, M.H., 200 n. 39
Willis, W.E., 197 n. 6
Winter, F., 100 n. 22
Wiseman, T.P., 55 n. 26
Wood, S.P., 54 n. 14
Xenophon, 172, 175 n. 10
Yohanan, R., 140
Zangenmeister, C., 27 n. 11-12, 31 n. 51
Zenon, 88
Zopyrus, 45
Zosime Veria, 60-62, 65 n. 19

Index Locorum

Aelian
Varia historia
  8.7: 130 n. 2
  9.9: 130 n. 3

Ambrose of Milan
Abraham
  1.4: 63

Apostolic Tradition
  26-28: 181, 198 n. 13

Apuleius
Apologia
  41.2: 41
Metamorphoses
  1.22-23: 47
  2.11: 54 n. 19
  10.17: 53 n. 12

Aristotle
Ethica Nicomachea
  5.7.1: 28 n. 13
Oeconomica
  2.2.3: 30 n. 42
Rhetorica
  1.13.2: 28 n. 14

Artemidorus
Onirocritica
  5.82T: 68, 77 n. 8

Athenaeus
Deipnosophistae
  2.47f.: 88
  4.145-46: 130 n. 1
  4.147f-148b: 130 n. 4
  4.148b: 133 n.53
  4.152f-153c: 133 n. 53
  4.161d-e: 53 n. 8, 54 n. 15
  5.195-96: 131 n. 16
  5.195d: 130 n. 9
  5.196-97: 100 n. 6
  5.196b: 100 n. 22
  5.204d-206c: 100 n. 22, 130 n. 6
  5.207: 131 n. 22
  5.207c: 130 n. 9
  6.275a: 53 n. 12
  7.289e: 87
  8.34: 79 n. 52
  12.537d: 132 n. 35
  12.538b-c: 133 n. 52
  12.538c: 100 n. 22, 130 n. 2
  12.541c: 100 n. 22, 133 n. 57
  12.542c: 130 n. 3

Augustine
Confessiones
  9.8: 41, 53 n. 7
Enarrationes in Psalmos
  127-128: 62, 65-66 n. 29
  130: 62
Serm.
  117: 62

Aurelius Victor
De viris illustribus
  5: 32 n. 57

Ausonius
Parentalia praef.
  79 n. 65

Cato
De re rustica
  134: 79 n. 38

Index Locorum

Catullus
  90: 53 n. 8

Cicero
Ad Att.
  8.14: 79 n. 61
  14.10: 57
  94.3-4: 53 n. 7
Brutus
  22.85-86: 28 n. 21
De imp. Cn. Pomp.
  8.17: 17, 28 n. 20
  16: 33 n. 61
De officiis
  2.73: 13, 27 n. 2
  2.74: 13, 27 n. 3
  3.69: 28 n. 18
Ad Fam.
  7.26: 57
  197.2: 55 n. 19
Leg. Agr.
  2.40: 29 n. 27
De legibus
  2.22.55: 78 n. 31, 79 n. 36, n. 39, n. 55
  2.24: 79 n. 52
De officiis
  1.106: 45
Ad Q. Fr.
  21.19: 38, 53 n. 7
Tusc.
  1.40.96: 98 n. 1
  5.41.118: 98 n. 1
In Vat.
  32: 40
In Verrem
  2.1: 98 n. 1
  2.1.36.66: 81
  2.4.54: 133 n. 57

Clement of Alexandria
Paedagogus
  1.55.1: 45
  2.1: 180
  2.2.1: 45
  2.13.1: 42-43
  2.13.2: 43
  2.31.1: 43-44
  2.31.2: 43
  2.31.3: 43
  2.33.1: 43
  2.33.4: 43
  2.39.2: 44
  2.53.5: 44
  2.54.1: 43
  2.54.2: 43
  2.54.3: 43, 46
  2.55.1: 42
  2.55.3: 42
  2.60.1: 42-43
  2.60.2-3: 43
  2.60.4: 43
  3.79.4: 43

Cod. Just.
  4.61.11: 33 n. 61

Columella
De re rustica
  2.21: 78 n. 33
  8.17.12: 34 n. 79

Consilium Veneticum
  Canon 12: 136, 142 n. 12

Digest
  1.8.1: 14-15
  1.8.2.1: 15
  1.8.2, *praef.*: 27 n.11
  1.8.3-4: 29 n. 26
  1.8.4-6: 29 n. 30, 33 n. 72
  3.4.1, *praef.*: 32 n. 55
  7.1.9.5: 28 n. 24, 30 n. 35
  9.2.29.2-7: 35 n. 98
  18.1.6, *praef.*: 28 n. 16
  19.1.12: 34 n. 88
  21.2.44: 35 n. 98
  39.4.13, *praef.*: 21, 53 n. 54
  41.1.1-3: 17
  41.1.14, *praef.*: 28 n. 16
  41.1.50, *praef.*: 30 n. 34, 33 n. 72

(Digest continued)
    41.2.1, *praef.*: 28 n. 24
    43.7: 30 n. 35
    43.8: 30 n. 35
    43.8.3, *praef.*: 30 n. 31
    43.8.8-9: 30 n. 34, 33 n. 72
    43.14.1, *praef.*: 29 n. 27
    43.14.1-7: 29 n. 26
    43.14.1.7: 29 n. 27, 30 n. 35, 31 n. 46, 31 n. 48
    43.14.2: 31 n. 46
    47.10.13: 31 n. 48
    47.10.13.7: 28 n. 24
    50.15.4.6: 29 n. 27
    50.15.4.7-8: 31 n. 48
    50.16.15: 28 n. 16
    50.16.16-17: 29 n. 28
    50.16.16.17: 32 n. 55
    50.16.17: 17
    50.16.96: 29 n. 25
    50.16.112: 29 n. 25

Dio Chrysostom
Euboean Discourse
    7.65-67: 47, 55 n. 26

Diodorus Siculus
    16.83.2: 131 n. 16
    17.16.4: 100 n. 22, 131 n. 16

Dionysios of Halicarnassos
Ant. Rom.
    2.40: 79 n. 66

Eusebius
Historia Ecclesiastica
    2.18: 164 n. 26
Hypothetica
    11.1-18: 154
Preparatio Evangelica
    8.5.10-11: 154
    8.6.1-8.7.20: 154
    8.11.1-18: 154

Festus-Paullus
    3L: 79 n. 42
    61L: 78 n. 30
    68L: 78 n. 28 & 29
    69L: 79 n. 43
    104L: 79 n. 44
    121: 29 n. 27
    187L: 80 n. 71
    218L: 79 n. 38
    296L: 78 n. 36
    377L: 78 n. 34

Gellius
Noctes Atticae
    4.6: 79 n. 38
    13.11.6: 55 n. 23
    15.2.4-8: 98 n. 1
    16.4.4: 78 n. 32
Varro
    13.11.2-3: 52 n. 4
    13.11.4-5: 53 n. 5

Homer
Il.
    22.338-342: 74

Horace
Epist.
    1.5.22-24: 53 n. 8
    2.2.184: 135, 142 n. 4, 142 n. 4
Satires
    1.6: 57, 64 n. 7
    2.6.63: 79 n. 49, 80 n. 72
    2.8: 50, 53 n. 8, 55 n. 26

Josephus
AJ
    13.171-73: 165 n. 32
    13.298: 165 n. 32
    13.311-13: 165 n. 32
    18.19: 161
    2.204: 141, 144 n. 72
    14.214: 142 n. 8

15.371-79: 165 n. 32
16.164: 144 n. 60
17.346-48: 165 n. 32
18.11: 165 n. 32
18.18: 165 n. 44
18.18-22: 165 n. 32, 166 n. 46
20.190: 119, 132 n. 36, 132 n. 36
BJ
1.78-80: 165 n. 32
2.113: 165 n. 32
2.119-161: 158, 165 n. 32
2.125-132: 142 n. 16
2.128: 165 n. 33
2.129-133: 159, 161
2.137-42: 164 n. 23
2.344: 119, 132 n. 36, 132 n. 36
2.567: 165 n. 32
3.11: 165 n. 32
5.145: 165 n. 32
5.4.4: 104, 130 n. 5, 131 n. 16
Vit.
10-11: 165 n. 32 & 38

Julian
Con. Gal.
305E: 143 n. 58

Justinian
Inst. Iust.
2.1.1-7: 29 n. 25
2.1.2: 19, 29 n. 27, 29 n. 29, 30 n. 37

Juvenal
Sat.
3.14: 143 n. 46
3.30 ff.: 29 n. 29
5 passim: 27 n. 7
5.76-77: 53 n. 7
5.85: 79 n. 47
6.542: 143 n. 46
6.594-601: 64 n. 14
11.117-27: 55 n. 23
11.133: 53 n. 8
14: 59, 64 n. 13

Lex Irnitana
LXXVII: 27 n. 4

Livy
1.33: 32 n. 57
2.9.6: 32 n. 61
29.37.3: 32 n. 60
39.43.3: 55 n. 19
45.41.12: 54 n. 17

Lucan
10.111-21: 130 n. 4

Lucian
Catapl.
7: 79 n. 47
De Mercede conductis potentium familiaribus
14-17: 39-40
15: 53 n. 8
18: 53 n. 5
Luct.
24: 68, 78 n. 10

Lydus
De Mensibus
4.24: 79 n. 62

Manilius
Astronomica
5.656-81: 34 n. 76

Martial
Ep.
1.41.8: 33 n. 61
2.37: 53 n. 8
2.50.3: 53 n. 8
3.58: 59
3.60: 183
3.82.11: 55 n. 19
3.82.15-17: 44
4.4: 143 n. 45
4.86.9: 33 n. 61
5.78: 53 n. 5

(Ep. continued)
  5.79: 53 n. 8
  6.89.1-2: 44
  7.20: 53 n. 8
  7.20.17: 53 n. 8
  8.33.23-24: 53 n. 8
  8.59: 53 n. 8
  8.59.13-14: 53 n. 8
  8.71.9-10: 53 n. 8
  10.87.12: 53 n. 8
  14.87: 131 n. 25
  14.120: 53 n. 8
  14.121: 53 n. 8

New Testament
Matthew
  5.13: 181

Mark
  7.3: 142 n. 21

Acts of the Apostles (Ap. Act.)
  19-29: 183

1 Cor.
  5.1-13: 179
  5.11: 164 n. 24
  10.16: 179
  10.27-28: 179
  11.17-34: 12, 167-75, 196
  11.23-25: 179

Galatians (Gal)
  2.11-14: 178

Philippians
  2.7: 42

Nonius
Varro
  49.15: 34 n. 79

Old Testament and Apocrypha
Leviticus (Lev.)
  6.15: 165 n. 40
  23.22: 13

1 Samuel (1 Sam.)
  2.35: 165 n. 40

1 Kings
  2.35: 165 n. 40
  4.4: 165 n. 40

1 Macc.
  2.42: 165 n. 41
  7.13: 165 n. 41

2 Macc.
  14.6: 165 n. 41

Ovid
Ars Am.
  3.755-56: 39
Fasti
  2.543: 79 n. 65
  2.553-616: 79 n. 60
  2.571ff.: 76, 79 n. 70
  5.485: 80 n. 73
  5.432ff.: 79 n. 69
Metamorphoses
  3.341-55: 45
  4.288-95: 54 n. 17
  5.47-52: 54 n. 17
  8.241-43: 54 n. 17
  8.655a-61: 55 n. 19
  9.702-17: 54 n. 17
  11.301-2: 54 n. 17
  13.753-54: 54 n. 17

Oppian
Hal.
  3.620: 34 n. 75

Persius
Sat.
   5.179-184: 134, 141 n. 2
   6.33: 79 n. 51

Petronius
Fr.
   37: 143 n. 45
Sat.
   33.6: 53 n. 8
   56: 182
   57: 183
   59-60: 183
   60: 132 n. 44
   65.4: 53 n. 8
   67.5: 47
   72.4: 53 n. 8

Philo
De Cherubim
   92: 144 n. 63
De vita contemplativa
   1a: 154
   34-35: 154
   34-37: 155
   40-63: 155
   64-66: 156
   68: 154
   69-72: 156
   73: 157
   75: 157
   78: 157
   80-87: 157
   89a: 157
   89b: 157
Legatio
   12: 144 n. 63
   361: 142 n. 10
Quod omnis probus liber sit
   75: 166 n. 49
   75-91: 154

Philostratus
Ap.T.
   5.33: 142 n. 9

Plato
Leg.
   7.824C: 19, 30 n. 37
   823: 28 n. 13
Symposium
   175c: 99 n. 7
   177d: 99 n. 7

Plautus
Pseudolus
   348: 79 n. 54

Pliny the Elder
Naturalis Historia
   5.17.4: 164 n. 9
   12.5.10: 133 n. 47
   13.91-99: 55 n. 23
   14.96: 58
   23-79: 147
   28.24: 53 n. 8
   28.26: 53 n. 8, 54 n. 15
   28.26-27: 55 n. 23
   31.39-45: 32 n. 70
   31.73-105: 32 n. 70
   31.73,77: 32 n. 56
   31.73,81: 32 n. 56
   31.89: 32 n. 5
   31.94: 35 n. 94
   36.184: 53 n. 8

Pliny the Younger
Ep.
   1.15.2-3: 53 n. 5
   2.6: 37, 183
   3.1.9: 53 n. 5
   3.5.11-12: 53 n. 5
   5.6.36-40: 109, 131 n. 25

(Ep. continued)
   6.20.2: 51
   9.17.1: 55 n. 23
   9.17.3: 53. n. 5
   9.36: 57, 64 n. 8
   9.36.4: 38, 53 n. 5
Pan.
   49.6: 44
   49.6-8: 133 n. 55
   49.7: 44

Plutarch
Aem.
   5.3: 54 n. 17
   28: 130 n. 9
Brut.
   34.4: 53 n. 9
Cat. Mai.
   25.3: 53 n. 6
Cat. Min.
   56.4: 53 n.9
Crass.
   19: 79 n. 50
Luc.
   39.4-5: 133 n. 47
   41.2: 52 n. 4
Moralia
   5A: 41, 53 n. 11
   14F: 54 n. 15
   38C: 53 n. 12
   42F: 54 n. 15
   45E: 54 n. 15
   50D: 54 n. 15
   99D: 41
   102E: 46
   113D: 46
   140A: 53 n. 7
   158C: 55 n. 23
   272C: 36, 52 n. 1, 53 n. 12
   439F: 53 n. 12
   447A: 53 n. 12
   458D: 53 n. 12
   461C: 53 n. 7
   511D-E: 55 n. 26
   528A-B: 53 n. 7
   554A: 53 n. 12
   638B-F: 53 n. 5
   667C-669E: 53 n. 5
   672F-673A: 53 n. 12
   679B: 52 n. 4, 55 n. 23
   679F: 53 n. 9
   697D: 38
   704B: 55 n. 23
   706F-710A: 55 n. 26
   725F-726A: 38
   727A: 55 n. 23
   728c-730F: 53 n. 5
   800: 50
Quaestiones convivales
   1.612D: 177
   1.617A: 177
   1.660B: 177
   1.2, 615d ff.: 101 n. 37
   1.3, 619b-f: 101 n. 37
   4.4.4-5.3: 142 n. 10
   5.5: 100 n. 22
   6.2: 143 n. 46
   7: 79 n. 48
   7.679A: 197 n. 1
   7.697C-E: 177
   7.8, 711b-d
Sert.
   22.2-3: 132 n. 37
Sol.
   21: 68, 77 n. 6
Sul.
   11.1-2: 132 n. 37

Polybius
   6.53: 76
   30.26: 130 n. 9
   31.25: 132 n. 37

Quintilian
Inst.
   1.2.8: 44
   8.3.66: 53 n. 8

Rabbinic and related literature

Misnah
`Abodah Zarah
  4.2: 143 n. 40
  5.5: 142 n. 11
Kerithoth
  3.7: 141, 144 n. 74
Ketuboth
  5.9: 143 n. 33
Pesahim
  10.1: 143 n. 53 & 56

Tosefta
Pesahim
  143 n. 56
Yom Tov
  2.15: 142 n. 7

Palestinian Talmud
Berakoth
  III 6a: 144 n. 70
Sanhedrin
  VIII 2.26b: 144 n. 64

Babylonian Talmud
`Abodah Zarah
  8a: 142 n. 11
  11a: 142 n. 19
Baba Bathra
  57b: 142 n. 28, 143 n. 36
  93b: 143 n. 44
Baba Kamma
  92b: 142 n. 14
Baba Mezi`a
  107b: 142 n. 14
Berakoth
  2a-b: 142 n. 16
  6b: 144 n. 75
  15b: 142 n. 23, 143 n. 41
  30b: 144 n. 73
  35a: 142 n. 22
  42a: 144 n. 73
  42b: 143 n. 38
  43a: 142 n. 25, 143 n. 34
  43b: 142 n. 30
  44b: 142 n. 18 & 32
  46a: 142 n. 27 & 29
  46b: 143 n. 39
  47a: 142 n. 21 & 26, 144 n. 73
  51b: 142 n. 31
  57b: 142 n. 1
Bezah
  23a: 142 n. 5
Gittin
  38b: 143 n. 48
Hullin
  86b: 142 n. 29, 143 n. 37
  104b: 142 n. 29, 143 n. 38
  105b: 142 n. 18
  106a: 142 n. 21
  107b: 143 n. 36
Ketuboth
  8a: 144 n. 73
Mo`ed Katan
  26b: 144 n. 69
  27a-b: 144 n. 66
  28b: 144 n. 68, n. 75
Pesahim
  100a: 143 n. 35
  107b: 142 n. 17, 143 n. 53
Shabbath
  10a: 136, 142 n. 15
  13b: 143 n. 33
  105b: 144 n. 67
  119a: 137, 142 n. 20
  122a: 142 n. 11
Sotah
  49a: 143 n. 40
Ta`anith
  30a: 143 n. 42

Midrash Ecclesiastes Rabbah
  1.3.1: 144 n. 73
  2.2.4: 144 n. 73

Midrash Esther Rabbah
  1.6: 142 n. 11

Midrash Lamentations Rabbah
  1.16.51: 143 n. 47
  3.17.6: 143 n. 38
  4.2.3-4: 138-39, 143 n. 43
  5.16.1: 143 n. 40

Rutilius Namatianus
  1.475: 34 n. 73

Seneca
De beneficiis
  3.26.2: 54 n. 12
Ep.
  78.23: 130 n. 13
  90.9: 130 n. 13
  90.15: 130 n. 13
  94.8: 53 n. 12
  95.47: 142 n. 3
  115.8: 130 n. 13

Prov.
  4.9: 130 n. 13
QNat.
  4.13.7: 130 n. 13
  5.16.6: 53 n. 9

Seneca the Elder
Con.
  9.2.2: 55 n. 19
  9.2.4: 53 n. 8
Suas.
  7.13: 91

Servius
Ad Aen.
  4.244: 33 n. 61
  5.78: 79 n. 45
  5.92: 78 n. 34
Ver. G.
  2.161: 29 n. 27

SHA
Aug.
  64.3: 46

Heliogab
  21.1: 133 n. 47

Solinus
  5.19: 32 n. 56

Soranus of Ephesus
The Gynecology
  66 n. 30

Strabon
  3.11: 35 n. 96
  3.4: 35 n. 96
  4.188: 29 n. 27
  4.4.2: 34 n. 87
  5.3.6: 132 n. 44
  7.320: 30 n. 42, 31 n. 44
  7.6.2: 30 n. 38

Suetonius
Aug.
  64: 58, 64 n. 9
  70.1: 100 n. 31
  76: 143 n. 45
Calig.
  23.2: 132 n. 40
  24: 58, 64 n. 12
  24.1: 47
  24.2: 78 n. 24
  59: 74
Clau.
  24.2: 53 n. 7
  32: 46, 58, 64 n. 10
Gramm.
  17: 78 n. 15 & 16
Ner.
  31.2: 130 n. 13, 131 n. 27, 132 n. 42
Tib.
  39: 132 n. 44
  75.3: 79 n. 58
Tit.
  2: 54 n. 18
Sev.
  4.6: 38

Vesp.
  19: 182
  21: 182
Vitellius
  13.1: 64 n. 6
  15.3: 132 n. 40

Tacitus
Annales
  3.2: 79 n. 46
  4.59.1-2: 132 n. 44
  6.5: 79 n. 47
  13.16: 46, 58, 64 n. 11
  13.57: 33 n. 70
  14.4: 55 n. 19
  15.60: 53 n. 7
Hist.
  2.95: 79 n. 46
  5.5.1: 142 n. 9

Tertullian
Ad Nat.
  13: 142 n. 3
Apol.
  39: 180
De Anim.
  4: 79 n. 64

Tibullus
  1.5.53: 79 n. 53
  1.5: 59

Valerius Maximus
  2.1.2: 54-55 n. 19
  9.1.5: 132 n. 37

Varro
De Vita Populi Romani frag.
  104: 79 n. 38
Ling.
  5.118: 47, 55 n. 23
  8: 105
  9.47: 53 n. 8
Rust.
  1.7.8: 32 n. 56

  2.11.6: 32 n. 56
  3.4.3: 133 n. 47
  3.5.9-17: 109, 131 n. 24
  3.13.2: 107, 132 n. 47
  14.1-2: 130 n. 11

Vergil
Aeneid
  5.77-80: 76

Vitruvius
De Architectura
  6.3.8: 117-18
  6.3.9: 96
  6.3.10: 86, 99 n. 14
  6.4.1-2: 131 n. 33
  6.5.1: 51
  7.3.7: 32 n. 56
  7.4.5: 53 n. 8
  8.3.7: 32 n. 59

Xenophon
Memorabilia
  3.14.1: 175 n. 10

Papyri
Dead Sea Scrolls
The Community Rule (or The Manual of Discipline)
  1QS 3.13: 164 n. 21
  1QS 5.2: 161
  1QS6: 144 n. 76
  1QS 6.2-6: 150-51
  1QS 6.13: 151
  1QS 6.16-17: 150, 152
  1QS 6.16-21: 152
  1QS 6.16-25: 161
  1QS 6.22: 164 n. 21
  1QS 6.24-25: 150, 153
  1QS 6.25: 164 n. 21
The Messianic Rule (or The Rule of the Congregation) (1QSa/1Q28a)
  1QSa 1.2: 161
  1QSa 1.1-3: 153, 164 n. 20
  1QSa 1.6-22: 153

(The Messianic Rule continued)
   1QSa 2.3-22: 153
   1QSa 2.11-22: 164 n. 20
   1QSa 2.17-22: 150

PcairZen
   59445: 88, 100 n. 21

Sel. Pap.
   no. 171: 88, 100 n. 21

Inscriptions
Johnson 1935
   no. 13.3 (Degrassi 732): 33 n. 61
   no. 15.7 (Degrassi 733): 33 n. 61
   no. 20.12 (Degrassi 738): 33 n. 61
   no. 25.11 (Degrassi (743): 33 n. 61

Lehner 1930
   14, no. 27: 31 n. 52

Lifshitz, Donateurs
   No. 66: 188, 202

Reynolds-Tannenbaum, 1987
The Jewish Dekania *of Aphrodisias*: 193-4, 203

Sheppard 1980-81
Kalecik:
   No. 11: 195, 205
Stratonicea:
   No. 1: 195, 204
Yala Baba Köy:
   No. 8: 195, 205

Thylander 1952
Tomb 15: 60-62
Tomb 64: 60, 65 n. 20
   - Funerary urn: 60, 65 n. 21
Tomb 87: 60, 65 n. 17

Väänänen
   No. 40: 61, 65 n. 23
   No. 41: 61, 65 n. 24
   No. 43: 61, 65 n. 25
   No. 42: 61, 65 n. 26

AE
   1888.65: 33 n. 61
   1913.91: 34 n. 86
   1919.10: 19, 30 n. 38
   1920.99: 34 n. 77
   1924.122: 33 n. 61
   1934.254: 28 n. 21, 33 n. 61, 35 n. 95
   1937.141: 32 n. 59
   1952.22: 31 n. 53
   1969-70.270: 32 n. 53
   1973.362: 34-35 n. 90
   1973.363: 35 n. 90
   1973.365: 35 n. 90
   1973.370: 35 n. 92
   1973.375: 35 n. 90
   1973.378: 35 n. 90
   1988.664: 30 n. 33
   1988.862: 33 n. 61, 35 n. 95
   1989.341: 29 n. 29
   1991.1024: 34 n. 83
   1994.1279: 34 n. 82

CIJ
   I 518: 134, 141 n. 1
   I 694: 187, 201

CIL
   1(2).589: 30-31 n. 43
   2.537: 34 n. 86
   2.681: 34 n. 86
   2.1168: 35 n. 98
   2.1169: 35 n. 98
   2.1180: 35 n. 98
   2.1183: 35 n. 98
   2.1944: 32 n. 53
   2.2242: 30 n. 32, 34 n. 85
   2.5929: 34 n. 77, 34 n. 81, 35 n. 98
   3.1209: 32 n. 59
   3.1363: 32 n. 59
   3.6065: 29 n. 29
   3.14356: 3a: 34 n. 84
   4.826: 34 n. 77

4.5659: 35 n. 94
4.7698b: 44
5.6670: 33 n. 61
5.8750: 34 n. 81
6.1080: 34 n. 81
6.1152: 33 n. 61
6.1872: 34 n. 77, 35 n. 98
6.200 iv, 61 and 66: 61, 65 n. 27
6.9854: 29 n. 27
6.29700: 34 n. 81
6.29701: 34 n. 81
6.29702: 34 n. 81
6.32049: 62
10.7856: 33 n. 61, 35 n. 95
11.390: 34 n. 82
11.391: 34 n. 82
11.3007: 33 n. 61
12.5360: 33 n. 61
13.8611: 31 n. 51
13.8723: 31 n. 51
13.8793: 35 n. 92
13.8815: 35 n. 93
13.8830: 20-21, 31 n. 51
14.409: 34 n. 81, 35 n. 98
14.2112: 76, 80 n. 76

CPJ
138 (P. Ryl. 590): 188-89, 202-203
139 (O.E. 368): 189, 203
I 139: 140, 144 n. 61
III 254-55: 198 n. 25
III 452a: 140, 144 n. 63
III 467: 140, 144 n. 62

IDR
3.2.285: 33 n. 61
3.3, no. 119: 32 n. 59

IG
XII 7.515: 92

ILS
140: 75, 79 n. 67
1461: 20-21, 31 n. 51
6914: 32 n. 53
7212: 76, 80 n. 76
8858: 30 n. 38
14.4328: 28 n. 24

JIWE
II 591: 134, 141 n. 1

SIG
1025.46: 182
1026.4: 182